the Great

Game *of*

Business

the Great Game of Business

THE ONLY SENSIBLE WAY TO RUN A COMPANY

JACK STACK

with Bo Burlingham

CROWN
BUSINESS

New York

Crown Business books are available at special discounts for bulk
purchases for sales promotions or corporate use. Special editions,
including personalized covers, excerpts of existing books, or books with
corporate logos, can be created in large quantities for special needs. For
more information, contact Premium Sales at (212) 572-2232 or e-mail
specialmarkets@randomhouse.com.

The Library of Congress has cataloged the Doubleday hardcover as follows:

Stack, Jack
The great game of business / Jack Stack.—1st ed.
p.   cm.
1. Success in business. I. Title.
HF5386.S77   1992
650.1—dc20   91-48148

The Great Game of Business is a trademark of The Great Game of Business,
Inc., a subsidiary of the Springfield Remanufacturing Corp.
SRC is a trademark of the Springfield Remanufacturing Corp.

ISBN 978-0-385-34833-1
eISBN 978-0-385-34834-8

Printed in the United States of America

Illustrations by Fred Haynes
Jacket design by Dustin Myers, 40 Digits

9 10

First Revised Edition

To Betsy,

for your incredible strength and love.

And to

Ryan, Katie, Meghan, Timmy, and Kylie

for everything you have taught me.

I don't want to leave your generation

worse off than ours.

I want to leave it better.

Contents

INTRODUCTION TO THE EXPANDED AND UPDATED EDITION

I think that in most people's hearts, they want to write a book. And most people can. But here's some advice: don't write a business book. Write a western or a romance instead—anything but a business book. Why? Because few people keep your typical novel. They read the book and then they get rid of it. They rarely dog-ear it, Post-it-note it, flag it, bookmark it, highlight it, or underline it. It's almost as if time stands still when you write a business book. It's unlikely that someone will bring a mystery or a romance novel back to you twenty years later and ask what you meant by what you wrote on page 121 or whether you're still doing the things you mentioned on page 67. When you write a business book, and profess to practice what you preach, you're permanently putting your reputation on the line. Plus, your readers might actually do something with the advice you wrote about. That's an awesome responsibility to live with.

Twenty years ago, Bo Burlingham and I wrote a book called *The Great Game of Business*. We weren't trying to do much more than document how we at Springfield Remanufacturing Corp. (SRC) in Springfield, Missouri, were operating our business, which was focused, at the time, primarily on remanufacturing truck and automobile engines. We were a classy garage shop. But what really made SRC different was that our business wasn't run in the traditional top-down, command-and-control way most other companies were (and still are). We had built a repeatable system that enabled our associates to run the company—a business of businesspeople, as I like to call it, where everyone gets a chance to grab the brass ring if they choose to do so.

WHAT'S IN A NAME?

The name we used for our leadership system, *The Great Game of Business* (also known as the Great Game, the Game, or the GGOB), has caused a lot of head scratching over the years, especially by people who think that it trivializes business by equating it with a game. Business is serious, they say, where people's lives, let alone life savings, are at stake. It's a fair point.

We used the word *game* for our system because we wanted to find a way to make business approachable and less intimidating to our associates working on the shop floor or in an office. Business is not an art or a science. It's a competitive undertaking with rules, winners and losers, ways of keeping score, and all the elements of luck and talent. It doesn't have to be an instrument of exploitation, or a tool of greed, and you don't need an MBA to understand it. Given all that, we figured there wasn't any reason we couldn't set up our company so that everybody could play the game together and share the rewards. We wanted to demystify business.

The truth is, when we still worked for International Harvester, we were great at building products like engines and tractors, but nobody had ever taught us how to build a company. I'll never forget a guy who worked on the factory floor running a drill press. His job was to literally figure out how to make the perfect hole by correcting for millimeter-wide variances. Nothing more; nothing less. You could imagine my surprise when someone told me that the same drill press operator was actually a self-made millionaire who had built his wealth through savvy real estate investments. Here was this incredible entrepreneur working under our noses and all I had this guy doing was drilling holes. What a wasted opportunity.

This haunted me for a long time because we had missed out on using this drill press operator's full range of talents. We only asked him to drill the perfect hole, not about how he thought we could build a better company. For thirty-three years, we only had him keep his head down thinking about control charts, measurements, and throughputs. He had given us his skills, but we lost the opportunity to tap his full intellectual capacity. What we didn't realize at the time was that by failing to tap the strengths of every individual in our company, we were heading toward a dead end by dumbing people down.

Our wake-up call came when International Harvester

told us it was shutting down our plant. When we took the opportunity to buy the company for ourselves in 1983, we knew we needed a smarter way to run our business. The old way didn't work. We needed something that was the opposite of the command-and-control model that we had been taught and that had been used for years and years. If we were even going to have a shred of a chance to make it on our own, we needed to find a way to tap the strengths of every individual in the company.

In those early days, none of us knew squat about business. It was really, really hard to break free from our old ways. Even though we owned the company, there was still an attitude of "us versus them" between the managers and the workers. You still had people pointing fingers and waiting for commands. We had plenty of job descriptions that could tell you the size, measurements, and tooling you needed to make the perfect hole. But nothing in that description was tied to the success of the company as a whole. That's where we fell short.

Even though we were owners, nothing really had changed. We were still experiencing the hangover from the Industrial Revolution. We weren't moving forward, we just kept going backward. It was an example of how devastating the command-and-control model truly was.

It wasn't until we appealed to everyone's competitive spirit that we began to see change take place. It's a universal law of nature that if you poll a group of people and ask them their opinion on just about anything, you'll rarely get everyone to agree. Except when it comes to winning. Everyone likes to win—and no one likes to lose. That's why we tried to open the business up using the analogy of games—things that people are interested in and have fun doing. Work is boring. But people love the idea of playing a game or competing. Call it a hook if you want. It was all born out of frustration about how to teach people the metrics of business. We wanted to find a way to get people to apply the same skills they were using to build the perfect tractor to also build the perfect company. We needed to change our focus so that the *company* was our product.

The GGOB became an accelerated learning process we used to bring about a cultural and behavioral change and take down the walls that our command-and-control system had created. When the lightbulbs started to come on, and we really began thinking about how we could build a great company together, the transformation was incredible.

By the time we wrote the original book in 1992, the results were already staggering. Revenues had grown from $16 million to $83 million, and the company's value had skyrocketed from $100,000 to $25 million. Just as important, our Employee Stock Ownership Plan, or ESOP, had grown to the point where hourly workers who had been with SRC from the beginning had holdings worth as much as $35,000. But beyond any specific numeric goal, we were very vocal in that first book about our goal that everyone who worked at the plant would have a chance to buy a house of his or her own.

That was a heavy objective for a bunch of guys and gals with grease in their fingernails and sweat on their brows. It also brought us a lot of attention over the years. I can't tell you how many times people who read the original book have asked me how that house thing worked out. I'm proud to report that the average ESOP account for our original hourly workers topped $400,000 in 2012. In Springfield, Missouri, that's a house, a lake house, a bass boat, and a pickup truck. The most important thing is that our employees know how to achieve their dreams. That's the real secret of the GGOB.

All the same, we never stopped marching forward. We've only gotten bigger and stronger in the years since the original book was published. We started this process a long time ago, but it's never finished. The more we play, the more we learn. The more we fix, the better we get. It's like working in a living laboratory.

A critical component of our success was that the more we taught people, the more they taught us. The more we opened things up, the more people wanted to know. It was contagious. In a command-and-control system, people don't ask questions because they don't know what to ask. But when you're collectively trying to build a great company, you ask hard questions. And when everyone respects the people asking those questions, you get stronger because you have to work harder to come up with the answers. It still surprises the heck out of me how transformative it is when the lights go on in someone's head and the person just gets it.

With the help of the GGOB, the people at SRC have continued to be profitable every year since we got our start back in 1983. SRC's combined revenues have grown to more than $450 million. Just as important, the company has created thousands of jobs while building more than sixty diversified businesses over the past thirty years. Most of the SRC companies remanufacture products for the agricultural, industrial, construction, truck, marine, and automotive markets. We've diversified into core management, failure analysis, reverse engineering, logistics, kitting and packaging, and warehousing and distribution. Most would advise you to stay within your "core competencies." To the contrary, we have been in banking, furniture, biotech, clothing, retail, and software. That growth and diversity has helped drive the share price of SRC's stock from $0.10 in 1983 to $348 today—that's a 348,000 percent growth rate, if you're counting. To frame that another way, if you had put $1,000 in a Standard & Poor's index fund back in 1983, you'd have about $8,434 today. If you had invested $1,000 in shares of Berkshire Hathaway, Warren Buffett's company, over the same time frame, your stake would be worth about $113,000. Not a bad return on your money. But if you had invested your $1,000 in the people of SRC back in 1983, you'd be worth $3.4 million today. That's incredible.

CHANGING PERSPECTIVES

The cumulative effects of the GGOB didn't just stop at the stock price. What I've noticed over the years is that when things are going well, and when people are feeling good about themselves, they begin to feel good about others as well. It's infectious when you get on a roll. You begin to do things first at home and then out in your community to make sure you don't lose that feeling. You begin to pay it forward, which is something the media somehow seems to forget when they start attacking successful businesses.

As an example of what I mean, I asked our human relations team at SRC to find out how many of our associates serve in volunteer organizations throughout our community of Springfield, Missouri. When they told me that we had more than 115 of our people serving in a range of executive positions that included everything from a school district board member to a United Way organizer, I was simply blown away. And that doesn't count all the folks like our chili cook-off king, those who coach soccer and Little League teams, and everyone else who gives back to the community in their own way. You build wealth, distribute it, and then continually recirculate it from generation to generation throughout your community. When you add it all up, isn't this what the brighter side of capitalism is all about?

I believe that people who invest their time in building a business are just as important as the people who invest money. That's not always a popular belief within the business community. A lot of people will say that because they risked it all, they deserve all the rewards. The investor who puts in $1,000 gets $2.9 million but the worker who spends thirty-three years on the line only gets his wages? To me, this is the darker side of capitalism.

What differentiates the GGOB is that it gives the associates in a company the chance to grab the brass ring and not just settle for arm-wrestling over wages. The people who invest their time should be given similar opportunities to reap rewards as the people who invested their money. The GGOB addresses the notion that the longer you stay with the company, and the more time you invest, the greater the chances are of reaping your rewards if the venture is successful.

THE ONLY SENSIBLE WAY TO RUN
A COMPANY

I think one of the key reasons the original book was so popular was because the people who read it said—"I knew it! I knew this was the right way to run a business but I wasn't allowed to do it. This book says it's okay to do it." Or "I was doing some of these things already, but I never made the connection as to why they were important. Now I get it!" That's heady stuff and got people really interested in what we were doing.

The result was that at the same time we were opening our books and teaching business to our associates, we were also opening up our company to other people from literally all over the world. We felt compelled to share and help other companies get started playing the GGOB because it had made such a difference to us. And the more we opened up our business to others, the more accepted the GGOB became within SRC itself. The fact that people from Europe, Africa, Asia, and South America would travel for thousands of miles to learn what we were doing helped validate our system, and it encouraged our associates to dig deeper. The more we shared with others, the better at the GGOB we became. The reciprocal effect was amazing.

At first, we would give tours. We just let people in and allowed them to talk to whomever they wanted. Then, we started holding seminars where we shared some of the tools we were using to teach our associates how to play the GGOB. Year after year, scores of people would come visit us and tell us, "Yes, this is exactly what we need."

Those seminars eventually grew into an annual conference we now call the Gathering of Games, an event that also celebrated its twentieth anniversary in 2012. In total, more than fifteen thousand people from more than five thousand companies from literally every industry you can think of—including health spas, pizza restaurants, hospitals, and even members of our government—have visited our facilities or attended our conferences and seminars over the past twenty years.

Eventually, in true SRC style, we also recognized that there was a real opportunity to build a new training and education company, which we also named the Great Game of Business, that could help teach and reinforce the rules of the GGOB both inside and outside of SRC. Today, the GGOB (you can visit the company at greatgame.com) sits at the center of a vast community of people spread around the globe who believe in the GGOB.

WHY THE GREAT GAME OF BUSINESS MATTERS

One message that I wish I emphasized more in the original book was how freeing the GGOB becomes for leaders. Too often I see leaders who are afraid to come out of their offices without their ties perfectly straight or who suffer strokes because they're so stressed out from feeling like they have to know every answer to every problem. People think that as leaders they always have to make the right decisions—something that terrifies them.

But leaders don't have to have all the answers. They need to know where to go. What I didn't know twenty years ago was the sheer impact that results from tapping the power of teamwork and collaboration by trusting, delegating, and ensuring that everyone knows his or her role. I just thought working together as a team was the right thing to do. It was common sense. But what I didn't realize at the time is that the GGOB allows anyone, regardless of his or her position inside the company, to make a difference. It frees people.

The GGOB also matters because it helps build leaders—and we have built an incredible group of leaders at SRC over the past thirty years. That's why we've been able to build such a diverse range of companies over the years. I can't tell you how many times I've heard from other businesspeople about how they had to bypass an incredible opportunity because they didn't have the people on board to do it. If leaders are so important, then how come we aren't teaching people to lead all the time? Why don't we have an everyday system that works on giving people the tools they need to become leaders? By using the GGOB, we can delegate information to make people responsible for making decisions. People appreciate their jobs more when they are given the opportunity to make a difference. The GGOB matters because we can use knowledge and communication to teach and build leaders. Then we give people who are ready the chance to lead.

Historically we've adopted this idea that people need to be managed, which is reinforced by business books and gurus who have never run a business. But I believe, deep in my heart, that people don't like to be managed. The idea of working a system instead of a hierarchy is that when you have a variance or a deviation, you attack the reason for the discrepancy, not the person. But the opposite is also true: when someone exceeds a standard, no one can swoop in and steal his or her recognition. That's because everyone sees where he or she fits in.

The GGOB then becomes the foundation for a company's reward and recognition system. Credit and acknowledgment goes to those who deserve it. Nobody is stealing accomplishments or results. You never see anyone taking credit for something someone else did. In this system, you have ownership of your results. That kind of behavior grows people. They then grow the company.

TO THE DOUBTERS

Despite the success of the GGOB at SRC and companies around the world, it's astounding how many people insist that this system won't work in *their* company. Believe me, I've heard all the excuses. They range from a fear of disclosing information to competitors to the notion that employees simply aren't interested or don't have the ability to think like businesspeople. It makes me sad that people have this fear. As George Gendron, the former editor of *Inc.* magazine, put it so eloquently: the reason people don't practice the GGOB is because they have too many secrets in their companies.

I believe these people are missing the opportunity of a lifetime to build a great company. A key theme of our second book, *A Stake in the Outcome*, was emphasizing what happens when you stop dumbing down your people and have them focus on more than just making products and services. If you ask people to build great *companies*, and give them the information they need to do it, you'll get great products and services as a result. The only way you can actually experience success is when your people understand the big picture, not just the small frames.

Two sure ways to kill a company are through arrogance and through ignorance. Keeping employees in the dark about the company's financial health only stirs the rumor mill. I believe that people have answers to all the questions that business owners don't want to deal with. Maybe you don't want to share the books because you don't want people to know your profits and how large or small they might be. But in the absence of real information, people will fill in the blanks with their own numbers. And they'll be wrong. When people lack facts, they fill the void with fiction, often mistakenly believing that a company's owners are lining their basement with gold bricks. It's been my experience that the numbers people make up are off by a factor of six times. At SRC, for example, we surveyed our associates before we began playing the GGOB and they thought our profits were between 40 percent and 50 percent when we actually made between 3 percent and 5 percent. Once they knew the truth, I had one associate ask why we were even in business.

But once the truth is known, you can see a behavioral change where people are much more willing to contribute to make things better. When business owners hide the numbers, especially when they're bad, they're doing a disservice to their associates and to themselves. When people unexpectedly get pink slips, as they walk toward the parking lot, they're wishing they could have done something about it . . . if they had only known.

I know because, once upon a time, I didn't understand the critical nature of the big picture. It was only after trying to find financing to buy our company that I realized that although I knew just about everything about how to rebuild an engine for a bulldozer, I didn't know anything about how to build value in a company. My "aha!" moment came when I learned to evaluate our business like an investor or a buyer would.

I also came to realize that almost anyone could be taught to be a businessperson and a leader. We invented the GGOB as a way to help our associates build confidence in becoming businesspeople by running a repeatable system built on three principles:

1. Every employee should be given the measures of business success and taught to understand them: **Know and Teach the Rules.**
2. Every employee should be expected and enabled to act on his or her knowledge to improve performance: **Follow the Action and Keep Score.**
3. Every employee should have a direct stake in the company's success and risk of failure: **Provide a Stake in the Outcome.**

If you explain to everyone how your business works—and why moving the numbers in the right direction leads to more reward and recognition—magic happens. This is how you create what I like to call "psychic ownership" within the minds of your associates. Because you have trusted individuals with the information, they feel a commitment and a sense of ownership to act on it. Why would people commit to action or making a decision if they haven't been given enough information?

While "opening the books" is essential to playing the GGOB, it is actually just a component of the overall system. I think a lot of people have come to use the phrase *open-book management*—which was coined in 1990 by John Case in *Inc.* magazine—interchangeably with playing the GGOB. And it stuck. In fact, in 2009 when *Inc.* dubbed me the "Father of Open-Book Management," I saw it as a kind of a curse.

The definition of *open book* by itself implies a company is merely sharing financial information with its associates. Sharing this information does not necessarily mean those associates understand or realize how their work affects the numbers. Just because you have a profit-sharing program at your company, for instance, isn't good enough until you teach everyone how to create profits.

I have run into many people over the past twenty years who pull me aside and tell me how frustrated they are because, as they say it, "I gave my people the numbers and nothing happened." I have to tell them they missed the point entirely. The GGOB isn't about giving people the numbers. It's the people who own the numbers and they're the ones who give them to the system. This all flows back to a Japanese business principle that says that no one knows a job better than the person doing the job. In other words, who knows the numbers better than the person actually doing the job?

Businesses also somehow got off track when they stopped asking people to make forecasts. There is a reluctance to put a name beside a forward-looking number. I don't know how you run a company without forecasting. We've found that the more information you share with people, the more they can plan and improve on the accuracy of their forecasts. The whole idea of a forecast is projecting where you want to go and making the commitment to each other to get there. You're not making up a number to please a boss—you're making a commitment to take a journey together. This is a beautiful thing. An accurate forecast takes the uncertainty out of the process and sets an expectation for yourself to live up to. If you can control a forecast, you can control the world. I remember one awed CEO who, after his associates started forecasting their results, told me: "I can't believe there is this much information inside my own company!"

With the GGOB, the players themselves track, forecast, and identify the biggest weaknesses standing in the way of a company's success. The secret to changing culture lies in the simple act of repetition, repetition, repetition. It's not only the planning. It's not only the bonus program. It's not just the equity sharing. It's the repetition. It's nailing down the routine and getting people to forecast accurately, week in and week out. That's how people learn and how cultures change. It's commonsense business management, and it works.

WILL THE GREAT GAME OF BUSINESS WORK FOR YOU?

Someone once told me that somewhere around ten thousand new business books come out every year. That's a lot of dead trees. I'm no saint because I used to read as many of them as I could. Whether it was Total Quality Management, Six Sigma, or Management by Objectives, I spent fifteen years looking for answers and ideas to run our business better. And every year, there was a new best practice to learn. Although there is value in what these processes can teach you, none of them are the whole solution on their own.

This belief was confirmed for me after I read *Beyond Performance Management* by Steve Player and Jeremy Hope. I wasn't all that surprised to learn that just 30 percent of change programs, according to the authors, succeed. And that includes the balanced scorecard, benchmarking, and customer relationship management programs; the authors spend an entire chapter on open-book management. As I said earlier, even open-book management is also not an end in itself.

It wasn't until I went through the process of borrowing capital that I realized that the financials never go away. They've been with us since the beginning of business. But so few people can read or make sense of them today. While managers like me were looking for systems to help us, the answer was right in front of us. You can't have a healthy company if you don't have a healthy balance sheet. How did we miss something as basic as this? That's why at SRC we embraced the financials instead of hiding from them. Better yet, we found a way through the GGOB to make the numbers a part of the very lifestyle and the culture of our company.

It breaks my heart when people read this book or come to visit us in Springfield and leave with only a piece of the GGOB. Some of the managers and executives like our bonus programs; others like how we run Huddles or our open-book philosophy. So they take that back to the office on Monday. And when they do, they see results—for a while. But often, after a few years, it gets boring and everyone goes back to running things the way they did before. The point is that you can't have an effective bonus program if you don't have a forecasting system that's taking people forward to where they want to be. You can't just keep score. You need to get people involved. It's like people read the book and then pull out whatever components appeal to them without recognizing that each of the components of the Great Game of Business is designed to work within a system as a whole. It's only when you combine all the steps that you truly get sustainability.

What we recognized at SRC back in 1983 is that we needed to quit trying to cover holes with Band-Aids and instead lay the foundation for a whole new operating system for the company. That's what the GGOB is all about. I'll be the first to admit that playing the GGOB isn't easy— especially if you've already been in business for a while. It takes real courage to put aside everything you've been taught or break free from the bad habits you may have fallen into.

Doubters over the years have also said that our system is too focused on the numbers and not enough on the "softer" side of running a business, like delivering great customer service or building a great culture. Let me tell you, we have some of the biggest and toughest customers around. But they don't just love our products and services—they love our people. When you focus on building a great company, you have to provide great service and products to make it happen. Our system helps us avoid arrogance by forcing us to go out into the marketplace and find out what our customers want from us, which we can then deliver in a timely fashion with an attention to quality. That's how we make customers happy.

Twice a year we go through a process we call high-involvement planning, where we ask everyone in the organization to sign off on the direction we're heading—a process we discuss in more detail in Chapter 8, "Coming Up with the Game Plan." We look at the economy, the industry, and the competition. We bring the marketplace to our people so they can make some tough decisions. They all vote on the annual plan. And they only agree with it if they believe in it. It all starts not in the boardroom, but with each of them.

Once you get someone's thumbs-up on a decision, it becomes a lot harder for him or her to criticize or play Monday morning quarterback later on. If our people want the Cadillac of health insurance plans, that's great, because they understand the impact that choice will have on their bottom line and on the company's stock price—something I guarantee that every single associate in our organization can quote for you every day of the week.

We have also been surveying our associates every six months for thirty years about how satisfied they are with their jobs and the company as a whole. Back in the early days, the scores told us we had some work to do. These days, our engagement scores average about eighty-five out of one hundred. The other fifteen makes us stop and think.

It's also fascinating and validating to hear from other companies out there who are playing the GGOB. Getting the chance to connect with managers and employees playing the game from literally all over the world is one of the great benefits of our annual conference. I've lost count of how many stories I've heard where a business has turned to the GGOB as a last resort, after they've used up every other quick fix they could think of, which then spurred them to outrageous results.

The best metaphor I can think of to explain what happens is this: I believe everyone has two flywheels inside their brain. One of the flywheels is our creative side, where we get great ideas for a business (or for a book). This flywheel turns constantly at 6,000 rpm. On the other hand, we have our financial flywheel. For most of us, this turns at 60 rpm. But to get a successful result, we need to get the financial flywheel humming along at a much faster clip. When you can do that, that's when you can achieve a remarkable outcome.

WHY WE WROTE ANOTHER BOOK

Tackling this update to *The Great Game of Business* was like performing a balancing act between messing up something that is good and is working, and cleaning it up. When Rich Armstrong and Steve Baker, the president and vice president of the GGOB, respectively, gently prodded me to think about writing a twentieth-anniversary edition of *The Great Game of Business*, I felt all the blood drain out of my face. Writing the original, and its follow-up, *A Stake in the Outcome* (which was published in 2001), with Bo Burlingham were unbelievably challenging—as well as ultimately deeply rewarding. It was not something I was sure I was ready to do again.

But Rich and Steve won me over. Why? Because I think that the world of business that I love is under attack. As I write this, not only are entrepreneurs and small-business owners still struggling to recover from our nation's most recent recession, we continue to slog through an uncertain political environment where no one seems to know how to create jobs. Back in the 1980s, media people like Tom Brokaw were telling us that global competition would be the downfall of the United States. That broadcast continues to haunt me. It's no different today as politicians and members of the media seem to compete for the chance to tell us how badly we are losing to our competitors in China and India.

But I wholeheartedly disagree with these critics. In fact, if you take an objective look at the economy over the past thirty years, you'll see that we've had an incredible run on productivity because a lot of folks dug down deep to make things happen—at least until we all got tripped up in 2008. And that stumble was caused, at least in part, by our society's lack of economic literacy and transparency. If we were all more economically literate and transparent, the events of 2008 might never have happened. Look, we have been very fortunate at SRC to have the kind of run we have had over the past thirty years. And we owe a great deal of that success to this system we have continued to tweak and improve upon over that time. I think the results I shared earlier speak for themselves.

If you're a business owner or an entrepreneur looking

for answers on how to weather this latest storm, or prepare yourself for the next one by growing your business and creating jobs, why do that alone? Why not appeal to the highest level of thinking on the part of your associates by trying the system described by the GGOB?

What's so gratifying to me is that while the GGOB was a foundation for us to save and create jobs, we are now creating opportunities for our children in the workplace. The culture continues, and the fire keeps burning. After thirty years, we now have associates working with us who don't know of any other way of running a company, since we've been doing it so long. These folks have grown up in a business of businesspeople, which has helped speed up the evolution and the GGOB at all levels of the company. We want to keep creating leaders who can build great companies. We need strategists who can make changes, start the diversification process, and sell. We need change agents with strong leadership skills. We need people who can build relationships. And we need people who are hungry to develop their talent.

It's both exciting and nerve-racking to watch our next generation of players hatch new plans and dream about the future. It's exciting because they literally get what it means to build and grow a business because they are simply executing on the system we have in place. It's nerve-racking because even though I might know better, I have to let them learn by making their own mistakes along the way—maybe stepping in only when they might be headed off a cliff.

WHAT'S NEW?

In this revised and expanded edition, we've tried to strengthen the original book by outlining the system and describing the implementation process better, and by providing an interactive "Get in the Game" guide, at the end of the book. Having the tools and resources web-based will allow us to keep the content dynamic and up to date. We've learned a lot over the past thirty years about how to help others weave the GGOB's principles into their organizational DNA. The result is that there is this massive community of players out in the workplace along with lots of resources that you can tap into for help in starting to play the GGOB. You don't have to tackle this alone.

The past thirty years have been a wild ride and I am truly humbled by all the hard work and sweat put forth by every SRC associate over that time. It reminds me that the second-biggest mistake I ever made, after writing a business book, was putting my picture on the cover of the original edition. Not only is that a tough thing to stomach (it's like watching yourself age in the mirror), it also doesn't give credit to everyone who helped the company reach the heights it has. That's why I made sure my picture is not on the front cover of the new edition. And that's why I'm dedicating this twentieth anniversary of *The Great Game of Business* to all the players out there, wherever you are. You truly have the *gotta wanna*. God bless.

—Jack Stack

DOES IT REALLY WORK OR IS IT
JUST A BUNCH OF HYPE?

Boy, I wish we had a dollar for every time someone has asked us that question. Then I wish we had five dollars for every answer we've given. Let's see—that would be a debit to "cash" and a credit to "other income." Overhead, labor absorption, and materials would be unaffected, so we have raw profit going straight to the bottom line. *Wonderful!!!* Our stock value would be enhanced and our jobs even more secure than they are now. See, you're already playing the Game and you've hardly begun the book.

Would it scare you if your employees thought like this? Would it scare you if *you* thought like this?

If you are skeptical about the Great Game of Business, welcome to the club. I myself was one of the biggest disbelievers in the beginning. There is a story later on in this book about an hourly worker, a young lady, whose introduction to the Game resulted in the elimination of her job as well as the demise of a product line. That young lady was me and I have been known to be less than quiet and mild-mannered when things don't go the way I want. If you think SRC didn't have their hands full teaching me the Game, think again!

Is it hype? As a converted disbeliever who has played the Game from hourly to the managerial ranks over the years, it is hype to the point to get you interested. After that, IT REALLY WORKS!

In fact, the Game touches everyone in a different way. There are many stories at SRC about what changed the disbelievers into believers, one by one. It would be difficult to find two people who were swayed by the same circumstances. And yet, overall, the Game serves to unite us as a corporation, sometimes against foes many times larger, allowing us to survive in this wild economy. At the same time, the Game gives us the means to challenge ourselves internally and create friendly competition between departments. Along the way, we even have fun, and there is laughter in the halls.

What does it take to play?

As we say at SRC—*"You gotta wanna!"*

Denise Bredfeldt, 1992
Former Director of Research and
transmission rebuilder, SRC

THE HIGHER LAWS OF BUSINESS

1. You Get What You Give.

2. It's Easy to Stop One Guy, But It's Pretty Hard to Stop 100.

3. What Goes Around Comes Around.

4. You Do What You Gotta Do.

5. You Gotta Wanna.

6. You Can Sometimes Fool the Fans, But You Can Never Fool the Players.

7. When You Raise the Bottom, the Top Rises.

8. When People Set Their Own Targets, They Usually Hit Them.

9. If Nobody Pays Attention, People Stop Caring.

10. Change Begins at the Top, or—as We Say in Missouri—Shit Rolls Downhill.

THE ULTIMATE HIGHER LAW

When you appeal to the

highest level of thinking,

you get the highest level

of performance.

chapter 1

WHY WE TEACH PEOPLE HOW TO MAKE MONEY

It's amazing what you can come up with when you have no money, zero outside resources, and 119 people all depending on *you* for their jobs, their homes, even their prospects of dinner for the foreseeable future.

That's pretty much the situation my twelve fellow managers and I faced in February 1983, our first month in business as an independent company. We were supervisors and managers at a little factory in Springfield, Missouri, that up until then had been owned by International Harvester. At the time Harvester was in big trouble, sinking faster than the *Titanic*, cutting loose operations like ours in a desperate attempt to stay afloat. When the company offered to sell us the factory, we jumped at the chance to save our jobs. It was like jumping into a leaky life raft in the middle of a hurricane. Our new company was loaded down with so much debt that the smallest wave could capsize us.

We were scared. We couldn't rely on traditional ways of managing because they wouldn't produce the kind of results we needed in time to save us. So we grabbed for something new, based on what we thought of as the higher laws of business.

///

THE FIRST HIGHER LAW IS:
You Get What You Give.

///

///

THE SECOND HIGHER LAW IS:
It's Easy to Stop One Guy, But It's Pretty Hard to Stop 100.

///

I don't know where I learned these laws. You don't hear about them in school. You pick them up on the street. But I know they are real laws of business, and they are the reason why we survived and have been successful ever since. It was out of these laws that we created the Great Game of Business. These two higher laws sum up our success; they emphasize how thoroughly dependent we are on one another—and how strong we are because of it.

I am often asked to say exactly what the Great Game of Business is. I have to admit I find this hard to do. It is not a system. It is not a methodology. It is not a philosophy, or an attitude, or a set of techniques. It is all those things and more. It is a whole different way of running a company and of thinking about how a company should be run. What lies at the heart of the Game is a very simple proposition:

> The best, most efficient, most profitable way to operate a business is to give everybody in the company a voice in saying how the company is run *and* a stake in the financial outcome, good or bad.

Guided by this proposition, we turn business into a game that everybody in the company can play. It's fun, but it's more: it's a way of tapping into the universal desire to win, of making that desire a powerful competitive force. Winning the Great Game of Business has the greatest reward: constant improvement of your life and your livelihood. You only get that reward, however, by playing together as a team, and by building a dynamic company.

Playing and winning the Game worked for us in a big way. From 1983 to 1986, our sales grew more than 30 percent per year, while we went from a loss of $60,488 in our first year to pretax earnings of $2.7 million (7 percent of sales) in our fourth year. We never laid off a single person, not even when we lost a contract representing 40 percent of our business for a whole year. By 1991, we had annual sales of more than $70 million, and our workforce had increased to about 650 people from the original 119. But the most impressive number was the value of our stock, worth 10 cents a share at the time of the buyout and by 1991 worth $18.30, an increase of 18,200 percent in nine years. As a result, hourly workers who had been with the Springfield Remanufacturing Corp. (SRC) from the beginning had holdings in the Employee Stock Ownership Plan (ESOP) worth as much as $35,000 per person. That was almost the price of a home in Springfield in 1991.

We didn't do this by riding some hot technology or glamorous industry. Remanufacturing is a tough, loud, dirty business. Our people work with plugs in their ears and leave the factory every day covered in grease. What SRC remanufactures are engines and engine components. We take worn-out engines from cars, bulldozers, eighteen-wheelers, and we rebuild them—saving the parts that are in good shape, fixing those that are damaged, and replacing the ones beyond repair. But in some ways engines are incidental to what we do. Our real business is education. We teach people about business. We give them the knowledge that allows them to go out and play the Game.

the basic rules of the game

People who run companies know that there are really only two critical factors in business. One is to make money and the other is to generate cash. As long as you do those two things, your company is going to be okay, even if you make mistakes along the way, as you inevitably will. I'm not saying safety is not a major issue, or quality is not a major issue, or delivery and customer service are not major issues. They are all major issues, but they are part of the process. They are not end results or even conditions of survival. In business, you can have great customer service and fail. You can have a terrific safety record and fail. You can have the best quality in your industry and fail.

THE ONLY WAY TO BE SECURE IS TO MAKE MONEY AND GENERATE CASH. EVERYTHING ELSE IS A MEANS TO THAT END.

Those simple rules apply to every business. And yet, at most companies, people are never told that the survival of the company depends on doing those two things. People are told what to do in an eight-hour workday, but no one ever shows them how they fit into a bigger picture. No one explains how one person's actions affects another's, how each department depends on the others, what impact they all have on the company as a whole. Most important, no one tells people how to make money and generate cash. Nine times out of ten, employees don't even know the difference between the two.

At SRC, we teach everybody those rules, and then we build on that simple knowledge and take people all the way to the complexity of ownership. We constantly strive to paint the Big Picture for the people out on the factory floor. We try to take ignorance out of the workplace and force people to get involved, not with threats and intimidation but with education. In the process, we are trying to close one of the biggest gaps in American business—the gap between workers and managers. We're developing a system that allows everyone to get together and work toward the same goals. To do that, you have to knock down the barriers that separate people, that keep people from coming together as a team.

THE BIGGEST BARRIER IS IGNORANCE,

which creates frustration. I really think the two are one and the same. In most companies, there are three levels of ignorance:

1. The ignorance of top management assumes that people down the ladder are incapable of understanding its problems and responsibilities.
2. The ignorance of the people on the shop floor usually means they have no idea why managers do what they do and chalk up every mistake in the company to a combination of greed and stupidity.
3. The ignorance of the middle managers means they are constantly torn between the demands of top management and those of the workforce. They really have the most difficult role in the company because they have to please two masters. If they side with their people, they're against top management. If they side with top management, they're in conflict with the workforce. Consequently, they can never please themselves.

What lies at the root of all this is a basic ignorance about business. Most people who work in companies don't understand business at all. They have all kinds of misconceptions. They think profit is a dirty word. They think the owners just slip it into their bank accounts at night. They have no idea that more than 40 percent of business profits goes to taxes. They've never heard of retained earnings. They can't conceive how a company might be earning a profit and yet have no cash to pay its bills, or how it might be generating cash and yet be operating at a loss.

That's the ignorance you have to eliminate if you want to get people working together as a team. But eliminating it is tough because most people find business incredibly boring. They don't want to hear about profits and cash flow. They really can't get too excited about making money for somebody else. Sure, they want a job they can count on, but beyond that they'd rather not get involved. Everything they've ever heard about business makes it seem complicated, confusing, hard to understand, abstract, maybe even a little seamy.

That's where the Game comes in. We tell people that they have the wrong idea about business, that it really *is* a game—no more complicated than baseball or golf or bowling. The main difference is that the stakes are higher. How you play softball may determine whether or not you get a trophy, but how you play the business game is going to have a big impact on whether or not you can support your family, put food on your table, fulfill your dreams. On the other hand, you don't need to be an entrepreneurial genius like Sam Walton to succeed in business. What you do need is a willingness to learn the rules, master the fundamentals, and play together as a team.

Everything we do at SRC is geared toward getting people involved in playing the Great Game of Business. We teach people the rules. We show them how to keep score and follow the action, and then we flood them with the information they need to do both. We also give them a big stake in the outcome—in the form of equity, profits, and opportunities to move ahead as far as they want to go. We do all this, moreover, by using tools of business that have been around for a hundred years or more. The most important of those tools are the financial statements.

IIII▶ the basic tools of the game

When people come to work at SRC, we tell them that 70 percent of the job is disassembly or whatever, and 30 percent of the job is learning. What they learn is how to make money, how to make a profit. We offer them sessions with the accounting staff, tutoring with supervisors and foremen, instructional sheets, and so on. We teach them about after-tax profits, retained earnings, equity, cash flow, everything. We want each of them to be able to read an Income Statement and a Balance Sheet. We say, "You make the decision whether you want to work here, but these are the ground rules we play by."

Then we provide a lot of reinforcement. Once a week, for example, supervisors hold meetings throughout the company to go over the updated financial statements. Each person writes the numbers down. Those numbers show how we're doing in relation to our annual goals, and whether or not there will be quarterly bonuses. The more people understand, the more they want to know. Competition and peer pressure, and the thrill of the chase send the numbers flying around. As people get caught up in the Game, they learn and they keep learning.

Suddenly, business makes sense to everybody. Capitalism makes sense. But to understand it, you have to look at the totality. You can't keep your attention focused on one job, or one department, or one function. That's what happens in most organizations: people develop a very narrow focus. The Game takes down walls. It forces people to realize that they're on the same team, and they win or lose together. And people really do love to win together. It's the best kind of success. It's much more fun than winning alone. You know that you're going to get rewarded, but so is everyone else. When you look at goals, like profit and cash flow, that makes people understand how they all depend on one another. It forces them to look at the business from the other guy's shoes and to have a broader perspective.

||||▶ ignorance can kill a company

What amazes me is that more companies don't do this. I worked at a giant International Harvester plant near Chicago for ten years. On Fridays I'd go to a staff meeting where the plant manager said, "We gotta make more money, we gotta be more profitable." But he never taught me *how* to make more money. We received plenty of orders—deliver a crankcase to such-and-such a line, cut down on accidents over there, get so-and-so's productivity up. I never knew anything about making money, and here I'd supervised hundreds and hundreds of people. Finally, it dawned on me that there was a better way, the way businesses have been run for a long, long time—with the financial statements. If people know how to use them, that's really the simplest way to run a business.

If people don't know, they won't understand, and they won't do the right things, and they'll blame you when the company fails. They'll say, "All this time you've been blowing smoke up our ass, telling us what a great job we've been doing. Now you come back and tell us the company is going to fail. We can't accept that. We really can't. Where did all the money go?"

▶ why we play the game

Reason #1 for Playing the Game: We Want to Live Up to Our End of the Employment Bargain.

I have always believed that you take on a big obligation when you hire somebody. That person needs to bring home money, put food on the table, take care of children. You can't take that obligation lightly. Of course, the individual has obligations to the company as well. Employment is a two-way street. But as much as possible I want it to be someone's choice whether or not he or she leaves the company. It really bothers me to see people laid off through no fault of their own. To prevent that from happening, we have a contract among ourselves. Everything we do is based on a common understanding that job security is paramount—that we are creating a place for people to work not just this year or five years from now, but for the next fifty years and beyond. We owe it to one another to keep the company alive.

That's really why we started playing the Game in the first place—we wanted some degree of job security for ourselves and the people with whom we work. One of the lessons we learned from the demise of International Harvester was that there is no security in ignorance. The only way to know if your job is safe is by looking at the financial statements. We had never dreamed that our jobs at Harvester might be in danger. This was a company that went back a hundred years, one of the thirty largest in the country, more than 100,000 employees. My dad had retired from it. I'd worked there for fourteen years. I just *assumed* my job was secure, and I had no way of knowing it wasn't, because no one ever taught me how to read a balance sheet. Then Harvester went down the tubes.

We had no such illusions, however, when we started SRC: we knew our jobs were in jeopardy from the start. To buy the plant, we'd had to come up with $9 million, of which we were able to scrape together a grand total of $100,000 from mothers, fathers, in-laws, uncles, and friends, not to mention our own personal savings. We borrowed the rest. This was like putting up $1,000 to buy a $90,000 house. You don't really own it—the bank does, and it will pull the plug the first time you miss a payment. In business terms, we had an 89 to 1 debt-to-equity ratio, which put us on a par with, say, the government of Poland. We were nearly comatose as a corporate entity. We couldn't afford to make a $10,000 mistake.

Looking at this situation, we realized there were two things we couldn't do. Number one, we couldn't run out of cash, because then our creditors would close us down. Number two, we couldn't destroy from within, which would be a danger if morale got bad. If either happened, we'd lose the company, and 119 jobs. Everybody had to know the company's financial pulse at every point. We had to tell people where the cash was and then make sure they were involved in deciding what to do with it. That's how the Game began.

We developed a system that, in effect, delegates the responsibility for job security by giving people a scorecard and a way to influence the score. The Game lets you see for yourself how safe your job really is and shows you what you can do to make it safer. It doesn't provide guarantees, but there aren't guarantees anymore. To tell the truth, there never were.

Reason #2 for Playing the Game: We Want to Do Away with Jobs.

How often have you heard this: "All we ask you is to do the job, nothing more." Well, I don't want people just to do a job. I want them to have a purpose in what the hell they're doing. I want them to be going somewhere. I want them to be excited about getting up in the morning, to look forward to what they're going to do that day. Maybe it's a matter of tricking people into wanting to come to work. I say "tricking" because I don't think it's a natural thing. Most people would rather be doing something other than work—I certainly would—but they feel they don't have any choice.

Companies reinforce that feeling. They not only tell people just to do the job, they set up the work so it is just a job. They say, "Drill as many of these holes as possible, as fast as possible, and don't think about anything else." That's one way to run a company. What you wind up with are workers who think a job is just a job. I call them the living dead.

I want to get rid of the living dead. I can't stand going into factories and businesses and seeing these faceless people standing around. They don't look healthy, and they don't act healthy, and they're a big problem for corporate America. I'm talking about the people who are there because it's a job, whose attitude is, "I have to be here, but I don't have to like it. I'll do it for my family, not for myself." What have we done to create those types of environments? We should be able to tell this person, "It's your obligation to be happy. Find somewhere to be happy. Don't sit around me and be miserable." Then we wonder why we have productivity problems. You can't have high productivity with faceless people. They're not happy with themselves, they're not happy with their jobs, and they bring you down.

On the other hand, you can't really blame them for feeling that way about their work when they're constantly being told to just do the job, nothing more. Why would anybody think a job was more than a job when that's all the company expects it to be? But if you set up the work to be a step on the path to something else, then it takes on a new meaning. It becomes more than just a job.

To do that, you have to get people to dream. You have to show them that there really are pots at the end of the rainbow, and you can get your pot if you want it and are willing to work for it. Business is a tool for achieving your highest dreams—your financial dreams, that is. Obviously there are some dreams business can't help with. It can't restore a person's health. It can't endow you with artistic talent. But it can help most people to achieve some success in life. It can give people hope. Once you understand the Game, you can take it as far as you want to. The only thing that holds a lot of people back, I think, is that they don't put the highway out in front of them. They limit themselves. We continually challenge people to tell us where they want to go, and what they want to do with their lives. When you do that, you open a lot of doors. You get rid of a lot of the frustrations people have. You also take their excuses away, which is essential.

To be sure, some jobs are bad, demeaning—the kind of job nobody wants to do. We had a job that involved cleaning certain parts with chemicals. There was a cleaning tank, and someone had to stand there all the time in a splash-proof raincoat and rainpants, even when it was 90 degrees outside. Nobody wanted the job, so we took a tip from the Japanese: we got rid of it. We said, "Let's robotize the jobs people don't want, let's computerize them, let's get them out of the market." But once you've done that, once you've gotten rid of the worst jobs, then what? There are still a lot of jobs in this world that involve putting washers on bolts. You can't walk away from it. The work is boring, but it has to be done.

The Game is an attempt to create an environment wherein everybody can take pleasure in their work, even the people who put washers on bolts. They can be doing something else at the same time. What we're trying to do

is to take people beyond the job, to give them the opportunity to use their intelligence and achieve something. In
effect, you steal a little bit of someone's brain while she's
applying the manual effort. You get in there, and you turn
on a light, and you create a stimulation. She may be putting washers on bolts, but at the same time she's thinking
about ways of making her environment better, her position
better, her life better. She's not just making a contribution
to an end product. She's making a contribution to her own
life. She's moving in a positive direction. She's going somewhere.

Reason #3 for Playing the Game: We Want to Get Rid of the Employee Mentality.

The big payoff to us for playing the Game is that we become a more educated, more flexible organization. We can
respond instantaneously to changes in the market. We can
turn on a dime for a customer if we have to. We can respond to problems in the length of time it takes to place a
phone call.

We can do all that because we have a company filled
with people who not only *are* owners, but who also *think*
and *act* like owners, not like employees. That's an important distinction. Getting people to think and act like owners goes far beyond giving them equity. Many companies
set up Employee Stock Ownership Plans expecting some
miraculous change of attitude in the workforce. Then
they're shocked to find that people still think and act like
employees: they insist on being told what to do, they won't
take initiative or responsibility, they make excuses and

blame other people for their own failures, they constantly pass the buck to someone else.

That's the antithesis of ownership. Owners, *real* owners, don't have to be told what to do—they can figure it out for themselves. They have all the knowledge, understanding, and information they need to make a decision, and they have the motivation and the will to act fast. Ownership is not a set of legal rights. It's a state of mind. You can't give people that state of mind in one fell swoop. You can only nurture it through a process of education.

And the process doesn't stop, because business is always changing—markets are changing, technology is changing, customers are changing, and the needs of the company are changing. So the demands of ownership are always changing. To keep up with those demands, you have to keep learning. The nice part is that, as you learn, you grow, you get more out of life, and you have fun.

The whole idea behind the Game is to create an environment in which people are learning all the time. They're seeing all kinds of situations. We're showing them both sides of every story, allowing them to make decisions, to fail with any incorrect decisions they make, and to learn from their failures and try again. The numbers are an important part of that. They serve as the bond, the basis of trust. By giving people the numbers, I can say to them, "If you don't believe me, look it up. See if what I'm saying isn't true. This is life we're dealing with. It may be frustrating, but so is life. There's nothing hidden here. It's all there in the numbers."

Reason #4 for Playing the Game: We Want to Create and Distribute Wealth.

One thing that scares me about our economy is the whole trend of downsizing. What's really going on is that companies are getting rid of people and replacing them with machines. They view people as a contingent liability. They're missing the fact that productivity depends on people. I don't disagree that machines can make you more competitive. They can absorb overhead. They don't take breaks. They don't go on vacation. They don't sit around wasting time. What machines can't do is figure out how to make money. Only people can do that. If you have people who know how to make money, you'll win every time.

But to get people to that point, you have to educate them. You have to teach them why it's important to make money and generate cash, and then you have to figure out a way to keep them focused on doing those two simple things. I think we're lying to people if we tell them there's any other way to improve productivity. That's important, because it's only by improving productivity that we improve standards of living. All the other ways of increasing output are inflationary. Sooner or later you have to pay the piper.

But if we can improve productivity, we can create a society that's continually getting better, a society in which people do more to help each other. As it is, we're becoming a society of haves and have-nots. What's happening is that the rich know how to play the Game, and they're playing it well. Meanwhile, the society as a whole has a declining standard of living, which will continue to decline unless we can figure out how to be more productive. So why can't we figure that out? Part of the problem is that we can't increase the standard of living without generating wealth, and we hate everybody who generates wealth—whether it's the oil companies, or the doctors, or the entrepreneurs. That's a big mistake. It isn't the *generation* of wealth that we should hate. What's wrong is the *distribution* of wealth. Our real problem is that we have not taught people how to share in that distribution.

To be frank, I don't think wealth is distributed fairly in this country or around the world. To me, it was inexcusable for Lee Iacocca to pay himself $4.5 million at the same time that he was laying off thousands of employees, and he was by no means the worst offender. On the other hand, I didn't think we could solve the problems by taking away Iacocca's millions. That's really just a drop in the bucket. The only way to solve these problems long term is to make people conscious of generating profits and understanding profits, where profits come from and where they go. Somebody's got to be out there teaching people about wealth— about retained earnings, about equity, about an earnings multiple and what it means and how it can affect them individually. If we don't do it, we will never increase the standard of living. We'll remain in this ignorant, dormant stage where we continually think a job is a job is a job. And the decline will continue.

NO EXCUSES

People always make excuses for the situations they get into. It's human nature. We blame the company. We blame other people. We blame external factors. We don't look at ourselves. If you want to be an effective manager, you have to take the excuses away. You have to create an environment where people can't blame anyone else for the situation they're in—where they see they make a real difference, where there's no gray area. It's very easy for people to think they don't make a difference. That's one of the biggest problems in business today. The bigger the company, the bigger the problem is. And then we compound the problem by not asking people to make a difference, by not insisting that they make a difference, by not creating environments in which they can make a difference.

But you have to begin by getting people away from focusing on the specific mechanical things they do, because there's more to business than that. Business is dealing with some of our most pressing social issues these days, like health care. This is the first time I can remember when people on the floor, even those at the job-entry level, are paying attention to fringe benefits. Health insurance has always been taken for granted. Now it has moved to center stage. It's an overhead item, a hidden cost, a cost people don't necessarily see. It's important for people to pay attention to the cost. But how do you take them from focusing on washers and bolts to focusing on health care if you haven't devised some system for explaining it to them, so that it all makes sense?

THE PAY-ME-NOW-I'LL-PERFORM-LATER MENTALITY

People want things. They want big bonuses. They want expensive fringe benefits. My position is, "Fine, you can have it, but can you fund it?" A lot of times they can't fund it, and they don't want to take the time to learn how. They want it first—they'll worry about paying for it later. That type of thinking destroys companies. "Pay me now, I'll perform later." It brings down company after company. You find that thinking in everybody from the CEO to the guy on the shop floor. You need to take the opposite approach: earn it first. In reality, nobody really minds paying for it once it has been earned.

The Game gives us a tool for showing people why it's important to earn the things they want, but we still find ourselves fighting against the pay-me-now-I'll-perform-later mentality. It can be a big problem in the workforce. My fear is waking up in the middle of the night, saying, "Okay, I gave you what you asked for. Now, therefore, I have to lay you off." If you give the benefit or the reward before it's earned, you're constantly in a catch-up game. If things go bad, you may be forced to balance off the benefit in some way, and the balancing is usually done with human hide.

The Game is one way to do that. We're teaching people how to take care of themselves. In the process, we're redistributing wealth—we're redistributing the earnings of the company back to the people who created them.

Myths of Management

You may wonder if it's possible to play the Great Game of Business anywhere—in a division of a giant conglomerate, say, or in a factory with a dominant union, or in a company that doesn't share equity with employees or have an intelligent bonus system. In fact, the Game started in a place exactly like that, in a very small department at the huge International Harvester plant in Melrose Park, Illinois. It was there that I learned most of what I know about managing, and everything I've tried to forget about leadership.

Melrose Park was one of the toughest plants in the country in the 1970s, when I worked there. We had racial incidents, death threats, burning effigies, bombings, shootings, aggravated assaults—you name it. Workers and managers were constantly at each other's throats. There were two or three walkouts a year—when things were going well, that is. In a bad month, there might be two or three work slowdowns as well. Every time we turned around, we heard another rumor that the factory was going to be shut down because of labor problems. Let me tell you, we had more than our share of losers. I know. I was one of them.

My father, who was a foreman at Melrose Park, had gotten me a job as a mailboy in the purchasing department. I was nineteen at the time. I'd already been kicked out of college and a Catholic seminary for disciplinary reasons. I'd lost a job at General Motors for playing poker on duty. I'd flunked my army physical because of an accident I'd had—someone had thrown me through a plateglass window. Having been rejected by the church, academia, the military, and G.M., I figured Melrose Park was my last chance.

For reasons I still don't understand and can't really explain, it turned out to be the ideal place for me. I wound up having ten jobs in ten years, by the end of which I'd had a pretty good education in management. People came up with a slogan for me: Have Shovel, Will Travel. Whenever there was a mess that had to be cleaned up, they would put me in the middle of it and let me dig my way out. The odd thing was that I often found I'd had a hand in creating the mess in the first place. I'd do something in one job, and I wouldn't even be aware of the effect it was having until I got my next assignment. Then I'd have to undo the problems I'd helped create.

But I did learn how to get things done. I did that mainly by ignoring most of the advice people gave me about how to be an effective manager. The practice of management, I discovered, is filled with myths that are guaranteed to screw up any factory or company as badly as Melrose Park was in those days. The real secret of an effective manager is to learn how to ignore them. You *have* to ignore them if you are going to get people to play the Great Game of Business.

Myth #1: Don't Tell People the Truth—They'll Screw You.

Being honest with people was unheard of at Melrose Park and at most other companies in the 1970s. The whole mentality was, Cover your ass. If your job was to get parts, you never told your suppliers how many parts you really needed, or when you really needed them, because they'd screw you every time, or so the experienced schedulers told me. They said, "Lie, kid, lie. If you've got enough parts to last you a couple weeks, tell 'em you'll be out of stock by Friday." It got to the point where nobody trusted anyone else's numbers, and for good reason. They were all lying to one another to cover their asses.

But I had an advantage: I didn't need to cover my ass. I didn't have a family. I didn't have any responsibilities. So when suppliers asked me what the situation really was in the factory, I told them the truth. I told them exactly how many parts we had in stock, and how long we could go before we'd start having problems on the assembly line. I discovered that the more honest I was with them, the more they relied on me. They had their own scheduling problems, and they were desperate for information they could count on. As a result, they protected me. I was their source, and they made sure they never let me down.

The same thing happened when I began dealing with people on the shop floor. There we had a situation where nobody believed the schedules they were given because, once again, everybody was covering their asses. Let's say the schedule called for the assembly line to make fifty Model X engines and fifty Model Y engines on a given day, but the people on the line didn't have enough parts to fill the quota for the Model Xs. Instead they'd do two days' production of Model Y. That way they kept the line up and running, which meant their asses were covered, but they totally discombobulated everybody else, who now didn't know what the line needed or when. So I went to the guys in assembly, and I said, "Look. From now on we are going to live by the schedule we put out, and we're going to schedule from the assembly line all the way back. If a part isn't here when it's needed, we're not going to make do with the parts we have. We're going to shut down the line."

Everybody was shocked. They said, "You can't do that. The assembly line is god. You can't shut it down." I said, "Oh, yeah? Just watch me." As it turned out, I only had to shut it down once. After that, people got in sync real fast. They decided that if I was willing to shut down the line to give them a schedule they could count on, they'd make sure they got parts there on time. As for me, I made sure they had everything they needed to meet the schedule. If one department got in trouble, we'd send other people in to help out. Sure enough, our production began to go up. When I started the job, we were doing about 100 engines a day. By the time I left a year later, we were up to 300 engines a day.

We established credibility, and you only build credibility by telling the truth. You simply can't operate unless people believe you and believe one another. That taught me an important lesson: lying and dishonesty are bad business.

Myth #2: Nice Guys Finish Last.

We've all heard how you have to be an S.O.B. to succeed in business. How you have to step on other people to get results. How it's okay to throw your weight around because it's a tough world and you win through intimidation. It's all a crock. I've worked on the shop floor. Believe me, nobody there wants to hear a guy telling you to bust your butt if he's rolling around in a Mercedes and beating up the people he works with. When you flaunt what you've got, when you intimidate, when you treat people badly, you lose power. I've watched guys like that throughout my life. I've learned it's just a matter of time before they get theirs.

THE THIRD HIGHER LAW IS:
What Goes Around Comes Around.

Whenever I see someone take advantage of other people, whenever I see a boss acting like an S.O.B., I know his days are numbered. People like that take themselves out of the game. They don't understand the game. They've no idea.

But there are enough jerks out there promoting this garbage to keep the myth alive. I think it's one of the reasons so many people hate management, which is a big problem because that keeps good people from becoming managers, and businesses need all the good managers they can get. Moving from a line job into management can be scary. One of your biggest fears is that people won't like you anymore. A lot of workers turn down management jobs because they're afraid of losing their friends. It can be a real identity crisis. They worry that, when you're a manager, you can only associate with other managers.

I had those concerns, too, when I first became a manager, but my reaction was to get angry at the guys who suddenly didn't want to sit around and bullshit with me anymore. The problem wasn't me. I hadn't changed. They were the ones who were different. Their attitude was, "You're the boss, and we can't sit with you anymore." Eventually I got fed up and called them on it. I said, "What is this? You mean, because I have a title, my underwear's different now?" I overcame the problem, and I forced them to overcome it, too. But it wasn't easy.

To tell the truth, it's seldom easy to make that transition from a line job into management. That's another myth: managers have it better than workers. There's a reason you get paid more when you become a manager. You're taking on more responsibility, and you're giving up some of your freedom. You're moving into a glass house. When you become somebody else's boss, everything you do gets scrutinized in a way it isn't when you're on the line. You have to set examples. You have to walk the talk. If you don't, you're going to fail as a manager. Being an

S.O.B. gets you nowhere. That's why I get angry at the loudmouths who talk about winning through intimidation. Not only are they dead wrong, but they are promoting one of the most destructive myths in American business.

Myth #3: A Manager's Job Is to Come Up with Answers.

It's very common for managers, especially new managers, to think they're supposed to have solutions for any problems that arise on their watch. That kind of thinking can get you into deep trouble. For one thing, it sets you up to fail because no one has all the answers. For another, it undermines your credibility because everyone *knows* that no one has all the answers. It also isolates you from people. A big pitfall of managers at all levels is the notion they have to be perfect. I know supervisors who can't hold a meeting because they're afraid someone might ask a question they can't answer. As I mentioned earlier, I know CEOs who can't leave their offices unless their ties are straight and every hair is in place. Managers like that wind up hating their jobs. They feel they have to live up to an image, to be an idol, to be a representative of a position.

At the same time, they're failing as managers, because they aren't doing what every good manager has to do: build confidence in other people. To do that, you have to show people you're human, you're not God, you don't have all the answers, you make a lot of mistakes. You send the wrong message if you try to be perfect, if you always want to solve the problems yourself. You're much better off sharing problems, using the people you work with to come up with solutions.

That's another lesson I learned at Melrose Park. At one point, I remember, the truckers went out on strike and shut down the highways. We couldn't get steel delivered from the U.S. Steel plant in Gary, Indiana, because snipers were shooting at the trucks. You need steel to build tractors. If we didn't get the steel, people would be sent home—they wouldn't get paid, they couldn't put food on the table. I was in charge of making sure we had the steel we needed, but I didn't have the faintest idea how to get it past the snipers.

So I brought five of my guys together, and I told them this one really had me in a bind. How were we going to transport two tons of steel from Indiana to Illinois without getting our heads blown off? Someone said, "School buses. They wouldn't shoot at school buses, would they?" Another guy said, "It depends who's driving the buses." Someone else said, "They wouldn't shoot at *nuns* driving school buses." That's exactly what we did: we rented a school bus and dressed guys up as nuns. They pulled into the steel mill, loaded the steel bars into the school bus, and drove the bus back to Melrose Park. We were always doing crazy stuff like that to keep the lines running. Nothing stopped us. We came up with the most outrageous things you ever heard of, and they usually worked. I didn't come up with the answers. We all did.

That's what I mean by sharing problems. It's a shared learning experience. It's a way of teaching each other. You all learn faster when you can teach each other.

In fact, I learned a tremendous amount from those experiences. Aside from sharing problems, they taught me about the importance of managing with the downside in mind, of having contingencies and trapdoors. Because failure is part of the process. You can't succeed if you don't fail sometimes. But if you're not prepared for failure, it's going to take you by surprise and knock you for a loop. So you have to manage with the understanding that things may not work out according to plan. You have to have your strategy backed up.

The secret is to make contingency planning a habit of mind. It was a habit I developed as I moved up the ladder and found the problems kept getting harder. I would teach people everything I knew, and it wouldn't be enough, so together we'd have to come up with one more trick. I learned I could respond better if I already had a fallback position, an idea about what to do if the unexpected happened. Maybe it was just a plan to call certain people together, people I could share the problem with. But at least I wouldn't be shocked. I wouldn't freeze. I could spring into action.

That was critical because the people in the factory were depending on us. When you have the responsibility to take care of other people, you do whatever it takes to get the job done.

///

THE FOURTH HIGHER LAW IS:
You Do What You Gotta Do.

///

You drop everything else. You stay night and day on that one thing. You figure out how to motivate, push, sneak, threaten, do whatever is necessary because people's livelihoods are at stake. Take the hill. You gotta take the hill.

You do that, not by coming up with the answers yourself, but by generating a level of creativity that allows the answers to come out. And there's nothing like a challenge to make people creative. What really turned us on was the thrill of doing something nobody thought we could do. We could see that most people gave up too early. They stopped before they got to the finish line. They did that throughout their lives, and that's why they got stuck in a rut. I began to realize that one thing a manager could do was to help them get out.

Myth #4: It's a Big Mistake to Promote People Too Quickly.

The common wisdom is that people should prove themselves before they get promoted. I always promoted people as fast as I could. Sometimes I promoted them right out of my department. I liked giving people opportunities, and I didn't want them to get bored and stale, but I had an ulterior motive as well: it made my job a lot easier to have friends all over the company.

Tunnel vision is a big problem in business. When people spend all their time in one function, they see every issue from a single perspective. They can't appreciate other departments' needs. Walls go up. Communication is terrible. That makes it harder to accomplish anything. I got around this obstacle by getting my people jobs in other departments. In effect, I instituted a program of cross-training for the people I worked with. They learned to see different aspects of the business, and I built up my own communications network. As a result, my department could function better. We had our own support system consisting of erstwhile colleagues who understood our point of view and could give us help when we needed it.

Because I was promoting people so fast, I wound up having a lot of positions to fill. What I didn't have was time to do in-depth interviews and evaluations. So I came up with my own method of hiring: I looked for people who had been captains of their intramural teams in college. To be a captain of your intramural team, you had to be picked by your peers. So I knew they were winners, and we needed people who could be winners right off the bat, because we were operating in a real losing situation.

Myth #5: Don't Worry About the Big Issues—Just Do Your Job.

Like most American companies, International Harvester operated on the principle that everybody should focus on doing the specific job he or she was assigned. The corollary was that you should only give people the information required to do their specific jobs; everything else should be treated as some kind of corporate secret. Somehow it had become common wisdom that this was a good way to run a business—in fact, the only right way to run a business. That is the biggest myth of all.

If you want to make things happen, you have to get people to *raise* their sights, not lower them. The broader the picture you give people, the fewer obstacles they see in their path. People need big goals. If they have big goals, they blow right by the little obstacles. But those obstacles will become mountains if you don't get people beyond the day-to-day issues, if you don't appeal to something they really want to do. That means letting them see the Big Picture. It means sharing all the facts with them. It means showing them the challenge, letting them experience the fun of the Game, the fun of winning. It means motivating people with humor and laughter and excitement, which go a heck of a lot further than yelling and screaming and throwing tantrums.

I learned all that in one of my first management experiences. I'd been put in charge of getting parts into the factory, and I began going to weekly management meetings, where I started hearing some of the company's secrets. At the time, we had a big contract to make tractors for the Russians. The secret was that we were in trouble on it. The Russians had negotiated a penalty clause whereby they could charge us for every day we went beyond the deadline of October 31. By October 1, we were still 800 tractors short of the goal, and nobody knew where we could get the parts needed to fill the order in time. The other managers said, "Keep it to yourself. This is real serious. Heads are going to roll. You just focus on getting us the parts. We'll take care of the tractors."

None of this made sense to me. For one thing, I didn't understand why we should focus on getting parts in the door when the real goal was to get tractors *out* the door. And I certainly couldn't see the point of keeping it all a secret. So I put up a big sign outside my office saying, OUR GOAL: 800 TRACTORS, and I told people the whole story. Everybody thought I was crazy. We were shipping 5 or 6 tractors a day, and there were only twenty working days until the deadline. At that rate, we were going to be short by about 700 tractors. To reach the goal, we had to average 40 tractors a day. We got out 7 tractors on the first day, 3 on the second, and people shook their heads. But when we looked closer at the problem, we began to see ways to improve the daily score. We discovered, for example, that some of the parts weren't making it to assembly—they came in and sat on the dock. That showed us it wasn't enough to get parts to the factory. We had to push them through the door and out onto the shop floor. We also figured out that a lot of tractors were just missing a few key parts. If we targeted those parts, we could dramatically increase shipments.

It was a case of taking a big problem and dividing it into a series of little problems, which is the best way to solve any problem. But at the same time we kept the Big Picture in front of everyone's eyes. And it worked.

Suddenly, our daily total jumped to 55 tractors, and people got turned on. They were amazing. This was a factory where you never went outside your department, where you needed a pass to go into someone else's area, but we had guys doing scheduling, production control, assembly, testing, shipping, the whole nine yards. They'd come into the factory after hours and crawl over the tractors, figuring out exactly what parts were needed and how many tractors were short those particular parts. Then we'd go out on the shop floor and talk to the supervisors and the hourly people. We'd get them to schedule their time as efficiently as possible and made sure we covered them.

The numbers kept going up. When we hit 300 tractors,

everybody took notice. We put up bar charts—showing exactly what parts we needed, where they were coming from, and how that was going to affect shipments. People could see the whole picture. They could see all the different pieces and how—if this fell in and that fell in—we just might pull it off. They began to *believe*, and let me tell you, there's nothing like it when people believe, when they think they really can do something everyone said was impossible. Individualism goes out the window. The team takes over. Nobody lets anybody down.

By the last week in October the pressure was intense. The executives would come down and watch what we were doing. With five days left, I put up a sign saying we'd shipped 662 tractors, and the place went wild. Would we make it? Would we just miss? By this point, everybody was involved. Assembly was going crazy. People couldn't wait to get the latest score. We worked right up to the deadline of October 31. On Halloween, the last sign went up outside my office window: 808 TRACTORS SHIPPED.

What a celebration we had! We put balloons all around the sign. We had a party. There were pizzas all around. Nobody could believe that we'd beaten the Russians out of their penalty clause. It was great, just great.

That experience taught me a big lesson. I saw these guys get hungry. I saw them push and accomplish things they never thought were possible. I saw satisfaction on a daily basis. I mean, they didn't know they were working! I thought, *My God, if I can get people pumped up, wanting to come to work every day, what an edge that is! That's what nobody else is doing. Suppose I could run the right numbers, so that a guy wakes up in the morning and says, "Man, I feel terrible, but I really want to go in there and see what happened."* That's the whole secret to increasing productivity.

And I learned something else as well. The experience absolutely convinced me that secrecy is baloney. I decided that, from then on, I was going to give my people everything I got. Eventually that grew into the whole idea of teaching people how to make money.

///

THE FIFTH HIGHER LAW IS:
You Gotta Wanna.

///

When you think about it, all these myths have one thing in common, what you might call the Big Lie. That is the notion that you can manage effectively by forcing people to do things they really don't want to do.

It is just not true. People only get beyond work when their motivation is coming from inside. That higher law—you gotta wanna—says it all. If people don't want to do something, it's not going to get done. Whatever goal you're talking about—owning your own company, being the best, building 800 tractors in a month. If you don't want it inside of you, it ain't gonna happen.

Management is all about instilling that desire to win. It's about instilling self-esteem and pride, that special glow you get when you know you're a winner. Nobody has to tell you. You just feel it. You know it.

chapter 3

THE FEELING OF A WINNER

How do you start the Great Game of Business? By creating a series of small wins—by showing people how it feels to be a winner. Believe me, that's one of the rarest feelings in business today. Even successful companies are filled with people who are depressed, scared, and dissatisfied. Such feelings are symptoms of a serious business disease, one that can quickly become life-threatening.

I am a great believer in judging a company by its financial statements, but you don't need a balance sheet to tell the difference between a healthy company and a sick one. In many cases, it's the difference between going to a ballpark and a funeral home. In a healthy company, you can see and feel the enthusiasm. People nod and smile and look you in the eye. There are often banners around, or balloons. Something is always being celebrated—a birth-day, an anniversary, a new record, whatever. The bulletin boards are fresh with the latest news. In a sick company, on the other hand, the bulletin boards are filled with an-nouncements required by law—OSHA directives, antidis-crimination regulations, and so on. People don't look at you. They aren't happy to see you. The premises are run-down. The stock is disorganized. No one is having fun. Everyone seems depressed. It's as if people are going to a funeral every day, and it may be their company's.

That's pretty much the situation I found when I came down from Chicago to take charge of the Springfield Renew Center, as it was called back in 1979. The previous plant manager had been overwhelmed by problems, and he'd let himself become remote and isolated. People were literally standing around on the shop floor because they lacked the parts and tools they needed to do the job, and nobody in corporate management seemed to care. The employees were so fed up that they were ready to bring in a union to light a fire under their bosses. The only real ques-tion was whether they'd go for the United Auto Workers or the Teamsters. If I'd told them I was there to get them involved in the Great Game of Business, they would prob-ably have run me out of town.

You can't just walk into any company or any factory and start teaching people how to read financial statements. I couldn't have done it then, and I wouldn't suggest that you do it now without first taking a good, hard look at your organization and the people who work there. There are at least two conditions that *have* to exist before people are ready to learn about business—about making money and generating cash, about using the numbers to follow the action and keep score:

1. **Management has to have credibility.**

    Without it, people won't listen to you, and they won't believe the numbers you give them. If you set up a bonus program or some other game, they'll think it's a gimmick, a trick, a scheme to get them to work harder for less money, so that you can get richer and they can get screwed. There must be a minimum level of mutual respect and trust. People have to feel that, whatever your faults, you have some sensitivity to them and their problems, you value their contributions, you'll offer them a fair shake. At the very least, they have to be willing to give you the benefit of the doubt.

2. **Employees have to have some fire in their eyes.**

    No company can play the Great Game of Business with people who feel like losers. Even if people believe the numbers, they won't respond to them if they don't care about what they're doing. To play a game—any game—you have to be in a game-playing frame of mind. You can't be demoralized and cynical. You must have enough self-esteem and pride to think winning is important, to want to have fun. I have always felt that having fun should be a job responsibility. Nobody can do a job well if he or she doesn't have fun doing it.

> Winning is a lot of fun, but people may not know
> how to be winners in their jobs. So you have to
> show them.

There are all kinds of techniques you can use to build credibility and light fires in people's eyes. Where you begin will depend entirely on your circumstances. When I came to Springfield, there was so little mutual trust and respect that I had to start at the most basic level—listening. In my first couple of months, I met with every single one of the hundred or so employees. I brought them into the conference room in little groups of three, four, or five at a time. I asked them what they wanted, what they felt, where they wanted to go, and what they wanted to do. We talked about life. We talked about dreams. We talked about winning. I asked them what tools they needed to do their jobs. People talked very freely, and they had harsh things to say about management. I asked them just to give us a chance.

Of course, most companies aren't in as bad shape as we were. Yours may not need the kind of intensive treatment we had to administer to the Renew Center before we could start teaching people the numbers. But there is no such thing as a management team with too much credibility or a workforce with too much enthusiasm. The truth is that we still use many of the techniques we developed back in those days, and we are still guided by many of the lessons we learned then.

||||▶ pride before ownership

For people to feel like winners, they must have pride in themselves and what they do. There is no winning without pride, just as there is no ownership without pride. Pride is all about caring. It is the sense of pleasure or satisfaction you take in what you do, or what you have. If you don't care, you're not going to do what is necessary to be a winner or an owner. So pride has to come first. The problem is that a lot of people don't know how to be proud of something. They were never taught to care as kids. So how are you going to get them to care about their work or their company? It requires a whole training program. But if people don't feel proud of the company they work for, they won't ever want to own it, and they won't ever feel responsible for it. Without that sense of ownership and responsibility, they won't play the Game.

In the first couple of years after I came to Springfield, I worked very hard to instill a sense of pride in the people who worked at the Renew Center. We used very simple techniques—an open house, for example. I had put one on at Melrose Park, and it was a huge success. We held it on a weekend, in the employee parking lots. We brought in tractors; people invited their moms, dads, and kids to come in and see where they worked. We created a lot of goodwill. It was a way of letting people feel important. I decided to do the same thing at the Renew Center. I wanted people to feel proud of their jobs. I wanted them to feel like giants. I wanted a kid to look up to his dad and say, "Wow, you really do this, Daddy? You're a welder? That's really important."

In preparation for the open house, we gave people buckets of paint and allowed them to decorate their machines and their work areas. Some of the guys got their wives, who were generally more artistic, to paint bold statements on the walls. We had American flags, Hell's Angel insignias, everything you can imagine. Some departments put up slogans, like "Machining—We Make It Work." There were signs and symbols everywhere, and none of it was color coordinated. It looked awful, but it was theirs. They were putting their own identities out there for everyone to see. When they brought their families in, they could say, "Here's where I work—this is my environment."

We also hoped the painting would encourage good housekeeping, which is important in a factory for reasons of both safety and efficiency. We figured that people would be more likely to keep the shop clean if it was theirs, if they put their mark on it. We also figured they'd want it to be clean for the open house. But what turned out to be the best thing for housekeeping were the tours we started having a few years later. When outsiders began coming in to tour the facility, people started taking extra care to keep their areas clean. They wanted to be proud of their work areas.

We used every technique we could think of to generate pride. We held fishing tournaments, baseball tournaments. A local radio station decided to raise money for charity by sponsoring a frozen carp–throwing contest. Contestants would be given frozen fish to throw as far as they could. So we entered, and sure enough someone from our plant won.

We never turned down a chance to compete. We took

part in relay races against other companies. We had some major event going on at least once a month. We wanted people to wear our colors all the time, and we changed them frequently. We were real big on hats, caps, and jackets; we created events in which people could win these things—housekeeping games, attendance games. We had attendance award dinners. If you had perfect attendance for a certain period of time, we would give you a plaque to take home, and we'd take you and your family out to dinner. I usually took them myself. Let me tell you, I ate out a lot for about two years. Then we had Christmas parties, and we gave out Christmas gifts. We always tried to surprise people. One year we'd give out turkeys, another year cheese balls. It was all part of getting people to feel great about the place they worked.

We still work hard at instilling a sense of pride and ownership, but now we rely more on things like our bonus program, the Employee Stock Ownership Plan (ESOP), the weekly staff meetings, and the games we play around the numbers. We got to the point where people were ready to learn financials, which allowed us to do much more than we could in the beginning. What changed were the methods, not the goals. You have to start very simply. You can't get much simpler than a paintbrush and a bucket of paint.

▏▎▍▶ creating a team

Winning is not just a matter of pride, of course. It is also a habit. Unfortunately, losing can get to be a habit as well. When people are in the habit of losing, you won't see fire in their eyes, only sand. If you want to light the fire, you have to begin by creating wins and celebrating wins—by making a big deal out of little victories and then building on the little victories to achieve bigger victories. It's a way of putting fun in the workplace—literally. We throw parties and hold celebrations at the drop of a hat. What we're really doing is creating a team.

That is, of course, one of the major purposes behind the Great Game of Business. In the early days, however, we couldn't set up games around the financial statements, because people didn't understand them and would have been intimidated by them. So we came up with other games, simple games, games we knew people could win. That way, we could begin to create the habit of winning. Every win would give us something to celebrate and allow us to start fires. Along the way, we learned some lessons about the kind of games and goals that work best:

1. BUSINESS IS A TEAM SPORT—CHOOSE GAMES THAT BUILD A TEAM.

You can set up all kinds of games in a company. Avoid the ones that are divisive. The best games are those that promote teamwork and togetherness, that create a spirit of cooperation.

Those aren't hard to find, especially in a company with a lot of problems. Any problem can serve as the basis for a game. In my first few months in Springfield, we started games around safety, housekeeping, shipping, you name it. I'd sit in a room with the other managers, and we'd say, "Okay, here's a problem. What kind of game can we set up around this one?" To deal with the shipping problem, for example, we bought a huge, gaudy trophy, which we called the "traveling trophy," and we announced it would be awarded each month to the department with the highest shipments. Later we added delivery as a criterion, because our delivery to customers was so bad. We began measuring housekeeping as well. We'd have inspections. We quantified the results by giving points, say, if the floor was swept clean, or by taking points away if there was stuff on top of the lockers. Then we'd give a plaque to the department with the most points at the end of the month.

At the same time as you're fostering team spirit, you can also be using the games to build credibility. One of the first issues I went after, for example, was safety. I chose it partly because I was really concerned. The plant had such a bad safety record that we had to do something fast. The safety issue also gave me an opportunity to send a strong message throughout the organization that we cared about people. Safety is basic. It's the first thing that can turn people against you. It can undermine everything else you try to do. We'd be sunk if people started thinking, "They say they care about us, but they're not concerned whether we get hurt or not." And if that were true, they'd be right.

So I took on each issue, and I made it very personal. I went into staff meetings, out on the shop floor, into the cafeteria. I talked to all three shifts. I looked at people, and I said, "We're going after safety because I want you to go home to your kids. I don't want anybody to have the responsibility of knocking on the door of your home and saying, 'I'm sorry, but your daddy's not coming home because he died at work.'" That really got through to people.

We organized a safety committee and set a goal of 100,000 hours without an accident. We put up four-foot-high scorekeeping thermometers all over the place, and we filled them in every two thousand hours we advanced closer to the goal. As the weeks went by, the drama began to build. On the afternoon when we hit the goal, we closed the plant down for a beer bust. We played the theme song from *Rocky* over the public address system while members of the safety committee marched around, handing out fire extinguishers. There was a parade of forklift trucks decorated in crepe paper. People stood around and cheered.

2. BE POSITIVE, BUILD CONFIDENCE.

Managers have a bad habit of focusing on the negative. I've seen statistics showing how managers tend to react quickly to anything that goes wrong and overlook everything that goes right. Let's say you have a hundred people, and one guy is constantly complaining. It's easy to start thinking morale is bad because of that one guy. He gets you down, and he may lead you to institute policies or make changes that put the other ninety-nine at risk. You may highlight problems that aren't there. And you may forget to praise the ninety-nine. You may miss a big opportunity to inspire people, to get results that you wouldn't have dreamed possible.

This is a serious weakness. One of a manager's main responsibilities is to build confidence in an organization. To do that, *you have to accentuate the positive. If you accentuate the negative, it eats away at the organization. It becomes a demotivator, and management is all about getting people motivated.* A manager who doesn't motivate isn't doing his or her job. You can't motivate if you're continually focusing on the negative.

So it's important to be positive in the way you set up your games. Take the problem we had with shipping. We were way behind schedule, but we didn't focus on that—we focused on what we needed to ship. We began by breaking the problem into its elements. We put on the board what we did last year, and how we were doing this year, and we decided what records we needed to achieve. Then we said, "Okay, here's what we did last year, and here's a new record we set last month. Now let's go out and beat it." We didn't want people thinking about the weight of the stone or the slope of the hill, but about what it was going to feel like when we won.

We made some mistakes. For example, we decided to give out a scarecrow to the department with the lowest housekeeping score. We got an old broom, put some eyes on it, made it as ugly as we could. Then we started handing it out. It didn't work. People quickly lost interest in the game. They got mad, and that defeated the purpose. When you make people mad, they don't want to compete, and they quit. Our mistake was we got away from accentuating the positive. So we dropped the scarecrow and just handed out the plaques.

3. CELEBRATE EVERY WIN.

Records are important, no matter how insignificant they may seem, because you can celebrate whenever you break one. Every record represents an opportunity for management to compliment people, to make them feel good, and to build confidence and self-esteem. People may be feeling depressed, bored, or whatever. If you don't celebrate, you've missed the chance to cheer them up.

You can also use records to change the mind-set of an organization, to get people to take responsibility for themselves. Workers often try to delegate problems up to their managers, especially when the managers are new. It's human nature. They will dump any problem on you if they think you'll accept it. And you do accept it for a period of time if you're still learning. You're going through your basic training. But eventually you have to figure out how to get the situation under control, and the best way is to get people into the game. Maybe they have a good day and set a production record. That's an opportunity. Seize on the record, make a big deal out of it, celebrate it. What you're doing is creating and celebrating wins. Celebrate every win, even the small ones. If you celebrate a small win, people will follow it up with another one, and another, and another. After a while, they don't even know they're doing it. They're taking care of themselves. They're solving their own problems. They aren't passing them up to you. They're having fun. *Then the manager's job becomes making sure the fun goes on.*

Once the games get going, people stop pushing their problems up to management. If you're caught up in a game, there's no time to push problems up. You want to go out and solve the problems by yourself. Otherwise, you'll get behind, and you won't win. So the games get people to focus on solving the present problems, which leaves the managers free to think about the future problems—and that's how a manager stays in control. If you focus on future problems, you eliminate surprises. You deliver consistency. You have a very happy work environment.

4. IT'S GOT TO BE A GAME.

You can go too far in trying to light the fire in people's eyes. If you do, you'll find that people stop having fun and start getting scared. Then you have to pull back fast.

That happened to me at one point. I decided that each of the managers should have a list of ten accountabilities he'd be expected to meet in the course of the year. They were really specific. I got them down to a gnat's ass. I made them so specific that they overlapped and conflicted. People had to step on one another's toes to win. It might have worked out if each manager had done 80 percent of what I asked for. But I had two guys who strived to be the best in every category, and so they walked straight into each other's territory. They almost killed each other.

The mistake I'd made was to think people would look at these accountabilities as guidelines, as opportunities to help the company and help themselves at the same time. That was naïve. In fact, individual evaluations inspire fear in a lot of people. They see an implicit threat in a list of individual performance criteria. The message is: if I don't do these things as well as I can, I'm not doing my job. They look at the accountabilities as a line in the sand. They say, "Okay, this is the line. Management is telling me what I have to do if I want to keep my job." That's pretty scary stuff. I'd just as soon keep that line as invisible as possible.

So these two guys got into a confrontation. One of them walked up to the other and said, "Hey, you may be meeting your goal, but I ain't making mine. If I screw up, I could be out the door. My family could be in jeopardy. I could lose my job." I heard them arguing. I could see that they took the accountabilities not as ideals to strive for but as minimum standards of performance. I realized my mistake. I took the accountability sheets, went out in the backyard, put them in a metal wastepaper basket, and set them on fire.

The point is that it's got to be a game. *I hadn't realized the fear I was building into the system. When you think about it, the fear came out of being alone. Security comes from being with other people.* There's a lot to be said for knowing that everybody's in the same boat with you, that you aren't an island, that you don't have to do it all on your own.

I learned two other important lessons from that experience:

5. GIVE EVERYONE THE SAME SET OF GOALS.

Don't send people mixed messages. Let them all have the same objectives, and make sure they have to work together to achieve them. Turn success into a group effort. That way, they can win together.

6. DON'T USE GOALS TO TELL PEOPLE EVERYTHING YOU WANT THEM TO DO.

Too many goals are useless. You should only have two or, at most, three goals over the course of a year. What's important is to make sure each goal encompasses five or six things. In other words, choose a goal that people can only meet if they do five or six things right. It goes back to the lesson I learned at Melrose Park when we had the deadline on the Russian tractors: you don't have to tell people to get the parts in on time if you can get them to concentrate on getting the tractors out.

As we'll see later, it's a lot easier to come up with those all-encompassing goals when people understand the numbers, and you can give them financial targets to shoot for. But, in any situation, there are usually one or two issues that affect a whole series of problems facing the company, the plant, or the organization. If you can identify those issues, you can use them as levers to affect several things at once.

Bad housekeeping, for example, is frequently a sign of trouble in factories, just as it is in office buildings or homes. Whenever I see too much stock on the shop floor, I know there are production problems. Excess stock creates uncertainty—people never know what to work on next. It also hurts morale by making the work environment messy, cluttered, cramped. But, by the same token, you can use the stock problem as a lever to turn things around. Figure out how much work you have to do each day to get to the point where you have just one day's stock out on the floor. Then put up a chart and set up a game. That takes care of morale, motivation, work space, housekeeping, everything. At the same time, you take the indecisiveness out of the shop floor. People will work on what's there. They won't allow problems to accumulate. They'll know how to schedule their labor. As a result, there will be a continuous flow to the production line because now there's a limited amount of stock—they have to make every piece count. Volume will pick up.

⟫ feeding the desire to play the game and win

Much of what we did back in the early years we still do today. We haven't had an open house in a while, but we have picnics all the time. We also set aside special days when people bring their kids into the factory. We do it for the same reason we held an open house back then: to build pride and self-esteem. We have more games going outside the company than ever. There are the bass fishing tournaments, the Corporate Cup relays, the golf league, the softball team, the bowling competitions. It amazes me to see all the events our people participate in under the SRC banner.

I know some companies don't allow athletic programs under company auspices. They're afraid of lawsuits if people get injured, or if there isn't the right racial mix, or whatever. It's such a waste. Those companies are missing a tremendous opportunity—an opportunity to instill pride. The problems can be handled. If you're worried about the liabilities, ask people to sign waivers. If you want a broad cross section of your workforce to participate, make sure everybody feels welcome.

By sponsoring outside competitions, you keep feeding the desire to play the game and win. At the same time, you provide a way for people to take out their anger and frustration in a nonthreatening environment, and you give them opportunities to win that they may not have in their jobs. We have a quality inspector who could be the most unpopular guy in the company—except that he's also the best bass fisherman. People respect him because he has the ability to catch fish.

We definitely encourage the managers to take part in these competitions. It's another way of knocking down walls. No matter how hard you try to be open, people are intimidated by the title, the door, the desk—all the symbols of power. Those are barriers you have to break down, and these outside competitions offer a way to do it.

One year, I lost the company's bass fishing tournament because I forgot to set my watch forward when the time changed in the spring. As a result, my partner and I came in an hour after the event had ended. If we'd been on time, we would have won that day's tournament, and I would have been the top fisherman for the year, which is a big deal around here. You get bragging rights all winter long. So you can imagine how stupid I felt coming in late. My partner was furious, because timekeeping was my responsibility. My mistake cost him about $500, which represented more than a week's pay to him. But I have to say, the experience created a real bond between us, and other people in the company just loved it. They sent me watches, made wisecracks, the whole bit. It was good for them, because they could laugh at me. It was good for the company, because it broke down some barriers. It was even good for me, much as I would have liked to win that fishing trophy. You make a bonehead move like that, and you can never get a swelled head. It's a good reminder that the company's success is not a result of your brilliance.

KEEPING WORK IN ITS PLACE

I really don't want people to work more than forty hours a week. That's enough. People should have balance in their lives. If they do, they'll be happier. Working all the time doesn't help the business, not over the long term. I've seen workaholics who've destroyed people. They become obsessed. They send out terrible messages. They make people feel guilty if they don't show up on Saturday. What a stupid message. People should be giving that time to their families. They should be watching their kids play soccer. If you make them come in to the office or the plant, you're creating a situation where they hate work. I don't want people to hate work. I don't mind people putting in some overtime to make some extra money, or to make sure they have their responsibilities covered. But don't do it at the expense of having a balanced life. I'm not denying that some people can get a tremendous amount done by working all the time. I just think there's a better way. When you're lying on your deathbed, you never look back and wish you'd spent more time at the office.

THE CHEAPEST BENEFIT AROUND

Sponsorship of outside competitions may be the best bargain in business today. For example, it costs us about $500 to sponsor a softball team consisting of twenty people from the company. They get together, outside the business, at least three hours per week for twenty weeks. That works out to about 42 cents per person per hour.

Or consider our golf league, which is open to workers, managers, members of employees' families, customers, and suppliers. Altogether there are about fifty participants, who spend at least four hours per week together for about twelve weeks. People pay their own course fees. The company pays $200 for the gift certificate that serves as the prize. That comes out to about 8 cents per person per hour.

In return, we get people talking about the business after hours. We get advertising and publicity. We get a spirit of camaraderie. We get barriers broken down between managers and workers, between people in different departments, between the company and families. We get an easing of the tensions and frustrations that build up on the job. We get better relationships with business associates.

Most important, we get pride, self-esteem, and a winning attitude, for less than 50 cents per person per hour.

chapter 4

THE BIG PICTURE

Nowadays we start teaching people the Game as soon as they come to work at SRC. We plunge right into the financial statements. Once people understand the numbers, once they see how the Game works, once they get it, business makes all the sense in the world. It puts everything they do in perspective. It makes them understand why they're here. It shows them what their contribution is and why it matters.

But you may want to start a little more gradually, as we did in the early years. It's a lot easier to teach people about making money and generating cash if they know what the company does and how they affect its performance. Paint the Big Picture for them. Tell them why you're in business using terms they already understand. Then the numbers will make sense when you get to them. You'll be able to demonstrate how they can serve as tools to stay connected to the Big Picture on a daily basis, to keep everybody focused on common goals. And that, after all, is the main reason the numbers are important: they constantly lead you back to the Big Picture.

Most of the problems we have in business today are a direct result of our failure to show people how they fit into the Big Picture. That failure undermines company after company. We put a guy in front of a radial drill and tell him to focus all his attention on drilling a hole as accurately as possible. So he does it. He drills the hole and he watches the forging go to the next station, and he sees something fit perfectly into the hole he's just drilled. Then we come back and tell him the company is in trouble because there's something wrong with the way he's using his time. He can't understand. What could be wrong? His job was to drill the hole, and he did it perfectly. So if something is wrong, it has to be someone else's fault. The problem is that we've never trained people to look beyond their machine tools (or their computers, or their telephones, or their dollies, or their trucks, or whatever they use in their jobs). So they can't understand how the holes could be perfect, and the company could be failing.

KEY POINT: The Big Picture is all about motivation. It's giving people the reason for doing the job, the purpose of working. If you're going to play a game, you have to understand what it means to win. When you show people the Big Picture, you define winning.

So these are the steps so far:

1. Create a series of small wins.
2. Give people a sense of the Big Picture.
3. Teach the numbers.

That's the rough sequence, at any rate. The truth is that we are always looking for more wins of any size, and we never stop reminding people about the Big Picture. You shouldn't either. Here are some ways to go about it.

* Give Everyone a Course in Your Business.
Sometimes you have to make a dramatic statement to get people to step back, see how everything fits together, and think about the broader purpose of what they're doing.

I thought we'd reached that point toward the end of my second year at the Springfield Renew Center. We'd turned the place around and were making money, but there were still a lot of walls between departments. I had been hearing a lot of petty complaints—the engineers were paid too much, the inventory people weren't doing any good. There were misconceptions about the organization, and how the different parts supported each other, and what we needed to do to be successful. I wanted to break through the pettiness and tell people, "C'mon. Let's wise up. These are investments that we're making for your future."

So, one day in October 1980, we shut the plant down and had everybody show up instead at the Hilton Inn across town, where they participated in what we called Employee Awareness Day. It began with workshops run by the different department heads. People divided up into small groups that went from room to room. They learned what each department did, and how it fit in with what the other departments were doing. The head of engineering explained how his department made it possible for us to take on new products and keep up with technology. The materials department put on a skit dramatizing what would happen if inventory got out of control.

At the end of the day, we all gathered in a big room for dinner, after which I got up to introduce the feature presentation, an NBC White Paper called "If Japan Can, Why Can't We?" I had seen it on television, and it really got to me. It was all about the Japanese challenge and America's lackluster response. It showed how U.S. productivity was declining, and the long-term consequences for our way of life. At the end, the announcer said, "If this trend isn't reversed, the next generation of Americans will be the first with a lower standard of living than their parents."

When the lights came on again, I stood up and said, "Do you want this responsibility? Do you want to be the ones who started this decline? We've got to do something about it, don't we?" I'd never seen anything like the response I got. People were cheering, crying, yelling, and hugging each other.

I knew then that they saw the Big Picture.

* Market Your Products to Your Employees.

Just because you spend a lot of time, effort, and money telling customers about your products, don't assume your employees understand those products. The chances are that most of them know about only one small part of the process. They can't possibly see the Big Picture if they don't understand what your company does—what products or services it delivers to customers, how it helps customers solve *their* problems and take care of *their* needs. The answer is to spend some of your marketing budget on your own employees.

That's a lesson I learned when I was put in charge of the assembly line at Melrose Park. Believe me, this assembly line had a lot of problems. Quality was awful. Scheduling was awful. Productivity was awful. And life on the floor was a total nightmare. The lines struck whenever they felt like it. Guys would come in with hangovers. The jobs were boring. Somehow I had to figure out a way to motivate these people.

Part of the problem, I realized, was that the work was meaningless to them. These guys had no idea that they were building the trucks that went out on America's highways and moved goods around. They had no idea that they were doing something important. The company was spending millions of dollars on ads, posters, brochures, and other material designed to get customers to believe in our products, but we weren't using any of it to generate pride in our own people. So we went to the sales and marketing people and asked them to help us out.

We brought in beautiful posters of the trucks and the tractors. We really put on a big campaign to make the guys on the assembly line understand and believe in the products they were making. And it worked. I'll never forget the day a guy came to me and said he'd been driving down

Mannheim Boulevard with his kid in the car and a big Harvester truck pulled up alongside them. He said, "I told my kid, 'Your daddy built the engine in that truck.'" And he *did* build it.

That marketing campaign helped us to turn the entire operation around. It got people thinking like members of a team, which is crucial on an assembly line. Each station has to coordinate with the other stations, or the line won't move. After we ran the marketing campaign, people began to look at the overall process. They got religion—big time.

The lesson was: market to the people who are producing the goods. In fact, you should sell your people *before* you try to sell the customer. It doesn't do any good to go out there and sell an empty product. You want to sell a product that has life in it—that has people in it.

* Move People Around.

People Express Airlines used to have a practice it called "cross-utilization," whereby employees would get experience in different parts of the business. The flight attendants would spend time handling baggage, for example, and the accountants would work in customer service. It was, in fact, an effective technique for getting people to look beyond their specialties and get a direct, firsthand sense of the Big Picture.

We do something similar, although we haven't given it a name. We encourage people to move around the company as much as possible. Many of our marketing people, for example, came off the shop floor. It goes back to a lesson I learned at Melrose Park, when I kept promoting people as fast as I could. I found out that people who had worked in two or more jobs had a whole different attitude about business. Cooperation was great. They were much better at seeing the other guy's perspective. They understood how different functions fit together, how they depended on each other.

Even if people don't actually move from one job to another, you can broaden their perspective by taking them out of their usual roles and putting them in direct contact with another part of the business. That's one reason we send hourly people out to deal with customers. I remember the first time we did it. We had built a huge transmission for a big contractor in Denver, a gold-mining operation. The transmission alone was seven feet tall and cost about $150,000. When it went down, the whole operation stopped, and the contractor was losing $5,000 an hour.

So we sent out the two guys who had built the transmission. They were really the only ones who could handle the situation. They took an awful lot of abuse from the customer, who was understandably pretty upset. The real payoff for us came when these guys got back. They told everybody what it was like talking to that customer. Suddenly everyone realized that there were real people at the end of this remanufacturing process, that businesses out there depended on the quality we produced. They saw that they had responsibilities not only to themselves and their company, but to the customer as well.

In a way, the experience put people in my shoes. We all feel bad when we let someone down, when we disappoint someone. But, in most companies, the only people who hear about it are the customer service reps or the executives, not the people who actually did the job. Now we send hourly people out to deal with customers whenever we can.

* **Draw a Picture.**

Don't just tell people about the Big Picture, show it to them. Put it in the form of charts and graphs. Use them to decorate the walls. Anything that can be measured can be turned into a picture—net profits, retail sales, sales per customer, output per week or per day or per minute, energy use, scrap, you name it. And those pictures can be very dramatic. At one point, we had a graph in the cafeteria that went right off the paper, all the way up to the ceiling. It was about overhead costs, and it sure got people's attention.

But the most effective pictures we have aren't charts at all. They are the stock certificates we distribute every year, as a way of giving people physical evidence of their equity in the company and how they have increased their holdings in the past twelve months. The certificates look real enough, although they have no intrinsic value: normally, an Employee Stock Ownership Plan doesn't issue stock certificates, just an annual statement. We do this strictly because we want people to see the Big Picture. It's a way of reminding people how we measure success. We're saying, "In this company, you get equity. When you play the Great Game of Business, that's the measurement of success."

* **Get Incentives from the Six-Year-Olds.**

A company is just a means to an end, and the end lies outside the four walls of the business. So the real Big Picture, the one that matters most to people, reaches beyond their paycheck out into the community. We put a lot of emphasis on community programs—Adopt-a-School, the Christmas drive for homeless children, the United Way, the Special Olympics, the Red Cross. We have a hard time saying no to anybody. For us, it's all part of the Big Picture.

Partly, it's a matter of giving back. We're grateful for all we've received—now we want to help other people. But we also benefit a lot as a business by having people involved in these activities. It has a profound effect on a person to visit a center for autistic children or to distribute Christmas presents to homeless children. It puts everything else they do in perspective, because they go as representatives of SRC. They feel good about themselves and good about the company. Often they wind up talking to other people about our policies and our philosophy of business. It's a big inducement to practice what we preach. They come back revitalized and pumped up.

Of course, a lot of companies do community outreach, but usually the CEO and the top executives are the only ones involved. We want everyone involved in our community activities. For example, we are active in the Adopt-a-School program. We take students at risk of dropping out, and we try to keep them in school. Our frontline supervisors go in and talk about how they got to be managers. They benefit so much by doing that. Maybe the supervisors have problems in communicating. So they go into a classroom where they can talk to kids and break down the power game and show how power can be constructive, not destructive. Or a kid from the school will come into the plant and hang out for a day with one of our hourly people, a guy who has become his or her mentor.

We got into the program when the Springfield Public School District approached us about taking on a local school for kids in trouble, kids who probably wouldn't graduate—because of pregnancy, drugs, alcohol, grades, whatever. They are put in a smaller school where they can get more attention, feel part of a team. SRC has a reputation for taking on really tough jobs. We like that. We're remanufacturers. We used to be at the bottom of the hill, too. We can identify with these kids. They're a new cause, a new challenge. We do anything the school asks of us. Money. Time. A new award program. We do interviews. We hire the kids. We try to keep them in school. We give them as much individual attention as we can. Sure, that may mean people have to spend some time away from their jobs, but they know how to cover their responsibilities, and what we get back as a company far exceeds what we give up.

And we can really help. I think the educational system needs the help of business. Every problem the schools are having we can analyze on a day-to-day basis. Businesses have an obligation to be involved, and we shouldn't be shut out.

The level of participation we get in all these programs is tremendous. Take the United Way. In Springfield alone, we get 300 people contributing something like $40,000. That's one of the highest levels in the city. Why? Because people see themselves as part of the team. They want to make SRC look good. It's all part of the winning image. They want to be the best.

And it all comes back to us when we do good things. People feel good about themselves and about SRC. They're coming to work at SRC for the right reasons—to be part of something, to be part of a winning team. There are many aspects to winning. Helping the United Way is one aspect. So is being a good parent. It's also how you treat members of the opposite sex, people from other religions and races. It's treating each other right, and having the courage to say you're wrong when you are wrong. That's all part of business, and it's all part of the Big Picture.

||||▶ go beyond quality

Educating people about the Big Picture runs counter to a lot of ideas that became popular in the 1970s and '80s—notably the quality movement. Back then I found that people who were into quality didn't care about anything else. One of my closest colleagues at SRC thought it was a big waste of time to teach people about the different parts of the business. "Why should a manufacturing guy like me care what the marketing people are doing?" he'd say. "All I care is that they do their job right. If I do my job right, and marketing does its job right, and all the other people do their jobs right, we'll have a successful business. I don't have to know how the marketers go about promoting sales. What matters is quality. You get quality by making sure people pay attention to details, not by telling them how the company works."

The argument sounds logical enough, but it's wrong. I knew from experience it was wrong. I had seen companies run that way, and they usually had terrible quality, not to mention a host of other problems. When people focus on their narrow specialties, the different departments go to war. They don't function as the parts of one company. They act more like competing factions. It becomes very hard to make money or do anything else very well. Quality isn't better. It's worse.

Besides, I couldn't see what was so great about specializing. I myself always preferred to look beyond the job I'd been given. Maybe it was boredom with the assignment. Maybe it was frustration with the constraints of the system. Maybe it was just curiosity. In any case, the more I learned, the more fascinated I was, and I found that other people were fascinated with the same things. I could use the Big Picture as a motivator—as a way to help people get more enjoyment out of their work.

I also found that the Big Picture made us more flexible as a company. The Japanese tend to focus on the details, on doing a specific job right. I want our players to be more versatile. I want the tight end to be capable of playing quarterback. I want to give people all the plays, not just the ones for their respective positions. That way, we can adapt more quickly when circumstances change.

Meanwhile, look what has happened to the quality movement. Ten years ago, quality was about manufacturing the product without defects. Now we talk about "total quality management"—quality of information, quality of support, quality of customer service. It's not enough to have the product with the fewest defects or lowest warranty rate. You also have to deliver it. People say now you really can't measure the cost of quality. The reason is that you need more than quality to be successful—you need delivery, safety, housekeeping, the whole bit. If you want to measure, you should focus on the area in which all these things have to come together: the income statement and the balance sheet.

By the way, my quality-control colleague is now the vice president of SRC and one of the most devoted practitioners of the Great Game of Business I know. He has turned 180 degrees around. But I still get some resistance from people who are caught up in the buzzwords of quality control. They hear me talk about the Game and ask, "Where's the continuous improvement? Where's the process improvement? Don't you use processes in your factory?" My response is to show them a chart of our market value per share for the last five years. I say, "Is that enough continuous improvement for you?"

> My own goal is to generate wealth for the people I work with, to distribute it in a way that makes the world a better place. It's one thing to want the world to be better; it's another to come up with the resources that let you do it. What I'm trying to do here is raise people's standard of living by showing them how to create wealth and keep it. That's my Big Picture.

▐▐▶ the danger of mixed messages

When you don't teach people the Big Picture, you run a constant risk of sending people mixed messages. I know one Fortune 500 company president who sent out word he wanted to improve customer service, so people began building up inventories at the product distribution centers. What he didn't tell them was that he was being evaluated according to return on assets—that is, net income as a percentage of total assets. As the inventories grew, so did the company's total assets, and the further the president was from earning his bonus. In the last quarter of the year, he suddenly ordered his people to stop all deliveries so that he could meet his goal. It was a disaster. Fourteen hundred suppliers were shut off without any warning. Literally hundreds of thousands of jobs were put on the line. That happened because the president sent the wrong message. He said he wanted better customer service when he really wanted a better return on assets. He didn't tell people the Big Picture, and everybody was screwed and demoralized.

Companies also send mixed messages by having a commissioned sales force, although in that case the message to the salespeople is clear: the more sales, the better. The trouble is, more sales may not be good for the company. Commissioned salespeople can cause chaos. While they're out selling everything they can, the producers can't keep up. So what happens? Eventually, the company goes out of business, leaving everyone out of work. Or it takes away the commissions, thereby demotivating the sales force. Or it fires the experienced salespeople and replaces them with younger, cheaper talent. It has to do something, because the salespeople are making too much money, and the company isn't profitable.

Compensation systems are the primary way that companies send mixed messages. But they may also do it with their performance evaluations, particularly if they use

Management by Objective. People can get very confused. They develop tunnel vision. They don't see the effects of their actions. Say you tell a person she's being evaluated on inventory turnover, and she drives the inventory down to nothing. So what happens? Your inventory carrying costs are very low, but the production people can't operate their machines efficiently, so manufacturing costs go through the roof. That's why you need to get everyone to focus on the Big Picture.

chapter 5

OPEN-BOOK MANAGEMENT

The more people know about a company, the better that company will perform. This is an iron-clad rule. You will *always* be more successful in business by sharing information with the people you work with than by keeping them in the dark. Let your people know whatever you know about the company, the division, the department, the particular task at hand. Information should not be a power tool—it should be a means of education. Don't use information to intimidate, control, or manipulate people. Use it to teach people how to work together to achieve common goals and thereby gain control over their lives. When you share the numbers and bring them alive, you turn them into tools people can use to help themselves as they go about their business every day. That's the key to open-book management.

It has also been the key to SRC's success. We would never have made so much money, or generated so much wealth, if we hadn't been open with our information, ideas, and numbers. To tell the truth, I doubt we would even have survived. And when I say open, I mean open. A business should be run like an aquarium, where *everybody* can see what's going on—what's going in, what's moving around, what's coming out. That's the only way to make sure people understand what you're doing, and why, and have some input into deciding where you are going. Then, when the unexpected happens, they know how to react and react quickly.

You don't have to be in a situation like ours to benefit from open-book management. It can work anywhere. You can practice it even if you're a frontline supervisor in a company mummified in secrecy. Sure, it helps to have upper management's support. But even when the top executives play by their own rules and are oblivious to everyone else, you and your people will be more successful and better off working from an open book.

▌▌▌▶ the language cure: how open-book management works

When I talk about open-book management, I'm referring to the practice of communicating with people via the numbers. This is a cornerstone of the Great Game of Business as we play it at SRC. I'm not saying that open-book management is a cure-all for business problems. It may not work at all if you haven't done some of the steps mentioned earlier. People aren't going to *believe* the numbers if you haven't established some credibility and begun to foster a sense of mutual respect and trust. And people aren't going to *act on* the numbers if they've never had the experience of winning, if they think of themselves as losers, if they walk around with sand in their eyes. And people aren't going to *care* about the numbers if you haven't given them a sense of the Big Picture by educating them about how the company works, where they fit in, and why it all matters.

Start with the basics. Once you've laid the right foundation, then it's essential to teach people the numbers, because numbers are the language of business, and you can't understand business, let alone play the Game, if you don't speak the language. Only the numbers can tell you how you are doing, show you where you need to focus your attention, allow you to identify and solve problems, and let you see how your own day-to-day actions affect everything and everyone around you—the people you work with, your company, your community, your family, your hopes and dreams. It's like having microscopic and telescopic vision at the same time. The numbers link the individual to the Big Picture. That, ultimately, is the whole idea of what we do.

Open-book management is the best way I know of to keep people focused on the important issues facing a company. It takes down walls. When you communicate with people through the financial statements, knowledge gets to them quickly, without being distorted by internal rivalries. If everyone is looking at the whole business, it's much harder for departments to make excuses at one another's expense. Production can't dismiss a problem by blaming sales—by saying, "We did our job, but those jerks screwed it up." If there's a problem, it has to be solved. Everybody has to work together to solve it. Maybe production is causing the problem in sales—say, by operating behind schedule, or by letting quality slip. Open-book management forces that information to come out. It can't hide.

At the same time, open-book management changes the way an individual looks at his or her work. Numbers can give meaning to your job, show you exactly where you fit in, and why you're important. We had a guy, Billy Clinton, who ran the warehouse at one of our plants. For a long time, he thought he was an insignificant nobody, a cog in the wheel. He thought his job was just to hold on to parts and products until somebody else needed them. He was a caretaker and a flak catcher. He didn't see that he was responsible for feeding the organization and that he had a real impact on how fast the organization was able to grow.

But when he educated himself in the language of numbers, he began to understand his role. He saw instantly how much money was lost when an assembly line went down. A couple of times, the line went down because nobody could find some parts that were supposedly in the warehouse. It dawned on Billy that the organization was depending on him to know exactly what was available. If his counts were inaccurate, we might run low on a critical part without knowing it. In effect, he and his people were keeping the assembly lines up and running by having accurate inventory counts. The plant really needed them to grow. I can't tell you what a revelation that is to somebody. Suddenly what he does has *meaning*. It's not work; it's not just a job; it's a responsibility. And it's food on his family's table.

▶ take the emotions out of the business

I knew a company that prided itself on its humanistic approach to business. The people were always going on whitewater rafting trips or mountain-climbing expeditions, and they set aside a part of every day for self-improvement sessions. The CEO played motivational tapes and threw regular Friday-afternoon beer busts to tell people how great they were doing: a terrific corporate culture. But they forgot one thing: you have to make money to stay in business. After a brief but glorious run, the company folded, and the people all lost their jobs.

I am second to none in believing that business ought to be people oriented. But no company serves its people well by elevating emotions over numbers. That's one of the things I like most about open-book management: it takes the emotions out of the business, or at least out of the decision-making process. Emotions can cloud the brain, but the numbers don't lie. Our people see that success in business depends on making sure one plus one comes out to two. It has nothing to do with standing in a circle and doing a real good job of falling into someone else's arms.

Don't get me wrong. I think emotions have a legiti-mate role to play in business. I'm all in favor of pom-poms,

celebrations, and inspirational messages. I just don't think
they should replace solid information about the condition
of the company. People should understand why those pom-
poms are there—why it's important to be motivated, what
the payoff is for getting yourself up. It's too easy to manipulate people with motivational gimmicks, and it's wrong. It's
not fair to take advantage of people's ignorance, to pump
them up and pat them on the back, telling them what a
great job they're doing and what a great company they
work for, while you keep them in the dark about the real
condition of the business. I worked for fourteen years at a
company that said everything was great and the company
would be here forever. It carried us along by appealing to
our emotions. Had I looked at the balance sheet, I would
have known that our emotions were misplaced.

Let people evaluate the situation for themselves. Don't
do it for them with rah-rah squads. You can communicate
more clearly with numbers. If I tell people one plus one
is two, that message gets through without distortion. The
challenge is to get people to appreciate what I really mean
by one plus one is two.

And when you have bad news to deliver, the numbers
are crucial. It's hard to share bad news. There's a natural
fear that people will be discouraged, that they'll give up,
that they won't be motivated to solve the problems. So the
person who is supposed to deliver the news tends to put it
in the best possible light, which often undercuts the message. But if the message doesn't get through, the problems
are only going to get worse. So somehow you want to send
the message clearly without getting people down. You can
do that with numbers. People hear the message backed by

numbers loud and clear. They say, "Boy, we've got to do something about that."

▶ magic numbers: why open-book management works

A detective in a major city once told me that to make anything happen, you had to have a set of "magic numbers." His magic numbers, he said, weren't the ones on the cash in his wallet but the numbers he carried in his head—phone numbers of people who could get things done. The people who work at SRC also carry a set of magic numbers around in their heads, and those numbers are our most important competitive tool. Here's why.

There are only two ways to make money in business. One is to be the least-cost producer; the other is to have something nobody else has. Unless you have a proprietary product or service, you have to be prepared to compete on price, and you can do that best if you are the least-cost producer. If you have the lowest costs in the market, you can undersell the competition and still earn a profit. By the same token, you don't have to worry too much about losing business to competitors who charge less. If your *costs* are lower, a price war is going to hurt them more than you.

On the other hand, it's always nice to be in a position to charge a little more. To do that, you have to come up with an edge that customers can't get anywhere else. Maybe it's quality, maybe it's a particular service, maybe it's a unique product, maybe it's a brand name. As long as you're the only one who has it—and customers want it—you can charge a premium for it.

The most successful companies, of course, strive to have both the lowest costs and something competitors don't have. Many companies manage to develop some combination of the two. But the underlying logic still applies. If you're making three-inch nails, you'd better have the lowest costs in your industry. If your product is the Polaroid camera, you have a little more leeway.

Few companies are in Polaroid's position. The vast majority do not have the luxury of charging what they want, or what the market will bear. We don't. In our business, we have to be a low-cost producer, because anybody can remanufacture engines and engine components, and thousands of other companies do. It's essential to keep our costs down, and there is no individual, or department, that can do it for us. People throughout the company are constantly making decisions affecting the level of our costs. Every minute of every day, for example, someone on the shop floor decides whether to rework a used part or replace it with a new one. In principle, we want to recycle as many used parts as possible. The more parts we save and reuse, the lower our costs—provided, that is, people don't spend too much time doing the salvage work. Suppose we're paying $26 an hour for labor and overhead, and a guy decides to rework a connecting rod, which would cost us $45 new. If it takes him one hour, the company makes money. If it takes him two hours, we lose money. And it has to be his judgment call, because no two salvage jobs are exactly the same. So people constantly have to decide whether it pays to put in the time and effort required to do a particular operation.

In this way, we're no different from every other business. Cost control happens (or doesn't happen) on the level of the individual. You don't become the least-cost producer by issuing edicts from an office, or by setting up elaborate systems and controls, or by giving pep talks. The best way to control costs is to enlist everyone in the effort. That means providing people with the tools that allow them to make the right decisions.

Those tools are our magic numbers. Every business has them. Specifically, they are the numbers that tell you whether or not your costs are lower than your competitors'. To know what your costs should be, you have to find out what your competitors' costs are—what their labor rates are, how fast they make their product, what fringe benefits they offer, what other incentives they provide, what they pay for material, what their debt levels are, and so on. Only then can you determine what you must do to be the least-cost producer. Your competitors' numbers provide you with your benchmarks. Open-book management is the means by which you share those benchmarks with the people in your company, the way you get everyone involved in the effort to become the least-cost producer.

Of course, while you're striving for lower costs, you can also try to come up with additional services—services that nobody else has. Maybe it's a total quality management system. Maybe it's some kind of additional marketing or sales support. The idea is to offer something that allows you to charge a little more. In most businesses, however, you're not going to be able to charge a lot more. So you can never stop trying to be the least-cost producer. That means staying on top of your competition and then educating your people about your competition, letting them suggest ways to get the costs down. You'll be surprised at what they can come up with.

In the process, you get an additional benefit: a highly motivated workforce with very little turnover and great consistency—which translates into higher quality for the customer. That's something our competitors don't have, something that allows us to charge a little more.

▶ improvements come in fractions; only surprises come in whole percentages

The best argument for open-book management is this: the more educated your workforce is about the company, the more capable it is of doing the little things required to get better.

Business is a game of fractions. If you look at the income statements of corporations today, you'll see that very few of them have pretax margins above 5 percent. So a 1 percent improvement in profitability is very, very significant, but it takes time to achieve it. Surprises, on the other hand, pack a bigger punch. Everybody hates surprises in business. The odd part is that nobody hates surprises more than the manipulative control freaks who practice old-fashioned, secretive, need-to-know management. That way of operating virtually guarantees a steady stream of surprises, because people don't have the tools they need to forecast and project, to live up to their commitments. To eliminate surprises, you have to be aware of all the factors that may affect your ability to deliver what you promise. Again: open-book management.

No surprises—at least no big ones. That's another job responsibility here at SRC. Surprises mean you are not in control of your function. Opening the books is a way of giving people control and thereby providing consistency, and people crave consistency, just as they hate change. The consistency lies in the system, in the fundamental rules of business. It's beyond me, it's beyond you, it's beyond everybody. The system will always be there.

THE SIXTH HIGHER LAW IS:
You Can Sometimes Fool the Fans, But You
Can Never Fool the Players.

The Great Game is not a gimmick. If you try to use it as if it were, it won't work.

⏵ overcoming your fear of disclosure

How do you get to the point where you can even think about democratizing the workplace—about giving people access to the numbers and therewith the means to control their destiny? Not by swallowing your pride and admitting that you don't have all the answers and can't make all the decisions. No, it's by swallowing your fear.

THE GREAT FEAR #1

WHAT IF COMPETITORS GET HOLD OF YOUR NUMBERS?

The notion of opening up the company's books strikes terror in the hearts of many CEOs, who shudder to think that the numbers might fall into the wrong hands—like their competitors'. I have to admit that, in the beginning, our numbers were so bad it didn't matter whether or not our competitors saw them. Then, as we began teaching people the numbers, we could see our company get stronger, and so we worried less and less about our competitors because they weren't strengthening themselves in the same way.

Imitators never worry me as much as innovators. By sharing the numbers, we were developing something our competitors couldn't match. They could see every single one of our numbers, but unless they adopted our methods, unless they started using their numbers to build morale and motivation, unless they enlisted their own people in the struggle to keep costs down, they weren't going to take us out.

This is not to deny that it's possible to use a company's numbers to compete against it. We try to find out all we can about our competitors' numbers. We always buy stock in any competitor that is publicly traded. You'd be foolish not to. The more knowledge you have about a competitor, the easier it is to decide what course of action you should take in a particular situation—when you should compete, when you should back off, where you might have a particular advantage or weakness.

It's also true that a company, particularly a private one, can hide certain things, although a lot less than most people think. For openers, you can get a lot of information from easily accessible sources, such as Dun & Bradstreet and the other credit bureaus. If you compete in the same arena as another company, you're going to find out a lot about it just by being streetwise. When you lose a quote, you can usually figure out why. If you're getting material from the same sources, your material costs should be the same as your competitor's. That leaves labor and overhead. It doesn't take much to find out another company's labor rates—you ask someone who works there, or the neighbor of someone who works there, or you hire somebody from your competitor's organization. Then you're down to overhead. So let's say we bid $10, and our two competitors bid $9 each. It won't take long for us to figure out where we lost $1.

But the main point is this: in the long run, knowing a competitor's numbers doesn't mean anything unless you are the least-cost producer or have something nobody else has. You have to go back to those two basic principles. Yes, a competitor may use our numbers to underbid us on a particular job, but then he has to deliver; he has to provide quality and he has to stand behind the product. Knowing your competitor's financials is at best a short-term tactical advantage, one that pales alongside the benefits that come from educating your employees about the numbers.

Besides, it's sometimes better to let your competitor get that particular job or account. If it's very complicated, very costly, and if he's really hot to get it, you almost hope he does. In the first place, he may bid so low that he loses money on it. He may also put himself behind in the race for the next job. So you quote high and hope the other guy wins with a very low bid.

THE GREAT FEAR #2

IS IT COMPETITORS YOU FEAR—OR YOUR OWN EMPLOYEES?

Sad to say, a lot of companies hide their financials not because they're afraid of their competitors, but because they're afraid of their employees. They don't think people will understand the numbers, and there's some truth to that. If you don't show employees how to use financial information as a tool to help the company, they might well use it as a weapon against the company. I still think you're better off in the long run being open with financial information. When the numbers are hidden, people make assumptions, and they're often crazy ones. Nine times out of ten, people think a company has a lot more money to spend on wages and salaries than it does. They're trained to think big, and they don't understand business. It's amazing, for example, how many people confuse profit with sales.

So share the numbers, even if you don't go the distance in educating your workforce. You won't eliminate all the suspicions people have about your motives, or their doubts about the way you run the company. You're not going to get rid of the stupid, ignorant remarks people make when they are not taught what the numbers mean. But at least you'll avoid some of the wild assumptions people draw when they have no information about the company's real situation—assumptions that can lead to very destructive behavior.

THE GREAT FEAR #3

WHAT DO YOU REVEAL IF YOUR NUMBERS ARE BAD?

The CEO of a screen-printing company came up to me after I had given a speech to a business group in California. "I love your message," he said, "and I love the way you run your business, but I could never let my people see all our company's numbers. They'd leave if they knew how bad we were really doing." I said, "Does that mean you only show them good numbers?"

He said, "Yeah, I show them good numbers to keep them motivated." I said, "Do they trust you?" He said, "No."

The truth is that you've got to give people the bad as well as the good. It's the *only way* to build trust, and you must have trust, if only because you're bound to make mistakes. We made a ton of mistakes during our first year as an independent company. I personally lost our biggest customer within two weeks of the buyout. Then we got into trouble over a large tax liability we had incurred because we didn't understand the tax laws. Next we had to cancel our bonus program midway through the year because it wasn't working. Meanwhile, we were barely meeting payroll.

People accepted our mistakes and forgave us for them mainly, I think, because of the trust we had established during the long period when Harvester was teetering on the brink of bankruptcy and we were trying to buy the factory. Throughout that time, the managers never lost faith, and we asked our people never to lose faith. Under ridicule, under humiliation, under everything you can possibly imagine, we never lost our composure, and we always told people the truth. I think afterward they realized we'd pulled them through a very tough time. So our credibility came more in the face of adversity than in winning.

That's a significant point. Too many CEOs only want to share the good news. It's a combination of the good and the bad that builds credibility. If you continually make the situation look good, it's a fairy tale. Life's not like that. And people know it. Of course, you'll lose credibility just as fast if you constantly make the situation look bad in an effort to resist employees' demands. People know life isn't like that, either. If you want them to believe you, give them the numbers.

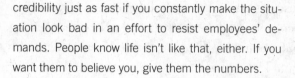 **how to be an open-book manager**

Sometimes I think what I'm really doing is conducting an orchestra. We have the violins over here, the cymbals there, the wind instruments beyond. I'm Lawrence Welk, going "ah-one and ah-two." My job is to keep the rhythm going. I keep things on schedule, on time. That can be tricky because conditions are always changing. You need to be flexible, but you also need structure. What's essential is to make sure that everybody is playing from the same scorecard. Our scorecard is a set of financial statements, notably the Income Statement and the Balance Sheet.

We mix all kinds of metaphors in explaining those documents to people. I usually tell them that the balance sheet is the company's thermometer. It lets you know whether you're healthy or not. An Income Statement tells you how you got that way and what you can do about it. For example, the Balance Sheet may tell you that you have a fever. The Income Statement tells you what created the fever, and what medicine will make the fever go away. You need both. They provide a check and a balance on each other.

When you use financial statements as management tools, you have to adapt them to your purposes. Don't rely on the kind of financial statements provided by CPAs.

Those statements are designed to give outsiders—investors, tax collectors, bankers—the information they want to know about a company. Employees need something a little different. The general form is the same, and the standards of accuracy should be just as high, but the detail has to be broken down in a way that sheds more light on *what's happening inside the company*. The point is to show each person how he or she affects the Income Statement and the Balance Sheet. You want to report the numbers accordingly, emphasizing the ones over which people have control.

How you do that depends entirely on your business, but here are some general rules to follow:

1. **Start with the income statement.**

    It is the best tool you have for drawing people into the action of the game because it is constantly changing. As a result, it lends itself to demonstrating cause and effect. You can use it both to monitor the action as it unfolds and to show people their role in determining whether or not the company makes money.

2. **Highlight the categories where you spend the most money.**

    Those are obviously the ones that are going to have the biggest impact on your company's profitability, so you want to monitor them very closely.

3. **Break down categories into controllable elements.**

    If labor is a variable expense, you want people

to see it vary. If you use trucks in your business, people should know how much you're spending there. In a sales organization, you'd keep a close eye on travel, entertainment, and other selling expenses; in a professional service firm, you'd probably want to break down billable hours. The whole idea is set up the income statement in a way that lets people observe the effects of what they do.

4. **Use the income statement to educate people about the balance sheet.**

While the action may center around the Income Statement, it is the Balance Sheet that tells you the real score—how secure jobs are, how much wealth has been created, where the company's vulnerable. You ignore it at your peril. Once people get the hang of the Income Statement, moreover, it's a fairly simple matter to show them how the changes there produce changes in the Balance Sheet. Use the same principle of breaking down large Balance Sheet categories to illuminate cause and effect.

Above all, develop a set of financial statements that works for your particular business. If you have a chain of clothing stores, your internal statements will wind up looking very different from those you would develop if you had a travel agency, or a hair salon, or a consulting firm, or a metal fabrication business. But the process by which you would come up with your statements would not vary much at all.

At SRC, we break out the various costs involved in the

manufacturing operation. Typically, these costs would be lumped together in the Cost-of-Goods-Sold line on the income statement. That may be adequate for a banker, but it doesn't tell us very much about what's really going on in production, where most of our people work. We want them to see exactly what effect they are having on profits, so we break down the Cost-of-Goods-Sold line into its basic elements—material, labor, and overhead. Every week, the various departments forecast whether, and by how much, they are going to be over or under budget for the month. Then, after the month's close, we produce a hundred-page set of financial statements showing exactly what happened where and how each person contributed.

Almost every element of the company is quantified, from the percentage of the budget spent on receptionists' notepads to the amount of overhead absorbed each hour that a person puts in grinding crankshafts. We constantly measure material costs, overhead, performance, and hourly rates. Labor ratios are calculated on a daily basis— by supervisors, group leaders, department managers, and the hourly people themselves. There are numbers for everybody, even the person who buys pencils, cleaning fluid, and the like. Every day, she punches her receipts into the computer, which matches them up against the standard cost file and gives her a printout. From that, she can see whether her actual purchases have been favorable or unfavorable to standard—that is, whether she's over or under budget. This happens all over the company. Sales numbers are posted daily: who's buying, what they're buying, how they're buying. The numbers are broken down not just by customer, but by product. Meanwhile, out on the shop floor, there's a constant flurry of "move tickets," telling stories of their own. Say a guy finishes ten engines. He would move them from his station to the warehouse, and a move ticket would go along. That ticket is punched to show the unit is now finished. Once the work order is completed, we'll calculate whether the product made money or lost money.

Visitors sometimes find all this a little overwhelming. I tell them to bear in mind that we didn't create this system overnight. It took us years to develop all the mechanisms we now have for keeping people up to date on the numbers, and we're still coming up with new ones. But we started out very simply. In the first year, our chief financial officer would put together a daily report like chicken scratch for the bank showing where our cash was, where our inventories were, where our receivables were, what we owed, and so on. That would be passed around the company. People got curious. They would come down to the front office in the morning and ask, "What do we owe today?" From there, the reporting system just grew and grew.

It expanded because people kept asking for more information. They didn't need an MBA to be curious about what was going on. Many of them had not even graduated from high school. But that didn't stop them from getting caught up in the Game. The more information we provided, the more they wanted to know.

DO YOU KNOW HOW MUCH YOUR
TOILET PAPER COSTS?

You've undoubtedly heard the time-honored manage-ment maxim, "Don't sweat the small stuff." It's the worst advice a business can follow. We sweat *every-thing*, although it took a little inspiration to get some of our costs under control.

By the end of our second year as an independent company, we had a budget system in place, but we were having problems with the minute costs of the business that were not directly related to making the product—everything from toilet paper to paint to pro-tective eyeglasses to heating and lighting. We hadn't been monitoring these so-called burden costs, and the spending was getting out of hand. So we said, "Okay, we'll divide the burden items up and give one account to each of the supervisors and other manage-ment people." It would be that person's responsibility to determine how big the budget item should be, not just for his or her particular area, but for the whole company, and then to make sure that we hit the target.

The idea was to give ownership of the burden num-bers to specific individuals. Before, nobody owned any of these numbers. The burden expenses were being dumped into catchall categories in the budget. Having those catchalls turned out to be a big mistake. If you have a catchall in a budget, people will dump anything and everything into it. The result was that people spent whatever they felt like on burden items, and the expenses went wild.

So we wrote the names of the burden items on slips of paper and put all the slips in a pot. Then we got everybody together and did a drawing. Each person drew an account with a dollar figure attached. A guy named Don Wood got toilet paper. After we finished the drawing, we told people to go out and do some investigating, then come back to the next meeting prepared to say whether or not they accepted the dollar figures we had put down. If not, they had to say why not and tell us what the actual figure should be. As it turned out, some people stuck with the number we gave them, some lowered it, and some raised it. We didn't really care, so long as they bought into the final figure, because from then on it would be each person's responsibility to follow that account and bring it home.

Don Wood took his assignment to heart. As he tracked the toilet paper account, he began to notice certain surprising but unmistakable trends. You would think, after all, that toilet-paper consumption would remain more or less constant from week to week or month to month, but that wasn't the case. Instead, there was a distinct pattern of variations. Being a curious guy, Wood began looking for factors that might cause a rise or a dip in toilet paper use. Sure enough, he discovered that the more time people spent working "on prime" (i.e., actually producing engines and engine components), the less toilet paper they used.

Conversely, toilet paper use increased whenever we hit a slow period in the business. At a staff meeting, Wood presented his findings in the form of a graph on which he had plotted toilet paper consumption in 1983 and 1984, along with the number of prime hours worked during each month of the period. He thereby demonstrated beyond dispute that the busier we were, the less frequently we went to the bathroom.

Aside from providing ongoing entertainment, the program worked. Don Wood came in under budget, and so did most of the other burden-item trackers. Their spirit was contagious. That was the year we went after overhead in the bonus program. At the beginning of the year, we had an overhead chargeout rate of $39 per hour, meaning that we spent $39 on overhead for every hour we worked on prime. The bonus goal was to reduce the chargeout rate to $32.50 per hour. In fact, we got it down to $26.32 per hour. Our profits soared, since every penny we took out of overhead went straight to the bottom line, and the value of our stock jumped from $0.61 to $4.05 per share. Somehow I don't think it was pure coincidence that all this happened the same year Don Wood came up with his toilet paper index.

Employees wanted to see exactly where they fit into the process: how much money they were saving the company, how much profit they had generated on a particular job, what their ups and downs were, and how well a particular idea had worked. Their questions told us what information we should be reporting. Management's role was to instill the desire to know. We did that by a variety of methods—through the bonus system, the weekly meetings, and all the other games we developed along the way. But the process got started as simply as can be: by sitting down and explaining to people how the bank was measuring us and how we were doing.

> The system is so damn logical. It takes the whole element of direct supervision out of managing. You don't have to pound a guy over the head because he doesn't want to work. You pound him over the head because he's missing opportunities that could put money in his pocket. It's a totally different style of management. You can communicate by pointing to the opportunities that are out there rather than by using threats and intimidation. It's a way to motivate people without lying to them or deceiving them. It's motivation with realism.

chapter 6

SETTING STANDARDS

Numbers have gotten a bad reputation in some quarters: no surprise when you look at how they've been used. Most companies use them as punishment—as tools to supervise, intimidate, or control. They don't use numbers as tools to build—to teach people to be more productive.

KEY POINT: The payoff comes from getting the people who create the numbers to understand the numbers. When that happens, the communication between the bottom and the top of the organization is just phenomenal.

You can't generate that quality of communication just by dumping numbers on people, however. You have to make the numbers both comprehensible and interesting. You have to bring them alive. After all, it is possible to quantify almost any aspect of business—inventory turnover, sales per employee, job safety, mailing costs, labor efficiency, productivity, telephone time per customer, energy consumption, and on and on. *The trick is to be able to evaluate those numbers, to make sense out of them, to know what to do with them.* For that, you need standards.

A *standard* is the number to shoot for in any particular category you are measuring. It may be a ratio. It may be a percentage. It may be an absolute number over a period of time. All that depends on the category. If you're measuring safety, you will probably look at frequency and severity of accidents. If you're monitoring how fast customers are paying their bills, it will be average days outstanding (i.e., the average number of days that receivables go unpaid). Whatever the category, you need a number against which you can compare your results and thereby determine how you're doing. That number is the standard—the level you can reach if you apply yourself and do a good job. It is the benchmark. I actually prefer the word *target* because it reinforces the point that these are not fixed, immutable goals. They are part of an ongoing contest of people against the realities of the marketplace. Standards are tools for challenging you to perform up to your abilities. As such, they can be revised as you get better, or as circumstances change.

Some standards are obviously more important than others, if only because some categories are going to have a bigger impact on your ability to make money and generate cash. To a large extent, that is a function of the business you are in. In a manufacturing operation like ours, for example, it is essential to have standards for labor efficiency and overhead absorption, because labor and overhead are critical to our ability to earn a profit. If you have a chain of clothing stores, on the other hand, you'd be more interested in having standards for, say, sales per square foot and inventory turnover—to determine how well you are using your people and your cash. A consulting company or professional services firm, by contrast, would tend to emphasize billable hours. A hotel might focus on its occupancy rate.

Within a particular company, moreover, people with different functions need standards that are tailored to their specific jobs and reflect the factors over which they personally have control. Rick Heddon, who ran the warehouse, may have been curious to know how the company's current quality compared to past performance and general industry standards, but he was most concerned about meeting his own standards for inventory accuracy and turns. Similarly, the salespeople are going to want standards for things like gross margins and selling expenses as a percentage of sales, while the purchasers will be much more interested in material costs. The number and variety of standards will vary from person to person and from job to job, but everyone in the company needs some way of measuring how he or she is doing on a daily, weekly, and monthly basis.

There is almost no limit to the number of standards you can come up with. Indeed, each individual can develop standards of his or her own. Anyone who really gets into the Great Game of Business will compile a substantial list over time. But don't overdo it in the beginning. You can start playing the Game with a couple of standards—say, one related to sales and another to productivity—and build from there. The whole idea is to throw a spotlight on some part of the action. Standards make the Game faster and more fun. They allow you to determine easily and quickly how you are contributing to the process of making money and generating cash.

For the open-book manager, standards are an essential means of making business understandable and manageable, of getting people over their fear of numbers and accustomed to taking control of the results.

> **KEY POINT:** Numbers like these are no more complicated, and need be no more intimidating, than the calculations millions of baseball fans do whenever they want to figure out their favorite hitter's batting average or their favorite pitcher's earned run average.

In business, however, people don't do the calculations because they don't understand the rules. Standards help you teach them. They allow you to show people the equivalent in your business of batting .400, or hitting sixty home runs in a season, or getting a hit in fifty-six consecutive games, or having an ERA of less than 1.00. And while you're educating people with standards, you're also giving them goals to shoot for. You're challenging them to see what they can do. You're getting them into the Game.

▶ numbers make the team

Most important, numbers like these help everyone play the *same* game. People need to have some way of keeping score. If you don't provide one, they make up their own. At Harvester, I noticed how an experienced foreman would do his own little Income Statement. He'd get to the factory early, walk the floor, count his stock, see where his machines were. Then he'd stand by the time clock and count the people coming in, after which he'd go back and set up an ad hoc Income Statement. I think most people come up with their own rough accounting systems that they use to get themselves organized and to figure out their priorities. The problem is the systems may lead them in different directions. That's why it's important to provide a set of standards everybody can use to keep track of what's happening. Then they all know when something goes wrong and they all see what they can do about it.

So how should you go about developing and implementing standards at your company? By choosing a category, picking a target, and going after it. Pretty much any target will do, as long as you can explain why it's worth aiming for. There is no single correct path to follow. Be guided by your own instincts, the specifics of your business, and whatever seems to work best. Come up with a number that seems reasonable. Don't worry about being precise. People can argue with it if they think it's wrong. Setting standards is a team effort and an ongoing process. Encourage people to debate each one. Let them negotiate. Over time, you'll get it right. Just start, stick with it, and learn from your mistakes. That said, here are some tips about setting and using standards from someone who has already made just about every mistake there is.

Tip #1: Do You Know Your Critical Number?

Every company has one. It is the number that, at any given time, is going to have the biggest impact on what you're doing and where you want to go. Exactly what it is will depend on a variety of factors: the kind of business you're in, the state of the economy, competitive conditions, your specific financial situation, and so on. Your Critical Number may have to do with sales, or cash flow, or quality, or recruitment, or operating costs, or a dozen other factors. Whether you're aware of it or not, it will make or break your company. It is the number you *have* to do well on if you are going to succeed, or maybe even survive. So it's vital that you identify it and come up with standards people can use to go after it.

The good news is that it's generally pretty easy to track down your Critical Number, assuming you know your business reasonably well. Pay attention to what keeps you up at night. Better yet, ask your people what keeps *them* up at night. If you're in the pit of a recession, all of you no doubt lie in bed worrying about sales. That's probably where you'll find your Critical Number. Or suppose you have a temporary services company and your business is going gangbusters. Then the number is more likely to involve, say, finding and keeping good employees. Or something may have happened to your company that makes one area of the operation particularly important. When the Kroger supermarket chain went private, for example, it took on an enormous amount of debt. Whenever a company borrows on that scale, cash becomes king. So the company gave all the store managers a lot of stock and told them that if they wanted to see the stock appreciate, they should focus on cash flow. Did they ever! They kept inventories low. They held off investments in capital equipment. They negotiated terms with their suppliers. They deposited their receipts quicker. As the company generated cash, it paid off its debt, and the stock shot right through the ceiling.

We were in a similar situation after the buyout, but since then we have tended to focus on our Cost of Goods Sold (COGS), which is our Critical Number under normal circumstances. That's where almost all the action occurs in our business. To know what's really going on, we have to look at all the different factors that affect the COGS line on the Income Statement, and monitor all the different variances. On the other hand, we also have to be aware that circumstances may change, sometimes abruptly, and bring another Critical Number to the fore. We've had periods, for example, when sales have taken off and we've had trouble absorbing the new work coming in. At times like that, you have to be very careful that you don't run out of cash. So the number we watch most closely is sales.

Tip #2: Build a Standard Cost System.

Sooner or later, your Critical Number will have to do with costs, and by then you'd better have a standard cost system in place. It's the only way of making sure that your costs are in line with the marketplace, that they aren't so high as to undermine your ability to compete. Remember, you can only make money in business by being the least-cost producer or by having something no one else has, and even in the second case you'd be foolish not to keep your costs down. To do that effectively, you must have a standard cost system that tells you what your costs should be in every aspect of your operation. Without it, you're going to have a hard time getting your people involved in controlling costs, mainly because they won't know what to do. In fact, they probably won't believe you if you tell them the company's costs are too high. And you'll find it almost impossible to teach them how to follow the basic rules of business: make money and generate cash.

I ran into all those problems when I first came to Springfield. I could see we were losing money on some products, but I had trouble convincing people on the shop floor because we didn't have a standard cost system in place. We had a person who was making transmissions, Denise Bredfeldt, and she was really proud of her work. Her quality was extremely high. But she had no idea whether or not she was making money. When I told her she wasn't making money, she couldn't believe it. I could see from the work orders that the material alone was costing us close to the selling price, but she was dumbfounded. She spent a long time in the cafeteria, going over her numbers, trying to figure it out. She finally determined that if she used fewer parts, did a little of this, a little of that, she could make some money. I let her do that for a while, but the prices of transmission parts kept going up. Eventually it became impossible for us to make a profit on the business, so we killed it. But the experience taught me a lesson. I realized there were probably a lot more people like her out there. That's when I decided we had to break all the products down—find out exactly how much material, how much labor, and how much overhead was going into each unit. I put together a team of five people who worked for a year figuring out how much we spent on everything we did.

Going through that process is a lot of work, but you have to do it if you want a true *standard* cost system. Most companies use what I would call an *average* cost system. They look at what they paid the year before and set that as the cost. Systems like that seldom are specific enough and never provide targets. If you have operated inefficiently and spent too much in the past, you simply build all those costs, problems, and deficiencies into the system. That kind of cost accounting is really an obstacle to improving productivity because it accepts and rewards inefficiency. If you are going to improve, you need to know how much you *should* be spending, not just how much you've spent in the past. That means going over every product, looking at every part, examining every process and operation, breaking each down into its individual components, and then coming up with standard costs for everything you do.

All this takes time and effort, but it is not nearly as difficult or mysterious as some people imagine. Even in businesses that are less standardized than ours—a graphic design company, for example, or a publishing house, or a consulting firm—you are still dealing with things to which costs can and must be attached. No two advertising campaigns may be exactly alike, but you create them out of the same components, and each of those components costs money. When you get right down to it, business is all about taking limited resources (time, talent, materials, energy, whatever) and turning them into products and services that customers want to buy. In any business, you can avoid a lot of trouble by knowing in advance what you can afford to pay for those resources and still earn a profit. That's the whole idea behind developing a standard cost system. You simply go through your company and figure out what all those costs should be. It has nothing to do with standardizing products. It has everything to do with being able to say to people with some certainty, "Look, we've got to operate at this level, or we don't have jobs."

CHECKLIST FOR
STANDARDIZING COSTS

- Is anything going to happen in the next twelve months to affect these costs?
- Am I overlooking any outside sources of information, such as industry groups or competitive wage surveys, that could assure me these costs are reasonable?

- Am I purchasing supplies in the right quantities? Using the right suppliers? Checking other sources?
- Is this specific operation really necessary? What would happen if I didn't do it?
- Have I created ways for people to contribute their ideas about reducing costs? Do people feel they are part of the process?
- Most important, will people buy into these standards? Have I given them every opportunity to debate the standards? Do people think the standards are theirs? This is where ownership starts. *Do people own these standards?*

IS YOUR CORPORATE PRESIDENT WORTH 27 CENTS?

A standard cost system is particularly important if you are part of a larger company, because operating costs may be the only things you control. That was our situation before the buyout. Corporate headquarters was charging us 27 cents of every dollar we shipped, supposedly to cover sales, marketing, accounting, and general administration. It was an arbitrary assessment. Frankly, it was ludicrous, considering how little we got in return. But we had to live with it. On top of that 27 percent, I added 13 percent for profits and taxes. In effect, we had to make a gross margin of 40 percent, which meant holding our operating costs (mate rial, labor, and overhead) to 60 cents of every dollar we shipped. To succeed, we had to educate people about manufacturing costs and get them involved in keeping those costs down. We couldn't have done it without a standard cost system.

A set of targets and the ability to keep track of how we were doing made it possible to succeed. You need them, too. If you don't know how much you *should* be spending, how can you determine whether you're high, low, or right on the mark? Ultimately, you want to find out everything there is to know about each product you're making, so that you can set up the strongest defense possible—so nobody can beat you, nobody can take you out. Developing a standard cost system is the first step.

Tip #3: Look for the Reality Behind the Numbers.

More than work, it takes creativity and imagination to develop good standards. There is a whole art to quantifying things, and it's one that's worth learning because the more quantifiable something is, the more you can do with it. But before you can be an effective quantifier, you have to develop an eye for the reality behind the numbers. You have to learn how to recognize what the numbers really represent, what sort of behavior produces the numbers, and what people can do differently to change the numbers.

That is seldom obvious on the face of it. Suppose, for example, you have a chain of retail stores, and one of them is turning its inventory much more slowly than the others. The number tells you that the store has too much cash tied up in slow-moving stock. The important question is, why? What's the reality that is causing the problem? Is the manager inexperienced? Disorganized? Lazy? Does he know his market? Does he order frequently enough? Does he have effective systems for finding out how much stock he has, and how much he needs? Does he use them? Perhaps the store also has unusually low sales per customer. Does that mean it has the wrong selection of products? Is it in the wrong location? Is the merchandise displayed poorly? Do the employees need training in customer service? Or do they need better leadership? Is anyone working on motivating them?

WARNING:

DON'T ACCEPT ANY NUMBER AT FACE VALUE.

Numbers are not magical, and they aren't sacred. They are important only as clues to the reality that produces them. To use numbers effectively, you have to strive constantly to understand that reality—to move from the abstract to the specific. Many a profitable company has gone out of business because people neglected to find out the reality behind the number on the bottom line. You can't pay your creditors with money that's tied up in stale inventory or uncollectable receivables.

To develop useful *standards*, on the other hand, you almost have to reverse this process. You have to understand what really happens in the workplace, how people go about their jobs, and then come up with tools they can use to measure their individual contributions to the common goals. That involves moving from the specific to the abstract. The trick is to do it in a way that does not confuse people, or disorient them, or send them mixed messages. The best kind of standard is one that makes so much sense to people it becomes second nature. It remains constantly in their consciousness. It is something they talk about in their normal, everyday conversation to explain how their work is going. Again, I like to use the baseball analogy. A batting average is an abstraction, but no one who plays the game has to think twice about what it means. If you're batting .047, you know you're in a slump. If your average is over .400, you know you're on a tear. You can use your average to measure how you're doing and to help yourself figure out whether or not you need to do anything differently.

||||▶ how we calculate our batting average

Every business should have its own counterparts to the batting average. We have several. One of the best is the *overhead absorption rate*. This is the number people on the shop floor use to determine how much overhead they cover, or "absorb," when they spend time working "on prime," that is, working on products (as opposed to taking breaks, cleaning up work areas, attending meetings, and so on). We calculate the absorption rate every year by adding up all the budgeted overhead costs and dividing by the number of prime hours required to meet our production goals. That tells us what we have to spend per hour on overhead to carry out our annual plan.

When I talk to executives from other companies, they find this hard to swallow. They can't believe that our hourly people know, or care, what they are doing to cover overhead. I tell them to come visit us in Springfield and walk around our shop floor. Everybody understands the overhead absorption rate. Why? Because it gives us a standard for determining quickly and easily if we are doing all we can to maximize our profits and earn our bonuses. We just multiply the absorption rate by the number of hours actually worked on prime, and we can see whether or not our production is high enough to cover our overhead expenses—that is, how much overhead we have absorbed. If we don't absorb all the overhead we have budgeted, we have to pay the difference out of profits, and that cuts into our bonuses, not to mention the value of our stock.

HOW TO CHECK IF YOU'RE MAKING A DIFFERENCE

Anything important to a business is worth measuring, and nothing is more important than creating an environment in which people feel they make a difference. You can't feel good about what you're doing unless you think you're making a difference.

So how do you measure whether or not people

think that? One way is to look at contributions to charity. It's a measure of morale. It's a sign of how people feel about themselves, the company, and the environment you've created. I've always been awestruck by our contributions to the United Way. The contributions per employee are always the highest in the city. Why? Because people feel they're the best. It all comes back to instilling self-esteem and pride, to the special glow you get when you're a winner. When the charity sends back your numbers and shows you where you stand in relation to everybody else, you know you're a little bit special. In this particular category, at least, you did make a difference. Is it because things may be going right out there? That's a scary thought.

Obviously, people at SRC care about overhead absorption because of the way we've set up the Game, but that's one of the benefits to having standards at all. A standard is useless if people don't care about it. The better the standards you develop, the more creative you will be in getting people to care.

Tip #4: Find Sources That Can Help You Develop Standards.

No matter what business you're in, there are benchmarks and standards, and the chances are that someone has already calculated them. You can usually find them out by digging around. Suppose you have to buy workers' compensation insurance for a new business. You need a way to measure safety. Well, the federal government has developed formulas for measuring safety, and the insurance companies use those formulas to set premiums. You can use the formulas as well to monitor your own safety in order to establish your own benchmarks. The better you do, the lower your insurance costs. Then you can use that to educate your people about their impact on overhead, to show them how they reduce overhead by improving safety.

Developing standards is an ongoing process of education. Never stop investigating what kinds of standards you should have and what the target numbers should be. There are dozens of ways to find out about both. Talk to the people who sell you equipment or material. Talk to all your suppliers. Conduct informal surveys. Join the industry associations. We have memberships in about twenty industry organizations, covering all aspects of our business. More important, our people play active roles. They give a lot, and they get a lot, and it all goes into refining our standards.

You can also learn a tremendous amount by studying great companies, especially if they're in your industry. Pick an overachiever, a superhero, and find out what it measures—just ask. Write to that company. Call it on the phone. Ask what industry events the executives attend, and go meet them there. If one of the executives is giving a speech, show up and stick around to ask questions afterward. Most people are happy to tell you what you want to know unless they see you as a direct competitor, and even then they are often willing to swap information. Or go to see those companies for yourself. You want to touch them, taste them, feel them. Find out how many shifts they're open, how many hours they're working, and what they do to make a difference. You don't need an appointment with the CEO. Talk to the guy who sweeps the floors.

Suppliers are a particularly good source of information. In the early days, we brought in suppliers to teach courses at the plant. Who knows more about the installation of bearings than the people who make them? In the course of teaching, they help you develop more standards and benchmarks. The sessions also reduce tensions with suppliers. You avoid the typical us-versus-them mentality. That's a big bonus. Your suppliers are your partners. You should treat them as your partners.

IIIII▶ how we developed standards on a new product

When we decided to start remanufacturing automobile engines in 1985, the first thing we did was to look for the best automotive remanufacturer in the world. We talked to all the machine tool manufacturers, asking them, "Who remanufactures automobile engines faster than anybody else, and how fast do they do it?" Three or four sources told us, "Dealers in Minnesota. Ten hours per engine." So then we had to find out what Dealers did to make engines that fast—what equipment they had, what their overhead rates were, how much they paid their people, and so on.

We started by calling up Dealers. They had moved to another state. It turned out they had had a strong union in the Minnesota plant. They were paying $14 an hour for assemblers. That told us right away why they had a ten-hour standard: it was the only way to compensate for their high direct labor costs. If they were paying that much for assembly, they had to come up with the most efficient processes for cutting down the number of hours they put into the engine block. That gave us a tremendous advantage right off the bat. Our automotive assembly plant was in an area where the going rate was $4.50 an hour. We reasoned that if we could build an engine in ten hours with workers making $4.50 an hour, we could establish a solid foundation for the business. Over time, we were able to increase the labor rate to as much as $10 an hour and create a standard of living that people could live with.

HOW STANDARDS CAN BRING OUT THE BEST IN PEOPLE

At one time, we had a problem with a competitor who tried to come in and take away our fuel-injection pump business. It all began when a new buyer was appointed at one of our major customers. Seeing an opportunity, our competitor went to him and offered to supply pumps at a price below ours. It was a smart move. The new buyer wanted to make a good impression in his company, and reducing costs was a good way to do it. So the buyer came to me and said, "Look. I don't have any choice here. Unless you reduce your price by 6 percent, I'm going to give the business to this other guy. I'll give you three months to get the price down to his level."

Now a 6 percent price reduction was basically the

difference between making money and losing money on the product. We couldn't imagine how our competitor was going to make money at that price. As it happened, we owned a share of his stock. We checked out his financials, and we saw that he had an unbelievable amount of debt on his balance sheet. I'm talking about a $100 million company that owed $56 million. When you borrow that much money, you can't hide it, even if you're private. Somebody knows. In addition, this was a union company, so we knew what he was paying his people. We also knew that our production times weren't unreasonable, and that our prices were in line with the marketplace. So it was clear that this guy was out to buy the account. He was subsidizing the product by using debt to cover his losses. His strategy was clear: he was going to get the contract at a loss, run us out of the market, and then raise prices later on. We explained all that to the buyer. We appealed to loyalty and everything else. But he insisted on the price cut, which was going to save his company money, at least in the short run. Somehow we had to come up with a way to reduce our costs.

So I went down to the pump room, where we make fuel-injection pumps. I told people what we were up against. These pumps sold for about $200 each. To cut the price by 6 percent, we had to save $12 per unit. I said, "I don't know how to get that kind of cost reduction, but if we don't do it, we're going to lose this contract, and that could cost some people their jobs." Then I put a picture of the other company's CEO on the wall, along with a copy of its financial statements. I said, "Here's the guy who's trying to take your jobs away from you, and I'm afraid I don't know how to stop him. I've already done everything I can, and it hasn't worked. It's up to you now." I honestly believed it would take a miracle to save the contract.

The people in the pump room were amazing. They formed a task force, and they put up a thermometer. They got together and talked about how they could save a nickel here and a dime there. They looked at their hardware. They questioned every material cost. They asked how a vendor could be charging us so much when you could get the same thing for substantially less at Ace Hardware. Every day they posted their savings. At the end of the three months, they had cut $40 out of the pump's cost—a 20 percent savings. I would never have thought they could do it. That was the one time people really surprised me. There isn't an engineer in the world who could have done what they did. They had to do it themselves. What's interesting is that they passed 10 percent of the reduction along to the customer, which passed it along to the marketplace, and the volume rose, creating more jobs. So people got to see the whole economic cycle. As for the competitor, he lost that one, but he's still out there, keeping us on our toes.

Moral: You need standards to show people the real world. You can't just go out there with wishes and goals. You need to give people a strategy to get there. You need to guide them. You have to show them the

goal is attainable, and here's how they can attain it. Unless you run into a situation that defies mathematics, like the fuel-injection pump problem. Then you're going for a miracle. And sometimes people can produce miracles, but it helps if they're well educated. I don't think the people in the pump room could have pulled it off if they hadn't already been trained on standards.

So that's basically what we did. We found out who was the best, we set a ten-hour standard, and we went after it. We couldn't make it, so we settled on twelve hours, and later knocked it down to eleven hours. We paid about $6.50 an hour, plus the bonus. Our salespeople say our prices are among the best in the industry. And we have all the business we can handle.

KEY POINT: Numbers are not a substitute for leadership. What's important is how you use them.

Never get so far into the numbers that you leave out the human factor. Use the numbers as a tool to get people to contribute more, not less. If we use them to create an environment in which people don't contribute, or can't contribute, that's worse than not using them at all.

Tip #5: Tell the Stories Behind the Numbers.

Once you've developed some standards, what do you do with them? How do you use them? More important, how do you get *other people* to use them? How do you demystify the numbers? How do you turn them into tools that people can use—that they *want* to use—to contribute more? In short, how do you educate people around the standards?

I have always found that the most effective way to do that is by telling stories. With standards, we can use the numbers to tell stories about what has been happening in the company and what we can do to change. We can bring problems out into the open where they can be addressed— where they *have* to be addressed. Once people understand a standard, they expect us to do something when we aren't meeting it. They know that if we don't, we won't make money or we may run out of cash, which would be a story in its own right.

Indeed, there are stories behind every number in the financial statements, stories of opportunities missed, unforeseen problems, mysteries unraveled, all of life's perfections and imperfections. Our weekly staff meetings are filled with these stories, which we tell to each other and then pass along to everybody else in the follow-up meetings we hold throughout the company. It's a way of animating the numbers, bringing them to life. When you use the numbers to tell stories, you can educate people without threatening or intimidating them. You can show where the numbers came from and what they mean. You can illustrate in a way people understand that they do make a difference, they do control their own destinies. It's their game.

For example, there's a story about the new plant manager who missed his overhead absorption target for two months by $45,000. At the staff meeting, he said his plant was going to absorb $270,000 worth of overhead for the month. He came in at $225,000. Everyone asked, "Where did the $45,000 go?" The next month, the same thing happened. So we sent in the chief financial officer, who figured out the guy was using the wrong formula to calculate his overhead absorption. Once he got the right formula, he realized that the plant wasn't meeting its standard because it was taking too long to make cylinder heads. Instead of doing it in four hours, it was taking them seven. Why? Because the people were brand-new. Why? Because the plant manager had promoted the cylinder-head people to new jobs, which had a chain-reaction effect everywhere else. Four departments wound up with brand-new people who had to go through learning curves, because there wasn't a job freeze in cylinder heads. So the plant missed its standards, and the people missed their bonuses. The real story was that people weren't learning the Game. If they'd known the Game, they would have understood why it was important for the cylinder-head people to stay put.

That's a story we can tell to demystify the numbers and give people a tool they can use to contribute more.

Tip #6: Look for the Profit in Problems.

Whenever you turn a loser into a winner, you get a double bang for your buck. Say you have a problem that's costing you $500,000 a year and you figure out a solution that winds up earning you $500,000. You don't have a $500,000 winner. You have a $1 million winner. When you can stop the bleeding and turn it into healing, you're twice as well off as before.

The financial system shows you where you can make more money just by telling you where you're losing it. Take the plant that was running $45,000 below its standard for overhead absorption. We knew we were running at $20 per man-hour in that plant. In effect, they were losing 2,250 hours a month. One person worked about 173 hours a month. So we had thirteen guys to worry about. We needed to find the thirteen guys on the bottom and get them working up to standard. Once we did that, we got more than the $45,000, because other people started improving their performance as well.

///

THE SEVENTH HIGHER LAW IS:
When You Raise the Bottom, the Top Rises.

///

You really want people to solve their own problems. If the problem gets bad enough, you can always go in and tell people what to do. But all you'll get is the routine. You won't get any creativity. So you hope you don't have to get to that point. It's much better to have an environment in which people can come up with solutions themselves. Standards are tools for finding solutions.

⬛⬛⬛➤ benchmarks can turn an operation around

When I was twenty-eight years old, I was put in charge of crankcase-cylinder-head machining at Melrose Park. It was a division made up of four departments, one of the seven manufacturing divisions in the plant, and this one was dead last. There were about 500 people in the division. I was the superintendent, and I had five general foremen working for me, all of them in their late fifties, and each had been promised the superintendent's job when it opened up. You can imagine how they felt when I got the job instead. As for me, I was scared.

I began going to regular Friday meetings with the plant manager, who would yell at us to get our productivity up. He had a report he'd wave around, showing how we were doing on productivity, and my division was always at the bottom of the list. So finally I decided, *If they're going to focus on this, I'm going to backtrack and figure out where this report comes from.* I started asking questions, and I learned that the reports were based on little cards our people filled out every day. So I went to the guy who was putting together the reports, and I said, "Look, is there some way we could get this information on a daily basis?" He said, "Sure. No problem." He began giving me daily reports telling us exactly what we did on each of the three shifts, and how we compared to the other divisions. He'd run it for me every morning, and I'd leave a copy of the daily standings lying around for the foremen to see. For a long time, the foremen ignored it, but then they began to notice, and finally someone asked to see the detailed report I was getting. That report showed productivity by person, just as it came off the cards. They saw that and said, "Holy cow, this is incredible." That was the opening I needed.

Once I had the foremen looking at the daily scores, I could create a little competition. I could generate some wins. There was some movement in the rankings. Some of the foremen rose. That's when I had the industrial engineer do a history of the best day each of my foremen had ever had. Let's say our division was doing $42 worth of production per man, per eight hours of work. But maybe one foreman had a day when his department did $62 per man. I set that as his benchmark. I went to him, and I said, "I'll tell you what. I'll buy your whole department coffee if you hit that again. I'll buy you coffee and donuts if you do it a second time. I'll have everybody over for pizza and a poker game at my house if you do it a third time." It didn't take them long to beat it. Everybody beat it. And they kind of got trapped, because if you can do it once, you can do it again.

Then they began telling me how they could really get their productivity up. We got some things changed, and the division went from about $42 per man up to the high $60s. Meanwhile, the rest of the plant was going up, too. It had been running about $50, but as our division moved up into the high $60s, the other divisions began to chase us, so the whole factory rose.

The big moment came when we took on the division that had always been at the top of the productivity rankings. Its superintendent was a guy named Nelson. His people were still the leaders, but we were hot. We really had it smoking, and we were getting a little cocky, too, so we went and challenged one of Nelson's departments to a contest. We bet $500 that our department No. 54 could beat his department No. 37 in productivity for the following week. It was intense. At one point, we had department 54 operating in the $70s, which was unheard of. A guy came up to me on the shop floor and said, "Hey, I've never done $76 in one day, but I'll do it today if you promise you won't let the industrial engineer change the standard on us." And we went out and beat them. We beat them by about 20 cents. It was unbelievable. Department 54 had a heavyset general foreman named Eddie Novak. He got on a little bicycle and—with his butt hanging over the seat—rode around ringing a bell, saying, "54 beat 37! 54 beat 37!" Let me tell you Nelson got off his rump, got in his cart, and went out to kick ass and take names. It was great.

What turned people on was the challenge, the fun of the game, the fun of winning. Humor and laughter go a heck of a lot further than yelling and screaming and throwing tantrums. But you can't set up a game like that if you don't have standards.

KEY POINT: If you can get people beyond the day-to-day issues, if you can appeal to something they really want to do, they'll blow by every obstacle.

LEADING WITH STANDARDS

Numbers are a critical tool for the CEO. I can see trends emerging before they become crises. That allows me to take action while things are still going good. I don't mean I tell people what to do. I mean I point out to them that a problem could be developing, and give them the opportunity to head it off. The numbers serve as a guide for me. Let's say one of our factories is having trouble with productivity. I can hold off, give the managers there a chance to come up with their own solution. I generally won't step in until the number begins to establish a pattern—say, when the same problem turns up for three consecutive months. Then I have to act to make sure the situation doesn't get out of hand and threaten everyone else in the company. But the nice thing about the financials is that they allow you to develop those trends. It doesn't bother me to see that we have problems. The important thing is whether people are working toward solutions. We're always going to have problems. The question is, what are we doing to fix the problems?

In business, you watch the numbers, and the numbers establish a pattern. As a CEO, you want to see those patterns, you want to master them. The benchmarks tell you where you are in a particular pattern. You get to the point where you can sense when something is wrong. It comes from having routines, from seeing the patterns. When something is out of the pattern, you react immediately.

It happens all the time. A number goes down. We focus on it. There's pressure on people to do something. Eventually the number goes up. I back off and go to another problem.

BEWARE ANY NUMBER THAT LOOKS TOO GOOD TO BE TRUE—IT PROBABLY IS

A man I know bought a door-making company that had been losing money. He came in, gave some pep talks to people, and set up a standard cost system. Then he sat back to see what happened. To his delight, his profits jumped $30,000 per month from one quarter to the next—or so his outside accountant told him. The guy didn't ask how this had happened. He just took the accountant's word for it. At the end of the year, the auditors came in and discovered the company was short $90,000 of work-in-process inventory.

The problem, it turned out, was that the wood came in ten-foot boards, while the doors were only eight feet long. Each board had to be cut to the right size. The excess wood was scrap, but the man had neglected to take scrap into account when he set up his standard cost system. So the scrap wasn't being written off. On paper, it looked as though there was extra wood lying around that could be used to make doors. In fact, there was a lot of scrap wood that wasn't of any use to the company.

Moral: Don't accept any number until you understand where it came from and you know it's real.

The numbers used in business are not sent down from on high. You get them by counting real things, and then by adding, subtracting, multiplying, or dividing. If you don't understand a number, keep asking questions.

KEY POINT: Businesses always have problems. Numbers tell you where the problems are, and how worried you should be.

MY OWN PERSONAL BENCHMARK

I always wanted to get SRC to the point where we could sell the company tomorrow, and everyone would walk away with at least $55,000, which was the median price of a home in Springfield in 1991. We'd have that kind of value and liquidity. That was my number, $55,000 per person. You need a number, or the goal isn't real. That seems like a good one because housing consumes such a tremendous percentage of disposable income. If your house is paid off, you can look to the future. You don't have to look back. You can have a whole new perspective on your life.

chapter 7

Skip the Praise—Give Us the Raise

There is no more powerful tool a manager can have than a good bonus program—which is why some companies will pay a consultant tens of thousands of dollars to design one. That's not necessarily a stupid investment. If a bonus program works, it can be an incredible motivator. It can get people producing at levels that make the cost of the program seem like peanuts, no matter how much you may have spent to set it up.

What a bonus program does is communicate goals in the most effective way possible—by putting a bounty on them. It says to people, "These targets are so important we'll give you a reward if you hit them." When you do that, you get people's attention very fast. You send them a strong message. You provide them with a focus. You give them a challenge and a very good reason for working as hard and as smart as they can to meet it: they're going to get paid.

We get all that and much, much more from our bonus program, and we didn't pay anyone a dime to come up with it. We call it "Skip the Praise—Give Us the Raise," or STP-GUTR—pronounced Stop-Gooter. Here are some of the things we like about it:

1. **Stop-Gooter is our most effective educational program. We use it to teach people about business.**

   If the goal is to improve the debt-equity ratio, people learn about debt and equity and how they can affect both. The same holds for pretax profits, or inventory accuracy, or the overhead chargeout rate. Whatever the goal, it gives people a big incentive to find out about some aspect of the accounting system, the company, and the competitive environment. Otherwise people won't have much fun, they won't earn the bonus, and they'll take a lot of flak from their peers.

2. **The bonus program serves as a kind of insurance policy on the company and our jobs.**

   That's because we use it to target our vulnerabilities. Every year, we figure out what is the greatest threat the company faces, and we get the entire workforce to go after it in the bonus program. In effect, we put an annual bounty on fixing our weaknesses. That gives everyone an additional reason to achieve the goals. These are musts, not wants, and so they are worth the extra effort. Interestingly enough, once a weakness is fixed, it tends to stay fixed.

3. The program brings us together as a team.

It ensures that everyone has the same priorities and that we all stay focused on the same goals. It eliminates mixed messages. When one department is having trouble, another department will send in reinforcements, and everybody understands why. Often people don't even have to be asked. They will help each other out spontaneously, sometimes at great inconvenience. That's because the program makes everyone aware of how much we depend on one another to hit our targets. We win together or we don't win at all.

4. The program helps us identify problems fast.

If we don't achieve a goal, we find out very quickly why we missed it. Everybody is looking through the numbers to see what the problem is. Maybe it's receivables: customers are slowing down their payments and conserving cash. Maybe it's productivity: people are new in their jobs and can't absorb overhead fast enough. The bonus program forces the problem out into the open. Once it's there, you can go to work on it. You can solve it.

5. Stop-Gooter is the best tool we have for increasing the value of our stock.

We always set it up to guarantee that the stock value will rise substantially if we hit our targets— and will be protected even if we don't. That's one of the most important messages we send through the program: "This Game is all about equity and job security." Short-term incentives like bonuses are fine, but we want to make sure people never lose sight of the long-term payoffs.

6. **Most important, the bonus program provides the structure of the Game.**

   It puts the ball in play. It sets the tempo. It keeps the action going week in, week out, all year long. It gives us a language, a way of communicating. It creates excitement, anticipation. It gets the adrenaline flowing. It makes sure that people stay involved, engaged, and on their toes. It is, in short, our most important motivator, which is its primary function. If it weren't raising the energy level, we'd stop using it, although I find it hard to imagine how it could fail to motivate. That's a question we constantly pose, "Is the bonus program motivating people?" But I have to admit that if anybody ever told me it wasn't, I'd think that he or she was a dirty liar—or that our education program was in deep trouble.

⫸ bootstrapping: the best reason for paying people with bonuses

I am a strong believer in operating a company, any company, as if its future were always on the line, as if something could happen at any moment to threaten its survival. Most companies do, in fact, follow that principle when they are starting up. They don't take the future for granted because they can't. They know they could run out of cash next week, and the game would be over. So they become extremely resourceful. They constantly look for an edge, for ways to cut costs and save money, for things they can do to get more bang for their buck. It's known as *bootstrapping*, and it's how every business should be run, not just start-ups. Bootstrapping is a mentality, a set of habits, a way of operating based on self-reliance, ingenuity, intelligence, and hard work. When you don't bootstrap, you grow fat and sloppy. You get into the habit of buying solutions to your problems. You take the future for granted. You assume you'll be in business forever. You let your costs rise, and you take your eye off the ball. You get caught up in a lot of issues that have nothing to do with making money and generating cash. The next thing you know, a competitor comes along and knocks you out of the box. Suddenly, your company doesn't have much of a future, and you may not have a job.

A good bonus system can help you build a bootstrapping mentality into your organization. It does that by putting a great deal of emphasis on job security—by reminding people what it takes to protect their jobs and by showing them how they can get more.

As I've said, there is only one sure way to protect jobs, and that is to be ruthless about costs. But least-cost companies face an unpleasant choice. If you want to come in below your competitors, you can (1) pay your people less or (2) make your product faster. That's about it. No humane person enjoys making such a choice. Who wants to have a business that provides people with the lowest standard of living in the market, or that forces them to work so fast it's unhealthy? Who wants a company that prevents people from taking care of their families and themselves, from leading a full and happy life? But what's the alternative if you're going to be competitive and stay in business?

A bonus system like ours offers a way around this dilemma. It allows the company to hold base salaries at a level that gives people a great deal of job security—that pretty much guarantees they'll have work so long as they do a decent job. But if people do a better than decent job, if they can figure out ways to improve, the company shares with them whatever additional money they generate by paying them bonuses. The more they generate, the bigger the bonuses. It's like getting a raise, maybe even a very substantial raise, over and above their regular salary, but in a way that doesn't jeopardize their future employment. We know we can survive the tough economic periods. We may not pay bonuses in tough times, but we'll keep going. We won't lose jobs.

In effect, we're creating a certain elasticity for the downtimes. We don't ever want to lay people off, and we don't want to cut wages either. Most of the salary a working person earns goes to cover his or her fixed costs—mortgage, tuition, groceries, transportation expenses. If you're forced to cut back in those areas, your morale is going to tumble. I don't know of anything harder than having to cut basic living expenses. We want people to be able to count on a certain level of income, but we also want to give them the opportunity to earn more. And they will earn a lot more as long as the company is in good shape and they are performing up to their capabilities.

if bonus programs are so great, why do so many of them fail?

Probably for a lot of the reasons our first bonus program failed back in 1983. It was a total disaster. For one thing, most people didn't understand it. They weren't motivated by it. They didn't know what they could do to achieve the goals. Not only that, but we'd chosen the wrong goals. We wouldn't have had enough cash to cover the bonuses if people *had* hit the targets. When we realized our mistake, we killed the program immediately, midway through the year, and went back to the drawing boards. That experience taught us how *not* to set up a bonus program. We've learned a lot since then about developing one that really works. In the process, we've come up with a checklist of what you should do, and what you should avoid, when you create your own bonus plan.

*** Put Everybody in the Same Boat.**
Every employee should be part of the same bonus program, from the chief executive to the people who sweep the floors and answer the phones. Give everybody the same goals and a similar stake in the outcome. At SRC, we calculate bonuses as a percentage of regular compensation. Whenever a bonus is paid under Stop-Gooter, each of us gets a check for an amount representing a preset percentage of our annual pay (salary, or wages, plus overtime).

We don't all get the *same* percentage, however. Under Stop-Gooter, most managers and professionals are eligible to earn bonuses totaling up to 18 percent of their annual pay. For everyone else, the maximum bonus is 13 percent of annual pay. The reason is simple: we want people to move ahead, to take more risks, and to shoulder additional responsibilities. If they do, it's important that they get rewarded. But, that said, we want everyone to go after the same goals and to be subject to the same rules.

That's because we want people to play together as a team, to pull in the same direction. It's easier to win that way. We don't want people or departments to compete against one another. We don't want to set up squads that try to beat one another. We certainly don't want to pit managers against workers, or vice versa. We want a compensation system that encourages people to understand one another's problems, that gets them to work things out. We want people to see how much we all depend on each other, regardless of where we stand in the company. At SRC, you win when everybody wins, when the company wins. I don't want a company-wide bonus program in which some people win and others lose. The only ones who lose should be our competitors.

The one exception to this rule is safety. You have to generate awareness of safety as an issue, because that's the only way to prevent accidents, and I don't have any problem doing that through internal competition. We don't include safety in our Stop-Gooter program. Instead, we run separate safety contests in which we divide the company into teams, deliberately mixing people across department lines. One year, for example, I was on a team with all the other people whose last name started with S. The idea was to see which team could go the longest without an accident, and we offered $62,000 in prizes. By reducing accidents, we managed to bring down our annual workers' compensation premiums by $100,000. So the safety program wound up netting the company 38 cents on the dollar. It was a win for SRC, and a win for everyone at SRC because the savings helped us on our Stop-Gooter goals for the year. But our main purpose was to get people thinking about safety and to keep them from getting hurt.

* Stick to Two or Three Goals—and Get Them from the Financials.
Giving people a long list of goals is like not having any goals at all. Build your bonus program around two or, at most, three goals per year. More than that just gets too complicated. The important thing is to choose the right ones. I want goals that keep people focused on the fundamentals of business: making money and generating cash. I also want goals that educate people about the different

aspects of the business, that teach people exactly what it takes to be successful, and that provide an incentive to do the right things. Finally, I want goals that make the company stronger by eliminating our weaknesses. As it turns out, you can get all that by choosing your goals off the financial statements.

We almost always base one of our annual goals on pretax profit margins—to ensure people stay focused on making money. The other goal has varied from year to year, depending on what we've seen as our biggest vulnerability at the time. As a general rule, however, we make a point of taking the second goal off the Balance Sheet—to make sure people also pay attention to generating cash. (I'll talk more about the process we use to select goals in the next chapter, "Coming Up with the Game Plan.")

Now, a funny thing happens when you choose goals from the financial statements. For every one you pick, you get about five or six others at the same time. Suppose we decide to go after *liquidity*, which you can measure by looking at what accountants call the *current ratio*. It's calculated by adding up all your *current assets* (i.e., those you expect to convert to cash within the next twelve months, such as inventory and receivables) and dividing by all your *current liabilities* (i.e., those you have to pay within twelve months, such as short-term debts and payables). The ideal current ratio can vary greatly from industry to industry, but you almost always want to have more current assets than current liabilities. A ratio of two to one is generally considered quite healthy.

Whenever you can quantify a goal, you can set targets. You can decide how big a bonus people will earn by improving the current ratio a specific amount. To hit that target, they have to pay attention to a whole range of factors: inventory levels, shipping schedules, operating efficiency, collection of receivables, negotiated terms with customers, and on and on. In the process, people get interested in various aspects of the business. Suddenly everybody wants to know about receivables. We have staff meetings where our accountant talks about which customers pay and how fast they pay. And people are interested because, if customers don't pay, we don't have the cash—the customers do. And we can't use that cash, say, to reduce our short-term debt. And if we don't pay down the debt, we don't hit the liquidity goal, and we don't get the bonus.

So the bonus game takes people down the money trail, and they see everything that happens when customers are slow in paying their bills. They get an education in business, numbers, and the accounting system. They learn how it all fits together. And they accomplish several goals in the course of going after one.

* Give People the Chance to Win Early and Often.

A bonus program is first and foremost a tool for motivating people. If it doesn't motivate, it isn't working. And what gets people motivated? Winning. There's really nothing like winning to make you want to go back and try again and do even better the next time. Set up your bonus program so that you put people on a winning track from the outset and then make it possible for them to keep winning right through to the end of the year.

That's the whole logic behind our system of payouts. After we choose a goal, we set the levels at which we will pay bonuses. There may be as many as five payout levels for each goal. With the profit goal, for example, the company's baseline is usually a pretax margin of 5.0 percent, while our top target is 8.6 percent. If we come in with a pretax profit margin below 5.0 percent, we don't earn any bonuses. If it's between 5.0 and 5.5 percent, we get into the first payout level, which pays hourly people bonuses equal to 1.3 percent of their regular pay. We hit the second level at a pretax margin of 5.6 percent, and the bonus rises to 2.6 percent. The third level starts at a pretax margin of 6.6 percent, and pays 3.9 percent of regular pay. So it goes until the company gets to an 8.6 percent margin or better, at which point an hourly employee earns the maximum payout on the profit goal of 6.5 percent.

Coming up with the specific targets and payout levels is largely a matter of arithmetic. (See "Bonus Math," page 176.) The numbers will, of course, be different for every company. You *must* do the math. The bonus system won't work if the math doesn't work. In making your calculations, however, do not lose sight of the fundamental purpose, namely, to get and keep your people motivated. Here are some general rules to bear in mind.

1. **Set the baseline at the lowest point that still guarantees the company's security.**

   Everybody must understand that the basic health of the company is paramount. Nobody should earn a bonus for doing the minimum required to protect jobs. We figure, for example, that a pretax profit margin of 5 percent is the lowest we can have without getting into trouble. (Remember, 40 percent of profits go to taxes, so that leaves us with about a 3 percent after-tax margin, which we need for working capital—replacing worn-out machines, handling swings in inventory, and so on.) On the other hand, you don't want to put the baseline so high that people get discouraged right off the bat. Keep the first payout level well within their range. At SRC, everybody knows we are capable of getting into the first level on either goal, because we set the baseline at a level we've already achieved in the past.

Notice that people are focusing *above* the survival point. Many companies set their goals too low, as if it's okay to break even. Then the company is in danger if people miss the goal. We never want to operate that close to the line. If our pretax margin is less than 5 percent, we all feel as though we've let one another down, and that's exactly how I want it. I would rather have people feel bad about missing the bonus than about losing their jobs because the company is not making money.

2. **Make sure people have the opportunity to take home a significant portion of the additional profits generated under the bonus plan.**

Bonuses won't motivate people if they think the company is being cheap or greedy, or if the rewards aren't commensurate with the effort they're being asked to put out. They must feel that the plan is both a fair deal and a way to earn some big bucks. Stop-Gooter gives a machinist on the shop floor a shot at getting an extra 13 percent on top of his or her base compensation—that's $2,600 for someone making $20,000 a year, or the equivalent of almost seven weeks' pay. As for the company, it gives back to people, in the form of bonuses, about half of the additional profits generated over and above the base of 5 percent pretax (assuming we hit the highest payout levels on both goals).

3. Make it possible for people to earn bonuses frequently enough to keep them involved in the Game.

One of the most common mistakes companies make is to have just one bonus payout per year. Then they compound the mistake by not announcing how much people have earned until long after the year-end, and not actually paying it for several weeks beyond that. What happens is that people ignore the bonus program until the final quarter—if you're lucky. More likely, they pay no attention to it at all and regard whatever they get under it as a gift. That kind of bonus is not a reward; it's a bribe.

We set up the Stop-Gooter program so that people have a chance to earn a bonus every three months. That makes sense because of our overall approach to the Great Game of Business. On the one hand, we want people to get used to a quarterly grading system: it's a time-tested way of evaluating companies, and it works. It fits in with the normal cycles of a business. It's a good short-term time frame. Moreover, the three-month period turns out to be pretty much ideal for the way we play the Game. The end of the quarter comes fast enough that we can keep people focused on it through our weekly meetings.

Not every bonus program should have quarterly payouts. Monthly bonuses might work better for some companies. I can also see having semiannual ones. Don't go longer than that, however, without at least locking in the money owed to people. Not only will the bonus lose its impact, but you may run into credibility problems, especially if the program is new. People are going to be skeptical when you lay out the bonus deal for them. They won't really believe it until they see the money in their hands. But once that happens, their attitude will change so fast it will take your breath away.

4. **Start with a small bonus pool and let it grow as the year goes on, so that people have the opportunity and the incentive to meet all the goals—and earn the entire bonus—right up to the end.**

By "bonus pool" I mean the total amount of money available to be paid out in bonuses during any given period. I'm saying the pool should start small and grow from month to month or quarter to quarter.

This is a very important point. If you are not careful, you might inadvertently build some subtle demotivators into your plan. Suppose you decide to give people the chance to earn 25 percent of the annual bonus in each quarter of the year, and they come up short in the first two quarters. That would take a lot of the steam out of the program. People might well get demoralized and stop trying. Suppose, on the other hand, they simply had to achieve the goals at any point in order to earn the bonus for the entire year—and they got everything done by the middle of the third quarter. Chances are that the company would be headed for big trouble before the year was through.

We avoid these pitfalls by increasing the stakes as the year goes on and by rolling any unearned bonus from one quarter into the pot for the next quarter. Here's how it works: the bonus pool for the first quarter is 10 percent of the total for the year. For the second quarter, it's 20 percent; for the third quarter, it's 30 percent; for the fourth quarter, it's 40 percent. Let's say we hit half of our targets in the first quarter and thus earn half of the available bonus. That amounts to 5 percent (half of 10 percent) of the total bonus we are eligible to earn during the year. We get paid the 5 percent we've earned right away; the unearned 5 percent is rolled over into the second quarter pool. So now, in the second quarter, we are going after 25 percent of the annual bonus pool (the 20 percent share for the second quarter, plus the 5 percent share left over from the first quarter). Suppose we don't hit any of our targets in the second quarter. In that case, the entire 25 percent gets rolled into the third quarter, which means we are now shooting for 55 percent of the annual bonus (the 30 percent share from the third quarter, plus the 20 percent from the second, plus the 5 percent from the first). Even if we hit all of our highest targets in the third quarter, there is 40 percent of the bonus pool available to go after in the fourth quarter. If we don't hit any of our targets, we still have a chance to earn the rest of the annual bonus (95 percent) before the end of the year.

As a result, people stay in the game right up to the last whistle. We can win one quarter at a time, or we can pull it out on a Hail Mary pass in the final seconds. Like the man said, "it ain't over till the fat lady sings"—and, by then, we have another game ready to go.

* **Communicate, Communicate, Communicate.** Above all, make sure people understand how the bonus program works and are kept up-to-date on how they're doing. Bad communication is the main reason most bonus systems fail. No matter how clever you have been, no matter how well you have chosen your goals, no matter how carefully you have designed your payout system, your program simply won't motivate people if they don't get it, or if they can't follow what's happening, or if they think you're hiding something from them. Don't expect them to give you the benefit of the doubt. I guarantee that they

will think you're manipulating the numbers if there is any doubt about the bonus formula, or if you lack a system for monitoring and checking the results.

Of course, if the bonus program makes sense, explaining it shouldn't be all that difficult. Start by teaching the teachers—that is, your managers, supervisors, and key employees. Develop a solid core of people who know what's going on and who can explain it to everybody else. It's a good idea to hold some meetings and produce some support materials (handouts, brochures, videos, whatever). But once your teachers are up to speed, don't wait. Go ahead and launch the program. Most people are going to learn about the bonus game the way people always learn about games: by playing it.

What's crucial is to have an effective system for keeping track of the results and communicating them throughout the company. Set a day and a time when the latest score will be announced each week (or, if that's not possible, each month) and then make sure you hit it. People will start looking forward to these updates. *Do not disappoint them.* If you are late with the scores, you will feed people's doubts and suspicions, dampen their enthusiasm, and undermine your chances of success.

How you communicate the results is up to you. Post them. Hold meetings. Put notices in with the paychecks. Set up an electronic ticker tape in the cafeteria, and flash the score at lunch. If your people are spread out geographically, send the results out by email or announce them by teleconference. Whatever you do, give people every opportunity to ask questions and get explanations. And go out of your way to make available the numbers on which the scores are based. Whether people actually check up on you or not, they want to know that they could if they had to. That's one reason for publishing complete, detailed financial statements every month. Ours run to a hundred pages, beginning with the monthly Stop-Gooter results. People could do their own calculations, if they were so inclined, from the numbers in the income statement and the balance sheet.

But keeping everybody up to date on the score is just part of the process required to make the bonus program work. In fact, the program should become the center of attention in your business. It should provide a context and a structure for everything else that goes on. If you've chosen the right goals, after all, achieving them should be everybody's top priority—by definition.

For the bonus program to play that role, there has to be a continuous, two-way flow of information between the people on the front lines and the managers who are overseeing the action. The top managers need numbers they can use to identify problems that should be solved, opportunities that should be pursued, and victories that should be celebrated. The frontline people need constant updates on where they stand, and they have to be shown what they can do to improve the results. The middle managers need tools to motivate and to lead, to set priorities, to draw the connection between meeting the standards, hitting the targets, and earning the bonus.

Obviously, we are talking about fundamental questions of management here. That's perhaps the most important benefit of a good bonus program. It provides a powerful incentive to make sure people throughout the organization have a clear understanding of their roles and the information required to perform them as well as possible. A company's ability to manage the flow of information will go a long way toward determining not only the effectiveness of its bonus program but its ultimate success in the marketplace.

At SRC, we manage the flow of information by playing the Great Game of Business. The principal mechanism we use is the weekly staff meeting, which is not so much a discrete event as the focal point for the entire process of exchanging information up and down the organization. I will take an in-depth look at that process in Chapter 9, "The Great Huddle."

* Don't Pay the Bonus Unless It Is Earned (But Do Everything You Can to Help People Win).
This is a simple point, but it is fundamental. The bonus program should be a tool for putting people in touch with the realities of the marketplace. A bonus should not be seen as a gift from management. It should be a reward people earn by doing a better job than their competitors who are out there vying for the same customers. You undermine that message if you pay the bonus when people come up short on their targets.

BONUS MATH, OR HOW IT ALL ADDS UP

If your bonus program isn't completely quantifiable, there is something wrong with it. People need targets and rewards they can count on. That means giving them numbers. Winning shouldn't be a judgment call or a matter of opinion. If it is, people won't believe you, and the program will fail.

But before you announce the targets and the payouts, make sure that the numbers add up. You don't want to launch the program and then discover that you've pointed people in the wrong direction, or given them incentives to do the wrong things. Above all, you want to be certain you can pay the bonuses you've promised. Otherwise you will have a disaster on your hands. If you fail to deliver the bonus when your people have delivered the goals, they'll never trust you again.

The math itself will depend on the type of bonus program you have, not to mention the specific circumstances of your business. But there is a certain logic to any process of choosing and checking the bonus numbers:

1. Set the profit targets and the maximum bonus payouts.

Before anything else, we decide on the baseline for profits, the top target for profits, and the highest level of bonuses we will pay on both goals. From that, we can figure out how much additional profit people might generate under the program, and how much the company will give back to them in the form of bonuses if they hit all their targets.

In our case, pretax profits have to be greater than 5 percent of our income before we pay any bonus on the income-statement goal. Above 5 percent, we start sharing the additional profits with people in the form of bonuses based on a percentage of their regular compensation. For simplicity's sake, let's assume that everybody gets the same percentage and that the most people can earn is an extra 13 percent of their annual pay, which they get if we hit the maximum level on both goals—6.5 percent for one, 6.5 percent for the other. Suppose we have sales of $70 million per year, and our payroll is $10 million. The most we'd pay out under Stop-Gooter would be an additional $1.3 million in one year (.13 × $10 million). We'd only pay that much, however, if we hit the maximum payout level on both goals. The maximum payout level for the profitability goal is usually set at 8.6 percent pretax profit. For purposes of this example, let's call it 9 percent. That means the company would earn an additional pretax profit of $2.8 million (9% – 5% = 4%, .04 × $70 million = $2.8 million). So after we have paid the bonuses, we will still have an extra $1.5 million left over for other purposes.

Notice we're assuming that we'll pay the maximum bonus on *both* goals, not just the profitability goal. A Balance-Sheet goal may not have any effect on your profits, but you'll have to pay the bonus on it if people hit it, so you must include it in your calculations. Obviously, if you do the calculating and don't like the results, you should go back and come up with different targets or payout levels.

2. Decide on a Balance-Sheet goal.
Meanwhile, we are choosing our Balance-Sheet goal with an eye toward making sure we'll have the cash to pay the bonuses people earn. You run a big risk if you

have an Income-Statement goal but not a Balance-Sheet goal: people may wind up making money without generating cash. Theoretically, all the money they make could go into inventory and receivables, and you wouldn't be able to pay the bonuses on time. That's one reason we like liquidity as a Balance-Sheet goal. It greatly increases the odds that we will have the cash we need to pay bonuses and do a lot of other things.

3. Set the targets on the Balance-Sheet goal.

The process we use for setting the Balance-Sheet targets is a little different from the one for the profit goal. First, we look at what would happen to the Balance Sheet if we hit the maximum target on the Income Statement. Then we start kicking numbers around on the Balance-Sheet goal in an effort to come up with a top target that will make those extra profits available for our use. In effect, we want to offer people a bounty for making sure the additional income doesn't get tied up in illiquid, nonproductive assets or liabilities.

Let's say our Balance-Sheet goal is liquidity, as measured by the current ratio, and we have $10 million in current assets and $5 million in current liabilities. So our current ratio is 2.00 to one, or 2:1. We already know that if people hit the top target on the Income-Statement goal, they will generate an additional $2.8 million in pretax profits. If they also hit the top Balance-Sheet target, we will pay $1.3 million in bonuses, which leaves us with an additional pretax profit of $1.5 million. About 40 percent of that goes to taxes, so we would have additional after-tax profits of $900,000 (.60 × $1.5 million = $900,000).

We'd really like to have all that in the form of cash. Let's say we use the $900,000 to reduce our current liabilities from $5 million to $4.1 million, while our current assets stay at $10 million. Now our current ratio is 2.44:1 ($10 million / $4.1 million = 2.44). We started out at 2.00. So, if we keep all the additional after-tax profit as cash, we'd have about a 20 percent increase in the current ratio. That's pretty much the maximum increase in liquidity we can expect if we hit a pretax margin of 9 percent and pay out the full bonus, 13 percent of payroll. It means we've taken all the money left over after paying bonuses and taxes, and used it to reduce our current liabilities.

Once we've done those calculations, we can set the targets on the balance-sheet goal. We put the biggest bounty, the 6.5 percent bonus, on that 20 percent increase in the current ratio, and we work backward from there. Since we want several payout levels, we decide to pay a bonus for every 5 percent improvement in the ratio. You might note that this gives people a strong incentive to reduce current liabilities rather than put the cash into current assets. If you increase current assets by $900,000 and leave current liabilities at $5 million, you wind up with a current ratio of 2.18 ($10.9 million/$5 million = 2.18). That only brings you up into the first level of the bonus payout.

4. Protect your equity.

The whole idea of a bonus program is to provide people with short-term incentives to achieve certain goals. That's fine. Everybody needs those kinds of rewards. But we don't ever want people to forget the real payoff for playing the Great Game of Business at SRC, namely, the generation of wealth in the form of equity. So we always go back and see what effect our Stop-Gooter goals are likely to have on the value of our stock.

If the company has a 9 percent pretax margin on $70 million in sales, it earns $6.3 million in pretax profits (.09 × $70 million = $6.3 million). Out of that $6.3 million, we pay $1.3 million in bonuses, which leaves us with $5 million pretax. We can use part of that money to build up the Employee Stock Ownership Plan (ESOP), which we want to do. So we reduce our earnings further by putting $1 million into the ESOP. That brings our pretax profits down to $4 million. We only get to keep about 60 percent of that amount, since 40 percent goes to taxes. So our after-tax profit comes to about $2.4 million (.60 × $4 million = $2.4 million). That's our retained earnings for the year, the money we have available to finance our growth, or pay down our long-term debt, or otherwise invest in ourselves. Let's say the company is worth about ten times its annual after-tax earnings, which is the common rule of thumb. In that case, SRC's value would be about $24 million.

You see, it's all very simple math. The bonus program generated $2.8 million in additional pretax profits. We gave out $1.3 million of that in the form of bonuses. We put another $1 million into the ESOP. We paid taxes on the remaining $500,000 and wound up with an additional $300,000 in after-tax earnings. That translates into a $3 million boost in the company's value. All because of the bonus program.

That can be very, very tough for a CEO. If people have tried hard and missed by a tiny amount, there is a big temptation to pay the bonus anyway. Resist it. Once you start changing the rules of the game, you step onto a slippery slope, and it is hard to go back. A couple of times, we have missed targets by .01 percent. In each case, it was agony. I never want it to happen again. So now, as we near the end of the quarter, our accountants come into the weekly meeting with sheets showing exactly what we must do to get to the next level on each goal. You can always come up with a few thousand dollars extra in some area, if that's what it takes.

▌▌▌▶ bonus power

The real power of the bonus program lies in its ability to educate people about business. Once they understand the math, they see how everything fits together, and how business can be a tool for getting them what they want. And it all *does* fit together. The system really works. You can't criticize it because it is simply a reflection of reality. You can criticize individuals. You can take people to task for the way they do business. You can go after the ones who are greedy, who only want to help themselves, who exploit other people for personal gain. But the fault lies in those individuals, not in the nature of capitalism.

chapter 8

COMING UP WITH THE GAME PLAN

The heart of the Great Game of Business is the annual game plan. By that, I mean a set of financial statements spelling out what you expect to do month by month for the entire year. Without a plan, people have nothing to which they can compare their performance, no means of recognizing problems, no targets they can use to organize, motivate, and challenge themselves. They won't know what they have to do to support one another, or whether they are doing a good job, or how to evaluate the numbers they're generating on a daily, weekly, and monthly basis.

Emotions will cloud the picture. Barriers will go up. As the leader, you won't know whether to celebrate or sound the alarm. No matter what you do, people will second-guess you. As for that bonus program, don't waste your time on it.

Without an annual plan, how could you ever come up with objective, quantifiable goals to shoot for? For that matter, how would you ever know if you'd reached them?

The annual game plan will tell you that, and keep you posted on other important matters:

> Is the company ahead of schedule?
> Is the company behind schedule?
> Is the company right on the money?
> Who is carrying the load?
> Who is falling behind?

But just as important as the plan itself is the way you produce it. You need more than a plan that is firmly rooted in reality. You also need one that people not only accept but agree to—without reservation. All the players must be ready to make the plan work. They have to *want* it to work. They must be willing to do whatever it takes to win. They must know they can count on everybody else to do the same, and that everybody else is counting on them.

You can only get that sort of consensus by opening up the planning process and bringing the entire workforce in. Set it up so people know they own the process, know they are responsible for what comes out of it. That's the game. Otherwise, the plan will become a club, not a tool they can use in their work, and they'll regard the goals as yours, not theirs—which defeats the purpose of having them. It is very hard to get anyone motivated to achieve someone else's goals.

///

REMEMBER, THE FIFTH HIGHER LAW IS:
You Gotta Wanna.

///

So how can that happen? How do you set up an orderly planning process that becomes part of the Game rather than an ordeal—that encourages everybody to participate, that makes sure each person is consulted about the decisions affecting his or her job, and that produces consensus on the final results? And how do you do all that without bringing the company to a total standstill? How do you engage people in thinking about next year's plans and goals without distracting them from accomplishing what needs to get done here and now? Most important, how do you make it *fun*?

Show people their stake in the process. When you put together your annual plan, you are designing the game you'll be playing for the next twelve months. This is everybody's big chance to say exactly how he or she thinks it ought to be set up. The whole idea is to come up with a game that people will play with a lot of enthusiasm—that they will care about winning.

First, decide what winning means. Ask people:

What do they think they can accomplish in the coming year?
How much can they increase sales and production?
Do they want to?
What concerns do they have about the company?

Are there problems that should be fixed?
Do they want more space?
Do they need new tools?
Do they want additional perks or benefits?

The planning process is a time to think about the future, to dream a little. It's also a time to think about what dangers may lie ahead, so that you can figure out how to minimize them. And it's a time for everybody to say what they are willing to contribute—what commitments they will make—to achieve the goals you all agree upon. At the end of the process, you want to be able to tell people, "Here's what we say we want, and here's how we can get it, provided we all just do what we say we can do." The front line has to block. The running backs have to hustle. The punt return unit has to get good field position. The team has to play in true team spirit.

There should be nothing boring about coming up with the annual game plan. Don't make the mistake of approaching it as an arduous but necessary ordeal. If it is, you've failed. The plan is the life of the company for the next year. If people are bored by the process of creating it, the way most people are bored by most planning processes, then there is little hope that they'll get excited about carrying it out—or that they'll even be able to. They won't take responsibility for it. They won't make the necessary commitments.

That doesn't mean you have to invent a whole new way of planning. We use a process you can find in any textbook on budgeting. There are four phases based more on logic than anything else:

1. Determine what your sales are likely to be in the coming year.
2. Figure out what it's going to cost to produce these sales and how much cash you can expect to generate as a result.
3. Decide what you want to do with the cash.
4. Choose your bonus goals for the year.

Simple stuff. What makes it all interesting, even exciting, is the drama that comes from having everybody involved. When we start out, we literally have no idea of where we are going to wind up. It's not as if the top managers have already decided the basic shape of the plan. I am as much in the dark as the guy who picks parts in the warehouse, and both of us are curious about what lies ahead.

WHY PEOPLE HATE BUDGETING

In my experience, most people approach budgeting with a mixture of cynicism and boredom. At best, they regard it as a meaningless exercise in which they feed back to top management the numbers it wants to hear. Alternatively, they feel they are being forced to help design the club they are going to be beaten over the head with for the next twelve months. Almost no one views budgets as tools for increasing productivity or making money. In fact, some trendy management thinkers say companies shouldn't bother with annual budgets at all. They argue that the business world has become too volatile to anticipate what's going to happen six, nine, or twelve months down the line, so what's the point of coming up with a plan you know will be irrelevant within a very short time? Not only is the argument wrong, but the conclusion is a big mistake. Yes, it's true that companies can often get by without budgets when they're small. And it's also true that developing a meaningful budget can be difficult if the company is still young and uncertain about what it's doing. But the volatility and unpredictability of business have been greatly overblown in recent years. Of course, the business world looks volatile and unpredictable if you don't have any method of forecasting what lies ahead, or if you base your plans on the wishes of top management rather than reality. In either case, you're bound to run into surprises—big, unpleasant surprises.

But the answer isn't to give up and accept those surprises as a condition of doing business. Most surprises, the worst ones, can be avoided as long as people have the tools they need. An annual game plan is an absolutely critical tool. By "game plan," I mean a lot more than the typical budget that tells people how much they can spend in each expense category. I'm really talking about a complete set of financials for the coming year—Income Statement, Balance Sheet, Cash-Flow Analysis, capital plan, inventory plan—the whole bit.

That may sound like a tall order, but it's not, provided you have the two other tools we've already talked about. First, you need a standard cost system

(Chapter 6), so that you know how much it will cost to produce what you expect to sell, and your people know what the plan is going to require of them. After all, the plan will only be reliable if people are committed to it. They can't make commitments if they don't know how much they will have to do, and how fast. That's what the standards tell them.

Second, you need a bonus program (Chapter 7), which will bring the game to life and give people a big incentive to win—that is, to make the plan work. If people are into the Game, they will care about the game plan, and they will help produce a good one, which is crucial. Lack of participation is the single greatest obstacle to coming up with a reliable game plan. If people don't participate, they don't commit, and they don't deliver, and so you wind up with those big, unpleasant surprises. When people hate the budgeting process, the failure of the budget is a foregone conclusion.

|||||▶ countdown to the new year

Step one in planning: put together a schedule. Without a schedule, there's a natural tendency to underestimate the time required, and you will probably let things slide. This year's demands always seem more pressing than next year's. As a result, you may wind up skipping important steps or be forced to rush to get done. Either way, nobody's going to have much fun, and you won't produce a good plan.

So how do you develop a planning schedule? Work backward from the new year. Figure out what you want to have when you finish, and how long it will take to produce it. Our annual game plan has eight documents:

1. Income Statement
2. Balance Sheet
3. Cash-Flow Analysis
4. Sales and marketing plan
5. Capital plan
6. Inventory plan
7. Organization charts
8. Compensation plan

You can undoubtedly get by with fewer—we did for years. The essential documents are the Income Statement, the Balance Sheet, the sales and marketing plan, and the compensation plan (which includes the specifics of our Stop-Gooter bonus program for the year). The Cash-Flow Analysis, capital plan, and inventory plan are tools that help us control the cash we generate. You, too, should have such tools, although you may not need so many. If your business doesn't have inventory, for example, you obviously don't need an inventory plan.

We give ourselves more than six months to produce the plan. We could probably do it faster, but we like to take our time and make sure everybody has a chance to contribute. The first two months are relatively low-key, a period of preparation. Mainly, we are thinking about the sales forecast. Given its importance, we want to come up with one in which we have a great deal of confidence. The real excitement begins in October, when we present the sales plan to the entire company, and from then on the pace does not let up until the end of our fiscal year, January 31— New Year's Eve at SRC.

ALL PLANNING BEGINS WITH A SALES FORECAST

There's a reason why the sales figure is at the top of the Income Statement. Without a sales line, you don't *have* an Income Statement. You can't feed anybody. There is no payroll to meet. The game is over before it begins.

Everything in business begins with sales, including the planning process. I often run into CEOs who say, "I know we need a plan, but I don't know where to start." I tell them, "Bring your entire staff together and—in front of everybody else—ask the salespeople what they're going to sell for the month." The response is always the same: "You know what they're going to tell me? They're going to say, 'What number do you want to hear?'"

There lies the root of the problem. You will never get your salespeople to forecast accurately if they think they are doing it for your sake. It's *not* for your sake, or at least it shouldn't be. Without a forecast, the entire company suffers, which is why the rest of the staff should be in the room. Let other people tell sales how frustrating it is to work in a situation where you never know what you're going to be called on to do next. It takes planning to live up to commitments, to support other people, to set and achieve goals. Nobody can plan without a forecast, and you can't have a game without a plan. The salespeople have to start the process. As soon as they say how much and what kind of business they're going to bring in, everybody else can begin to figure out what it will take to fill those orders, and you can lay the groundwork for the game.

Yes, the forecast is a commitment, a big one, and it takes some courage for the salespeople to make it. But without it, none of the other commitments are possible. Insist on sales forecasts, and make sure they are stable forecasts. You will never come up with a reliable plan if the forecast is constantly changing.

KEY POINT: If you don't stabilize a sales forecast, you can't control your company. If you control a forecast, you control the world.

Month Six: Hold an Early Sales Meeting

Toward the end of July, we reserve several rooms at a beautiful resort in the Ozarks and bring all the sales and marketing people together for a two-day meeting. (Remember, this is supposed to be fun.) Each of the salespeople makes a presentation about his or her expectations for the next eighteen months. The head of the department gives an overview, and then other people discuss how they are coming along on their individual goals, what they are planning to do in the rest of the current year, and how they see the following year shaping up. *Every* member of the sales team gets up and talks.

Managers from other parts of the company are present. We listen to the sales presentations, and we play a game of what-if. We do everything we can to poke holes in salespeople's strategies. We're not trying to be mean or argumentative. On the contrary, we want to help them make the strongest possible forecast, because it will serve as the foundation for our entire plan. So it's in everybody's interest that we identify any problems, false assumptions, unrealistic expectations, or hidden risks. Like these:

> What is it going to cost to deliver on these sales commitments?
> Do we have the capacity? The skills? The equipment? The money?
> Can we get the parts we need?
> How fast does this customer pay its bills?
> How vulnerable are we to competition in that market?
> What if interest rates rise?
> What if this deal doesn't pan out?
> How likely is it that the customer will increase the order?
> How likely is it that the customer will cancel?
> Can we handle that?
> What's our fall-back position?

Those are the kinds of questions you have to put to your salespeople. Ask the toughest ones you can think of, and ask early enough in the process so that there is time to come up with new answers or devise new contingency plans.

Your company may not have a sales force per se—if you have a professional service firm, for example. In that case, go through this same exercise with whomever is responsible for bringing in customers. If that happens to be you, get together a group of friends and colleagues and have them grill you about your expectations for the coming year. One way or another, you want to wind up with the best sales forecast possible, and that means doing whatever you can to tear it apart before you embrace it.

Month Five: Put Together the Sales Plan; Work on the Standard Costs

After you've dissected the preliminary sales forecast, you need some time to come up with a better, stronger, smarter version. We generally allow ourselves two or three months, which gives us a chance to do a thorough job without neglecting our current needs. During that period, the sales and marketing people digest everything they've heard at the July meeting and figure out how they should modify the sales plan. They do research, revise strategies, raise or lower estimates, go over schedules with customers, rethink contingencies, whatever. Meanwhile, they continue to probe the market, looking for fresh clues of what the coming year has in store. Toward the end of September, they pull all the information together in a new, improved sales plan.

By then, we've also pinned down a lot of our costs—almost all of them, in fact, except the ones that depend on the final sales plan. We had one person, Doug Rothert, whose entire job was to figure out what our standard costs should be. In the course of the year, he reviewed every single cost or expense in the company. He was an accountant who served as our head of production for a while, and he helped to set up our original standard cost system. Then he spent most of his time wandering around the company, talking to people about what they were doing, working with them to come up with better, more accurate standards. That's what I mean by getting your accountants into the Game. He also kept an eye on the areas in which we'd had trouble meeting our standards or met them so easily we'd left them in the dust—either one could have been a sign that the standards needed to be revised. By the end of September, he'd talked to almost everyone in the company and had a fairly clear idea of how he thought our standard costs should've been modified in the coming year.

Goals, on the other hand, have only been discussed informally at this point, although we do know what issues people are concerned about, and what things they'd like to see happen. I personally meet with all employees at least once in the course of each year. In late spring, I hold a series of meetings around the company, in which I talk with people in groups of 20 or 30 and try to get a sense of what's on their minds. Sometimes I'll ask them to give me lists of suggestions for improving the company. We conduct a lot of surveys as well—for example, asking people to rate the ESOP in comparison to the various benefit programs. We can use the responses to guide us in developing a game plan that people will feel enthusiastic about. Then there's the feedback we get regularly through the staff meetings, not to mention what we pick up at the numerous company events. So all this information is floating around, giving us food for thought as we draw closer to goal-setting time.

Month Four: Present and Debate the Sales Plan

In October, the process moves into high gear, as the sales department comes out with its revised forecast. There is an extended staff meeting, during which the plan is presented to the managers and middle managers who are going to take it to the rest of the workforce. Everybody gets a five-page document detailing what we think our sales will be in the next fifteen months—the last quarter of the current year and the entire following year. The forecast is very specific, showing exactly how much of each product is scheduled to be shipped to each customer in each month. That's important. A vague forecast is useless. People can't respond to it, and you can't base plans on it. Spell out precisely what you expect to sell, how much, and when. It's better to be wrong than to be vague.

Once the sales plan has been presented, we encourage everyone to go at it, to rip it apart, to expose any weaknesses or inconsistencies. The debate happens in two stages. First, the middle managers take the plan back to the frontline supervisors, who go over it carefully, paying close attention to the implications for their specific areas. (Can they handle the level of production in the plan? What's the significance of the changes from this year to next? Do they make sense?) At the same time, we are converting the dollar figures into pieces—for example, the actual number of fuel-injection pump nozzles we'll have to produce month by month to meet the plan. The supervisors can then take those numbers to the people on the shop floor and get them involved in the debate. (Do we have enough people to take care of this? Are we overstaffed? What do we need in the way of equipment? How is this going to affect quality?)

This step—converting dollars into things—is important. You can only get people to contribute by putting the forecast into a form they can readily understand and react to, a form that corresponds to what they do every day. Obviously, that form will vary from business to business and from job to job. In a chain of restaurants, a sales forecast has different implications for the cooks, the waiters, and the people who buy the ingredients. In an airline company, the pilots will want to know how many flights they'll have to make, how long the flights will be, and how often they'll leave. The customer service representatives should know how many calls they'll be expected to handle, the purchasers how many meals they'll have to order, the people on the counters how many tickets they'll have to write, and so on.

Spell it out for people. Show them exactly what they will have to do to fulfill the sales plan. Make it easy for them to participate in the debate. If they don't have a chance to contribute, they won't take responsibility for the plan, and you may make mistakes that could have been avoided. The company-wide discussion of the sales forecast should not just be a public relations exercise. Listen to what people say. We definitely want people to take a hard look at the numbers and to insist on changes if the forecast is unrealistic. Sometimes there are major changes. In the fall of 1990, for example, people raised very tough questions about the sales department's optimistic predictions for the coming year. Weren't we going to be hurt by the recession that was already causing problems for our customers? What made us immune? No one had a convincing response, so we knocked down the sales forecast by about 15 percent—much to our subsequent relief. The recession hit us hard in the third quarter of the next year.

At the end of October, the middle managers get back together with the salespeople to report what they've heard from the front lines and to come to a consensus on the forecast. By then, some people have already begun to speculate about goals, but the serious discussion has to wait until our accountants take the numbers from the sales forecast, plug in the appropriate standard cost figures, and come up with a detailed plan for the next year.

Month Three: Agree on the Costs of Executing the Sales Plan; Start to Target Wants and Worries

November is when we settled on the standards for the coming year. The accounting department distributes an in-depth, month-by-month analysis of what it will cost to produce and deliver the goods in the sales forecast. Again, there is a debate, although it tends to be quite focused at this point. Most standards do not have to be changed very much (if at all) from year to year. When a standard is modified, there should be a specific reason. In our case, we may have new machinery that has increased productivity. Or perhaps someone has come up with a way to save money on parts. Or we have figured out a more efficient production process. Or we're facing stiffer competition in a particular market and have to cut costs in order to protect jobs.

Whatever the reason for the change, it has usually been analyzed and discussed by the time November rolls around. In any event, the person in charge of standards goes over each one with the individuals affected. The supervisors and middle managers literally have to sign off on the changes before the budget can be approved. I personally review every change greater than 10 percent. We want to make sure that the standards are fair—that they are attainable and that they keep us competitive in the market. We also want to know that all the players accept the standards everyone else is going to be expecting them to meet. That way, the motivation for achieving the standards comes from inside. When you choose your own targets, you can't blame anyone else if you miss. Of course, some people may complain anyway, human nature being what it is. They may blame the accounting department for giving them standards they couldn't meet. At that point, you want to be able to remind them that they saw and approved all the standards in advance.

There's another reason to get approval of the standards. In giving it, people are making specific commitments to one another for the next twelve months. They are agreeing to carry their weight by meeting the standards. Those commitments

are the basis for the Game. Without them, there
is no Game, just a different form of manipulation
and coercion. Commitments are vital. You have to
achieve consensus on the plan.

///

Of course, you're much more likely to achieve consensus if you've laid the necessary groundwork by developing a
standard cost system along the lines we discussed in Chapter 6, on pages 133 to 137.

This is also a good point to launch the general discussion of goals, since you will soon be deciding how to spend
the cash generated under the plan. Ask people about their
worries and their wants.

Are there things that need fixing?
Should equipment be replaced?
Do they want new offices or factory space?
What do they see as the greatest threats to their
jobs?

Perhaps it's the possibility of a recession: you may want
to reduce your debt. Perhaps it's delivery to customers: you
may want an increase in finished goods inventory. Perhaps
it's quality: you may want to introduce new processes.

It doesn't matter where the dangers may lie—in the
economy, the marketplace, or the company itself. You want
people to look over the entire landscape and talk about their
most pressing concerns and urgent desires. After all, you
will have a limited amount of cash with which to address

those concerns and fulfill those desires, so it's important to find out which ones are most important to people.

We do that by having a company-wide discussion that begins in November and continues intermittently for several weeks. We raise the issue in staff meetings, and the people there take it back to the rest of the organization. Pretty soon, we begin to get feedback. If there seems to be a pretty broad consensus, we can begin to draw up lists. If more discussion is needed, we hold additional meetings either at the company or off-site. In any case, we keep talking until there is general agreement about how we should be spending our cash and what we should focus on fixing in the coming year.

Month Two: Figure Out What to Do with the Cash; Zero in on Bonus Goals

As soon as you have all the numbers for sales, production costs, and other expenses, you can put together an income statement for the coming year. Break it down month by month, so that you can see exactly what you expect to do and when you expect to do it. From the Income Statement, you can construct a preliminary Balance Sheet and Cash-Flow Plan, which you can then use to focus the discussion about cash.

We generally do this in December. We draw up a set of pending financial statements and present them at one of the staff meetings. We say, "Look. If we execute this plan and meet our standards, we should be able to generate this much cash. What do you think we ought to do with it?"

The middle managers will take the information back to the rest of the company.

At this point, you have to start making some decisions. Use the Balance Sheet as your guide. It will show you the different places cash can go. For example, how much do you want to put into plant, property, and equipment? That's a particularly important question in a capital-intensive business like ours, but almost every business has to answer it. Can you get by with the equipment you already have, or is now the time to replace some of it? Do you have enough space in your present facilities? Should you buy that building across town? The answers to such questions will serve as the basis for your capital plan for the year, which should also be broken down by month so you can see *when* you're spending the cash, as well as *how much* and *what for*.

Cash can also go into inventory, assuming there is such a thing in your business. If you're not careful, you may wind up with more cash in the form of inventory than you need. So you should also have an inventory plan. What additional parts and supplies do you need to produce at the rate required by the sales plan? When do you need them? How fast are you going to be shipping finished products? Again, break out the numbers by month.

Wherever cash can go, you need a plan. Understand that I am speaking here only of categories on the balance sheet—of assets and liabilities—not of expenses and costs that show up on the Income Statement. In your business, you may spend a lot of money, say, on entertaining customers, but you should already have taken those expenses into account in putting together your projected income statement. At this point in the planning process, you are really figuring out how you want your balance sheet to look at the end of the year. If the cash you've generated is tied up in buildings, equipment, and inventory, it won't be available for bonuses, dividends, buying back stock from people, paying off debt, whatever. That doesn't mean you shouldn't increase inventory or invest in buildings. Perhaps you think having more inventory would improve customer service, or expanding your facilities would do wonders for morale. By all means, do it. But how you spend your cash should be a conscious decision.

The money shouldn't disappear just because no one is paying attention. And believe me, it will disappear. Not that people will steal it (although theft is a lot more likely if you don't have a plan). Rather, the cash will be spent on things you didn't really want and don't really need.

Decide in advance where you want the cash to go. Look at your business and identify where cash can be absorbed. There are only so many possibilities: inventory, equipment, office furnishings, vehicles, whatever. Then come up with a plan based on your real needs in each area. Once again, make sure you get a lot of input from the individuals affected—the warehouse people, the engineers, the men and women who are using the machines, their supervisors and department managers. They are the ones who will have to live with the consequences of the decisions, so it's essential that they help make them. Don't undermine the consensus you achieve on the overall game plan by forgetting to ask people whether or not they have the equipment they need to play.

Keep your projected Balance Sheet and Cash-Flow Statement in front of you while you're figuring out what to do. In December and January, we continually play with both of those statements, calculating and recalculating the numbers to see what effect different plans will have on our ability to pay bonuses, put money into the ESOP, or buy back stock. If cash looks tight, for example, we may hold off purchasing that new computer or building an addition on the factory. We may also consider choosing a bonus goal aimed at increasing our liquidity.

In fact, there is a close relationship between our decisions about how to spend the cash and what to target in the bonus program, since both must take into account the long-term health of the company. Before we make those decisions, we want to have a consensus about our wants and weaknesses. By the middle of December, that consensus is beginning to emerge. As we put together the capital plan and the inventory plan, we also come up with a list of possible bonus goals, based on the feedback from the company. We may even start trying out formulas, plugging in various numbers to see their effect on the Income Statement and the Balance Sheet. But we wait until the very end of the process to make our final decisions on the goals. We want all the information out in front of us when we do. These targets will be our top priorities in the coming year. We will all be doing everything we can to hit them. When we choose them, we are saying, in effect, "These are our Critical Numbers. We have to do well on them to have a good year." By January, we are ready to make that choice.

Month One: Decide on the Bonus Program; Submit the Final Plan

There are, as I noted in the last chapter, two types of goals in the bonus program—one from the Income Statement and one from the Balance Sheet. Since we put so much effort into achieving these goals, we want to be sure we are making ourselves stronger in the process. Consequently we spend a lot of time thinking about our weaknesses before deciding what our goals will be.

Our approach is based on the simple premise that every business has different strengths and weaknesses, which vary from year to year. The weaknesses are a threat to job security. People may go out and work hard, but—because of these weaknesses—their jobs may be jeopardized by outside forces. So how can you minimize the danger? One way is to use the bonus program.

Target your goals to shore up your weaknesses as a business. Of course, you're never going to eliminate weaknesses. You can't avoid making mistakes. Nor are you going to succeed at everything you do. We all have to be able to fail from time to time. That's the only way we learn. So it's important to give people the leeway to fail, the leeway to make mistakes, without jeopardizing job security. We do that, first, by identifying the factors that pose the biggest threats to job security, and then by selecting bonus goals that keep everyone's attention focused on wiping out those threats. In effect, we are promising to pay ourselves a reward for doing the things required to protect our jobs. We are putting a bounty on our weaknesses each year. We are saying, "WANTED: A $29 PER HOUR CHARGE-OUT RATE." Or "WANTED: A 20% INCREASE IN THE CURRENT RATIO." And, if we bring it in, we pay ourselves very well indeed.

There is no reason other companies can't follow the same approach. The first step, obviously, is to identify the threats to your business. That's actually quite easy: ask your people. They know. They will tell you. Get them to talk about the things that most concern them as they look around.

> What does the company do badly?
> Where is it vulnerable to competitors?
> What are the dangers they see in the economy?
> How might the company be at risk?

I guarantee that you will come up with a comprehensive and revealing list of dangers.

That's an important list to have in any event, because it tells you the issues you should be paying attention to—through the bonus program or otherwise. To turn a threat into a bonus goal, however, you have to go a step further and quantify it. You have to come up with an absolute measure that leaves no room for doubt as to whether or not a goal has been achieved. People must have total confidence in the results of the bonus game. They must know that the score is accurate, fair, and objective—that it could not have been manipulated by anyone. That way, when they win, it is their victory, and when they come up short, they have only themselves to blame. You never want to be in a situation where you miss the target by a tiny amount, but it's really a judgment call. Then you're in a real bind. If you give out the bonus anyway, it's a hollow victory. If you don't, you create a lot of resentment. In either case, you undermine the bonus program as a motivator.

This is the main reason we have never made quality a bonus goal, although it always appears on our list of potential threats. We can't figure out how to measure quality so that the results wouldn't be subject to manipulation. As a result, we address the quality issue through other programs, and we use the bonus program to go after things we can quantify using the financial statements. We chose the liquidity goal, for example, because people thought there was a recession coming. That was their major worry. So we wanted a goal that would make us strong enough to get through a serious downturn. The more liquid a company is, the more flexible it can be in a bad economic environment, and you can measure liquidity with the current ratio—that is, the ratio of short-term assets (including cash) to short-term liabilities. Improving the current ratio became one of the goals.

In fact, the two goals tend to reinforce each other and thus may address similar concerns. At one point, for example, people were worried about an internal threat—our inability to keep track of the parts and supplies we had on hand. Inventory accuracy had fallen to 40 percent. In other words, our records showed that we had the parts we needed, but when we went to get them, they often weren't there. Inventory is a financial asset and therefore a Balance-Sheet item, but it has a big impact on production. If the part isn't there when you need it, production stops until you can get it. That affects the Income Statement. Our standard cost guy told me we'd see great increases in productivity if we could achieve an accuracy level of 95 percent. Sure enough, when the accuracy rose, the profits rose. It was unbelievable. We got a tremendous boost in overhead absorption and a big drop in the chargeout rate, which helped us to meet the income statement goal as well.

In many cases, of course, the real challenge is to figure out how to quantify a target that everybody agrees is worth going after. The process is the same one described in Chapter 6, when I discussed the art of quantifying as it applied to developing standards and benchmarks. That's exactly what you're doing here. Once you know what people are concerned about, and what they want, you look for the benchmarks for which they can aim. By putting those benchmarks into the bonus program, you are creating a powerful tool for educating people. You can use the excitement of the bonus game to show people how, by reaching these financial benchmarks, they can attain their personal goals. And not just their short-term goals, either—how they can attain their long-term goals as well, their dreams.

But to do this, you must completely *throw open the goal-setting process and let people choose their own goals. Then you can spend the rest of the year talking to people about not letting themselves down.* You don't have to ask them to do this or that for the company. You can get them focusing beyond the company, on something that is more important to them than the company—namely, their own lives. They're protecting their jobs; they're achieving their dreams. They're not doing it for you. They're doing it for themselves. If they leave money lying on the table, they are the big losers. Your role is to help them succeed.

For us, the selection of the Stop-Gooter goals is the culmination of the entire process of developing an annual game plan. Everything else we do is geared toward putting the pieces in place so that we can say, "These are the biggest concerns we have, and the things we want the most, and here's how we're going to go after them. This is a month-by-month plan we can follow over the next year to attack the threats to our job security and, at the same time, take care of some of our wishes."

AN INVITATION TO SKEPTICS

I know some people will say, "These targets sound very nice and orderly, but business just isn't that predictable. You must constantly be running into unexpected opportunities and problems. What if a new customer shows up in May and throws all your plans out of whack? What if you suddenly find yourself with tough, new competition and you have to revamp your entire cost structure? You can't have a plan that is good for an entire year. It's just not possible in this day and age."

I'd like to invite all you skeptics to attend one of our monthly seminars and sit in on a staff meeting. Call us at 800-386-2752. We'll set it up. You can watch as we go down the Income Statement, line by line. You'll hear person after person reporting numbers that are off the projection by $100 or less. Monthly sales vary less than 5 percent, even in a volatile year. Frankly, it's unreal how close people come to the projections.

But, even if something happens to throw the projections off, never change the annual game plan in the middle of a year. If the plan is a disaster, as our first one was, cancel it. Otherwise stay with it. Changing the plan is like changing the location of the holes in the middle of a golf tournament. To be sure, you can't anticipate everything. There will be unexpected developments. For example, one year we brought in some new business in the middle of the year. We hadn't expected it, and it cost us money to take it on, and we didn't reap the benefits until later. That was the year we didn't earn any bonuses. The new business was a factor, but not a major one. We went over our sales projection by about $4 million, which meant we would have had to have another $200,000 in pretax profits to get into the first payout level. We missed it by about $700,000. So it goes. You never change the plan, regardless of the surprises that come along. Stick with it no matter what.

That happens in January, the final month of our fiscal year. By then, everyone in the company has had a chance to talk about the various goals under consideration, and we've reached a consensus about two or three. We've also played with the numbers enough to figure out the appropriate levels and payouts, as described in Chapter 7. So we put together the compensation plan, which is the last section of the game plan. The various sections go into a big, black, three-ring notebook, affectionately known as "The Bible." We present copies of the new Bible at the next staff meeting. We say, "Do you like it? Is there anything you want to change?" Occasionally there is, although we try to do most of our arguing early in the process. We prefer not to make big changes so close to the wire.

///

THE EIGHTH HIGHER LAW IS:
When People Set Their Own Targets, They Usually Hit Them.

///

The final step is to submit the plan to the board of directors. They do another round of what-ifs. Where are the contingency plans? Where are the trapdoors? What if this doesn't work? What if this doesn't happen? We go over the checks and balances. We reexamine our internal controls. We make sure we have everything set up to run the right way. Then we launch the plan. We come back in the last week of the fiscal year and say, "Okay, here's the new game."

chapter **9**

THE GREAT HUDDLE

THE NINTH HIGHER LAW IS:
If Nobody Pays Attention, People Stop Caring.

People have to see the effects of what they do, or they won't care. It doesn't matter if the effects are good or bad. If you go out every day, and nobody notices whether your work is good, bad, or indifferent, you'll stop caring.

**OUR GREAT HUDDLES TELL PEOPLE
WE CARE. WE SEND THE MESSAGE OUT
EVERY WEEK—WE WANT TO KNOW WHAT
YOU'RE DOING.**

If you want to watch the Great Game of Business in action, come to one of our weekly staff meetings. They start at 9:00 A.M. every Wednesday in the conference room of our building on Division Street in Springfield. There are usually about fifty managers, supervisors, and other people from around the company in attendance, as well as an assortment of curious outsiders—customers, auditors, bankers, suppliers, visitors from other companies, and so on. As the group gathers, people stand around joking with one another, exchanging news, sharing fishing tips. Everybody seems to be relaxed. But there is a certain buzz in the air, the sound you hear in a theater before the lights go down and the curtain goes up, or in a ballpark as the pitcher finishes his warm-ups and the lead-off batter steps to the plate.

What we are all anticipating is the weekly ritual of calculating the score. This is where we learn how we are doing on our Stop-Gooter bonus goals. We figure it out right there in the conference room. People come to the meeting with the latest numbers from their departments. For every entry in the Income Statement, someone has a number representing the most accurate, up-to-date assessment his or her team can make as to what the entry will be when the month closes. After a brief introduction by me (or whoever is chairing the meeting in my absence), we go around the room, and people announce their numbers, while everybody else scribbles them down on the scorekeeping forms—really, blank Income Statements. There are "oohs" and "aahs" and good-natured digs. We can all see how the reported numbers differ from the ones in the game plan, which are printed on one side of the form, and from those given in the last meeting, which we've written down on the previous week's form. (A sample form is found on page 237.) So every announcement provokes a response. Is purchasing getting great deals or what? How did production manage to absorb so much overhead in a week? Where did all those automotive sales suddenly disappear to? Who said we couldn't turn around that warranty problem?

There is bravado. There is daring. There is trepidation. Some people are confident, even bold. Others are a little bit nervous. Everybody is on show, and nobody wants to let their colleagues down. People love to be heroes, but—to be a hero here—you and your department have to perform. You have to come in with a good number. When we finish, the chief financial officer announces the tally: our income (or losses) before taxes for the month, assuming these numbers hold up. Then we move on to the other news.

||||➡ what's going on here

The Wednesday meeting is the focal point for everything we do at SRC. It is where all the numbers we generate come together, where they get added and subtracted, totaled up, and sent out so they can be used by people in the company to do their jobs. It provides each of us with the information we need to play our position in the Great Game of Business. That's why we sometimes refer to it as the Great Huddle.

**WHEN WE COME OUT OF THE MEETING, WE
CAN SEE THE WHOLE FIELD BEFORE US.
WE KNOW WHO IS WHERE, AND HOW THE
GAME IS UNFOLDING, AND WHAT EACH OF
US HAS TO DO TO MAKE SURE WE KEEP
MOVING CLOSER TO THE GOAL LINE.**

As with any meeting, however, the real payoff comes from what happens *before* and *after* the Huddle. The meetings are, in fact, just one link in a chain of communication that is constantly moving information up and down the organization. From the Huddle, the numbers flow back to the rest of the company in a series of follow-up sessions held over the next couple of days. Within thirty-six hours, virtually everybody in the company has the latest information about where we stand and what we have to do to improve the score, and people are using that knowledge in their individual jobs. They, too, can see the whole field. They are linked up to the Big Picture. They know what it will take to close in on the Stop-Gooter targets, earn a bonus, protect their jobs, increase the value of their stock, and generate wealth. How they do it is up to them. Maybe they run plays they've used before; maybe they come up with new ones. One way or another, they are moving in the right direction and in the *same* direction. We are all working together to make those fractional improvements that determine whether or not we succeed as a business.

This *is* the Great Game of Business. This is how we play it, week in, week out. This is where we put into operation all the principles of open-book management, where we apply all the lessons we've learned in previous years, where we use all the tools we've developed—the standards, the game plan, the goals, the payout levels, the different ways of winning. This is how we constantly regenerate the pride and the sense of ownership; this is how we create mutual trust and respect, build credibility, light the fire in people's eyes. Above all, this is how we drive ignorance from the workplace, teach people how to make money, and show them why that's important. As we go from one Huddle to the next, and see the numbers change, and hear the stories behind them, we are learning about business, life, and the pot at the end of the rainbow. Not just the people on the shop floor, either: *all* of us are learning, all the time. And we are also having fun. There is action. There is drama. There is excitement. There is the thrill of a good game.

None of that would happen without our weekly Huddles. They serve as our organizational switchboard. They are the means by which we stay connected to one another. They set the pace and the tone and the mood of the entire company. When I see what our Huddles do for us, it amazes me that so many companies get by without having regular staff meetings at all.

COMMUNICATING IS ONE OF THE MOST DIFFICULT CHALLENGES IN ANY BUSINESS, BECAUSE PEOPLE HEAR WHAT THEY WANT TO HEAR.

If they don't hear anything, they speculate. They read the tea leaves. They start rumors, often unintentionally. Show me a company without regular staff meetings, and I'll show you a company with a rumor mill, not to mention a host of other problems. Rumor mills cost money, lots of money. They are the most expensive form of corporate communication around. They breed fear, mistrust, divisiveness, unrealistic expectations, and ignorance. They take all the problems a company has and make them worse. For that, you pay through the nose.

Bad staff meetings are better than none at all—but not much. When I came down to be the plant manager in Springfield, there were morning staff meetings. All the managers got together and had coffee and rolls. The main thing we talked about was who would get the rolls for the next meeting. People didn't know what else to discuss. More common is the type of staff meeting I used to attend at Melrose Park. Every Friday morning, the various department heads would meet with the plant manager, who would lecture us for a couple hours. He'd talk about the results he wanted but then didn't provide any tools for achieving them. He'd yell at us about problems but offered no help in getting them fixed. He'd give us background on what was going on in the company but told us to keep it a secret. We sat there and listened. He wasn't looking for our input. He wanted to do all the talking.

That's a major problem with most staff meetings: the boss is the only one communicating. Those meetings waste everybody's time, including yours if you're the boss. For openers, you're not getting the information you need to be a good leader. You sure aren't getting help from your staff. You're not even getting your messages across. Every one of them is being interpreted and distorted in ways you would never suspect. The main message you send, moreover, has nothing to do with what you say. It comes from your actions. When you dominate staff meetings, you are telling people you don't value their contributions, you don't think they make a difference. That's probably not the message you intend to deliver. You may not even believe it. But it's what they hear.

On the other hand, it's not enough to get the attendees to contribute, or even to have good meetings per se. You may have great staff meetings with your managers, but if you don't bring the rest of the organization into the loop, you will lose a lot of the benefits. People will feel excluded, maybe even resentful. Instead of teamwork, you will get ignorance and suspicion. The barriers will go up.

Bear in mind that I am talking here about the regular staff meetings that companies use for internal communication. Every company, including ours, will have all kinds of other meetings, and some of them won't be—and shouldn't be—open, participatory, or part of a process involving anyone except the participants. But the regular staff meeting belongs in a category by itself, because it plays a special role, or at least it ought to. Its most important function is to *build the organization*. It should be drawing the company together. It should be helping to educate people about the business. It should be providing managers with the tools they need to manage, and frontline employees with the tools they need to do their jobs. It should be sending clear, unambiguous messages. It should be encouraging communication at every level. It should be unifying people around common values and goals.

We get all that from our Huddles. The entire company depends on them and looks forward to them. They have become so popular, in fact, that we keep outgrowing the rooms where we hold them. When we tried having them every other week for a while, there was a big outcry, and we quickly switched back. It's not just that the meetings themselves are good, although we do try to make them as interesting, as exciting, and as efficient as possible. *The real test of a staff meeting is its value to the people who aren't there.* They, too, should be participants. They should know that they have a direct effect on what happens at the meeting, and that what happens at the meeting will have a direct effect on them.

Our people know that because of the system we have developed for keeping them informed and involved. To some extent, that system reflects our particular experiences and idiosyncrasies as a business. But the principles are universal, and the basic elements—the steps of the process—can be adapted to any company in any industry. The best place to start is with the Game.

Games are built around cycles, or rather cycles within cycles. In major league baseball, for example, there is a cycle every inning. You repeat the inning cycle 9 times per game and then repeat the game cycle 162 times per season—at which point you can think about starting another season cycle next year. In football, it's four downs per possession, four quarters per game, sixteen games per season. Every competitive sport follows the same basic pattern. The Great Game of Business is also built around cycles. The way we play it, there is a cycle every week, every month, every quarter, and every year. We tend to think of each weekly cycle as a separate game, consisting of four distinct stages.

The Great Huddle is the *first stage* of the game.

The *second stage* comes on Wednesday afternoon and Thursday, when the people in the Huddle return to their departments and go over the numbers with the other members of their respective teams, who fill out scorecards of their own. These follow-up meetings are more like coaching sessions, or "Chalk Talks," than Huddles. In each one, the group leader is analyzing the numbers, telling the stories behind them, passing along other news from around the company, and discussing what plays the team should be running in light of the latest score.

In the *third stage* of the game, the players go back on the field and run the plays they've discussed in the Chalk Talks. What they are doing is applying the information from the Huddle to the nitty-gritty circumstances of their jobs. Maybe cash is tight; so they cut back on expenses and are more careful with supplies. Maybe they have to absorb more overhead to get into the next payout level on the profit goal; so they put off their housekeeping or administrative chores and focus on production. Whatever the situation, they do what they can to improve the score, using the standards as a guide. Meanwhile, the coaches are out there motivating and facilitating—making sure the players know where they're going and have what they need to do the job.

The *fourth stage* begins shortly before the next Great Huddle. By then, the score has changed, but the changes may not be readily apparent. The managers need to study and identify them, and they need to do the scoring. What each team does will send ripples through the company, affecting every other team's results. When the production people cut back on supplies and expenses, for example, the benefits show up in the numbers reported by engineering. So it's time to regroup. Now the information flows the other way, from the frontline workers and supervisors to the managers who report the numbers in the Huddle. On Tuesday afternoon and early Wednesday morning, there is another series of meetings, sort of pre-Huddle Huddles, at which the managers of a department get together and revise their estimates from the previous week. They go over all of the entries in the income statement for which they are responsible and decide what they now think each one will be when the month closes. At 9:00 A.M. on Wednesday, they are back at the conference room, ready to recalculate the score and start another game.

That is the basic cycle we use in playing the Great Game of Business. It sounds time-consuming, but in fact no one spends more than four hours in the various meetings per week, and 95 percent of our people attend only one meeting that lasts an hour or less. We go through this cycle four or five times per month, depending on the number of weeks. After the month closes, the accounting department pulls together the actual numbers and distributes the monthly financial statements. From that, we can see how close each of us came on our final estimates, and how the various teams performed. Meanwhile, we have already begun the next monthly cycle.

Of course, any game is more fun if the stakes keep rising as you go along. That happens from week to week, as we get closer to the end of the month. It also happens from month to month, thanks to the bonus program. Since the payouts are made quarterly, we can fall short in the first two months and still make it up in the third. Alternatively, if we have a great first month of the quarter, there's a lot of pressure not to let the bonus slip away. So we not only have a game a week and a game a month, but we also have a game a quarter, with each succeeding month a little more exciting than the one before.

And there's more. Remember, we've designed the bonus program so that

✓ we're going after a bigger percentage of the total annual bonus in each succeeding quarter, and

✓ we always have a shot at any portion of the bonus we've missed in a previous quarter.

As a result, the stakes keep rising from quarter to quarter, the excitement continues to build, and everybody stays involved right up to the end of the year. That gives us an annual game as well.

What makes it all possible is the communications system centered around the weekly meetings. That system ensures that all of us are always up to date on all the latest scores, in all the games. We are following the action.

WHEN EVERYBODY FOLLOWS THE ACTION, EVERYBODY IS READY TO PLAY.

||||➤ tips for having truly great huddles, and getting the most out of them

If you want to play the Game the way we do, you clearly need some sort of system like this one to draw people into the action. That doesn't mean you need one just like ours. On the contrary, your system will inevitably look, sound, and feel very different, as well it should. Companies are as diverse as people, and nothing is more distinctive than the way you communicate. You have to develop a language and a style with which you and your people feel comfortable, that fits your personality as a business. You will also have to adapt other companies' techniques to your circumstances, and you may well have to invent new techniques of your own.

Take, for example, the case of the trucking company whose president visited us and came away determined to set up a weekly meeting process similar to ours. The only problem, he said, was that 90 percent of his workforce was constantly on the road, hauling freight all over the country. It was impossible to get them together for regular weekly meetings. (I suggested he provide them with portable fax machines and cellular phones.) I know someone else with a chain of about a hundred wholesale distribution centers in forty states. He practices his own version of the Game, and he doesn't have weekly meetings at all. Instead, he distributes the numbers on a monthly basis, sending a complete set of Income Statements to each of the centers, where most of the action occurs in his business. Then he follows up with a lot of intensive education. It's a different system from ours, but it works very well for him.

CHATTER

My dad was a professional baseball player before he worked at International Harvester. He coached me in baseball, and he taught me that it was important to be ready to react to whatever might happen. Partly that was a matter of being physically ready. If I was playing second base, I had to be leaning over, standing on my toes, ready to move to either side. But at the same time I had to be talking to myself, keeping my head in the game, achieving the highest level of attention possible.

That's chatter. It allows you to react quicker, dig down further, and push off harder when you're called on to perform the task. It's a way of getting ready to make the big play. The same technique is used in other sports. In karate, it's the scream. In discus throwing, it's the grunt. You can also find it in business. The Japanese do it with their singing and exercising. For us, it's the language of finance and numbers. It's the talk about overhead absorption, labor utilization, and so on. What's the split? What are the receipts? What's the standard? Are you beating your standard? You hear it all the time—not just in meetings, but on the shop floor, in the cafeteria, up and down the corridors, even over beers after work. It's a way that people keep themselves in the game, ready to move in any direction, to do what is necessary to win. It helps them to contribute at their maximum level.

I can always tell how well a company is doing by the amount of chatter I hear. It's a sure sign that people are motivated, excited, and engaged. Chatter can't be faked. If people don't feel it, they won't do it. By the same token, you can't force chatter on a company, although you can encourage it. Some companies try to do that with morning pep talks. High-powered sales organizations often have their own songs that people sing together before they go out on calls—IBM under Thomas J. Watson Sr. is probably the best example. Other companies promote chatter through their language and culture. They invent phrases that become part of the company's identity and serve to keep people focused on the common goals.

But such techniques only work if you have prepared the ground beforehand, if you have established credibility, if people know why it's important to get their heads into the game, and they participate willingly. Don't try to generate chatter without first creating the right conditions. Companies that do are engaging in the worst form of corporate coercion. They are using fear and manipulation to force a certain behavior on people. Not only is that wrong, it's futile. You gotta wanna. Chatter happens when people are focused on winning, not when they are thinking about losing their jobs.

We generate chatter through the weekly meeting process. Out of the Huddles and the Chalk Talks comes an awareness of the numbers, a familiarity with certain phrases. Once we have the language, we can use it. Managers can start talking in terms of the chargeout rate, the debt-equity ratio, absorbing overhead, improving inventory accuracy, and so on. Pretty soon, other people start talking in those terms as well, and you have chatter.

You also have education. You have an environment where people learn almost by accident. Words float around all the time—accounts receivable, current ratio, and so on. An individual may not understand the word, but she becomes familiar with it. She remembers it. Then she winds up in a situation where it all comes together. She says, "Aha! Now I understand." That's one effect of the chatter. Some of it sinks in. One of the warehouse managers told me his people are improving inventory accuracy because they've begun to see how it helps assembly absorb more overhead. That's dynamic chatter. *The chatter comes from knowing that what you're doing is important to somebody else.*

The truth is that every business is going to face unique challenges in developing an effective communications process. If you need help in overcoming them, my advice is that you begin by explaining the problem to your people and asking them for their ideas. Beyond that, let me offer some lessons that we have learned over the years and that you may find useful as well.

* Keep It Regular and On Time.

The most important thing about our weekly meeting is that everybody knows it begins at 9:00 every Wednesday morning. It's not 10:30 on Tuesday this week, 3:00 on Wednesday next week, then back to 9:00 after that. It's always same day, same time, same place. That way, people can count on it. They can plan for it. They can develop a routine around it. They don't have to spend a moment thinking about where or when the meeting is going to take place. They can focus all their attention on the Game.

* Hold It Frequently Enough to Stay in Control of the Numbers.

I always talk about our *weekly* meetings, but for a while we went to one meeting every two weeks. We changed because I thought people were bored. When we got to the part of the meeting where we exchange news, most people had nothing to offer. That made me mad. I thought they weren't trying, they didn't care. On the other hand, it occurred to me that we might be trying too hard. Maybe we needed a break. Finally, I said, "What the hell, let's go to biweekly meetings."

It was a disaster. Nobody was happy, which was surprising. You'd think people would prefer to have fewer meetings, but they were more interested in knowing the score. The change totally disrupted our routines. People lost track of what was going on, what they had to do to achieve the goals. Two weeks was just too long to go without a meeting. We didn't know where we were from one meeting to the next. In some categories, the estimates in the meeting turned out to be off by as much as 30 to 40 percent from the actual numbers in the month-end statements. I could see the walls going up between departments. People started blaming one another for their problems. The chatter stopped. It was like withdrawal. We were really shaking. So we switched back.

I'm not saying you shouldn't have biweekly staff meetings. Other companies may find them just right, but for us it was a big mistake. The lesson: develop a routine that lets you control the numbers, and then stick with it.

* Put a Name and a Face on Every Line in the Income Statement.
A major benefit of the Huddle is that it humanizes the business. It gets rid of the invisible enemy—the "they," as in, "They screwed up," or "They're out to get us," or "They don't know what they're doing." The invisible enemy destroys company after company. It sows suspicion and ignorance and divisiveness. You have to hunt it down and eliminate it before it eliminates you. We go after it at every chance we get.

One way we fight the invisible enemy is to divide up responsibilities for the financials, to attach real people to every number and every line. When we go around the room on Wednesday morning, the numbers aren't coming from "them." We are hearing directly from Pam in scheduling, Jeff in sales, and Irene in production. So we don't respond as we would if we were just getting numbers, say, from accounting. When "they" have bad news, we get angry. When Irene has bad news, we ask if she needs help. There's a personal connection. We want to support each other. When one person is down, someone else steps in and picks him or her up.

To establish those connections, you have to personalize the income statement. That means going through the process I described in Chapter 5. Break down the major categories on the income statement into controllable elements, and then assign each element to someone in the company. That person will then be responsible for reporting the number in the meeting. In most cases, he or she will be the manager whose team has the greatest impact on the number. If most of your people work in production, have a representative from that department report on labor costs. If most of them are involved in selling, give the responsibility to someone from sales. The whole idea is to match the numbers with the people who have greatest control over them and to spread the reporting responsibilities as widely as possible. Be sure to include representatives from every area of the business.

* Invite Anyone with Something to Contribute.

Our weekly staff meetings are open to everyone in the company, but the people who show up usually have a specific reason for being there. They have a number to report or a piece of news to deliver, or it's important for them to see what happens. Most of the participants are middle or top managers with departmental responsibilities. On the other hand, we don't want to be exclusive. There should not be any mystery about the meeting. It should be a familiar part of the landscape. So we make a point of inviting a lot of people in the course of a year. Occasionally they wish we hadn't. From time to time, a manager will bring a frontline supervisor into the meeting—say, the head of the cylinder head department. Whenever we see that, we know there's a bad number to report, and the manager has decided to let the person responsible come in and explain it himself. It creates a little incentive not to have a bad number again.

* **Have a Fixed Format, But Don't Be Boring.**
Our meetings generally last about an hour and a half, during which we cover an enormous amount of territory and still manage to keep people on the edge of their seats. We do it by having a simple format that never varies, while making sure that the content is interesting and the pace is fast. I usually start the meeting with a few brief comments designed to set the tone and establish a theme—more about that later. Then we go around the room twice. The first time we do the Income Statement in the manner I described before. That's always interesting, provided you know what's going on, and all the participants do. (Outsiders, on the other hand, tell me we go too fast for them to follow the action.) When we finish, we know how we are doing on our pretax profit goal.

Then we do another circuit during which people report any news or other information they feel the group would want to hear—new customers, important milestones, industry awards, fishing results, golf results, individual accomplishments, whatever. This part has the flavor of a town meeting, with each member getting up to tell us a little bit about what's happening in his or her neighborhood. There is much joking, commiserating, congratulating, and laughing. We are renewing the bonds of our community.

Meanwhile, the chief financial officer is quickly putting together a Cash-Flow Statement, using the numbers that people have just announced. We need that to see how we are doing on our Balance-Sheet goal. (The Cash-Flow Statement shows us how much cash we have, how much we are generating, and where it is going—all of which will help determine whether or not we hit our Balance-Sheet targets.) When we get to the CFO on our second pass around the room, we take out another scorecard, this one a blank Cash-Flow Statement. He announces the numbers, and we fill them in. So now we have a reading on both goals. If we are near the end of the quarter, the CFO will also distribute a handout showing where we stood as of the last meeting and what we would have to do to hit our targets. That's to avoid any agonizing near misses in the future. If we're .01 percent short of our target, there is always someone who can find $1,000 worth of savings and push us over the top.

After we finish the second pass, I close the meeting with a summary of the results. Often I will come back to the theme I talked about at the start of the meeting, or I may pick up on something one of the other participants has said. My purpose is simply to highlight whatever I think our common focus should be, based on what we've just heard and what is going on around us, the environment in which we are operating.

Then we adjourn.

* Be a Leader, Not a Boss.

If you are running the meeting, be careful to avoid the trap of being the person with all the answers. I never want people to think they are reporting to me so that I can tell them what to do. What's important is for me to keep putting back in their hands the responsibility and the tools for earning more. It's easy for me to come in after the fact and say, "You should have done this or that." But, if I do, they'll start leaving the decisions up to me. So I refrain from that type of backward criticism. Instead, I keep looking forward, and I encourage them to do the same. *I want people to be ahead of me,* to drive as far ahead of me as they can. I need tools to help them do that, just as they need tools. We're all using the same tools: the financial statements. So we're all moving in the same direction. We're a big team of horses, pulling a wagon, all in step. There aren't any more mixed messages, just the results on the financials.

This doesn't mean you should be passive. On the contrary, you should lead, and you should teach. Look for opportunities to plant seeds in people's minds. Highlight the important points. Push to get at the stories behind the numbers—the stories that show where the numbers came from, that connect the numbers to real faces and real events. Tell those stories every chance you get, because it's from the stories that people will learn.

One big opportunity to plant seeds comes at the start of the meeting. I spend a lot of time thinking about what I want to say, where I want to focus people's attention. Maybe it's the state of the economy or some other national issue. Maybe it's a local event—say, a big employer in town going out of business. Maybe it's a strategic question we are facing, or a recent success we can celebrate, or trends we have been watching. I'm looking for a subject that will give us a context, a perspective, something we should bear in mind as we go through the numbers and share the news.

After my opening remarks, I let other people do most of the talking until the end. Mainly I want to keep things moving. When people report especially good numbers, I cheer along with everybody else. When a bad number is bad, we stop and get an explanation. Good or bad, we want to hear the stories behind the numbers. By the time we finish, certain themes have emerged. We can see where we're weak and where we're strong, what we've done well and what we must improve to hit our targets. I talk about those themes in my summary. They are the messages contained in the numbers, the ones we need to emphasize when we take the results back to the rest of the company.

* Make Sure the Numbers Get Out.

Never forget: what happens after the Huddle is more important than what happens in it. The whole exercise is a big waste of time if the information stays with the people in the room. That's why we put so much emphasis on the Chalk Talks. We hold as many as necessary to get the word out as fast as possible. In a small department, there may be only one Chalk Talk. In a large department, there may be as many as eight. The head of production, for example, meets with all seven of the frontline supervisors on the shop floor. They then go back and hold similar sessions with their respective teams. In each meeting, people are not only getting the numbers and the news, they are also figuring out what they can do to improve the score. For instance, the production chief will talk with the supervisors about the allocation of resources in the factory. (Do we have enough parts to ship that order? Should we put an extra person in disassembly? Can we do anything about the problem in turbochargers?) The supervisors will talk with their people about specific ways they can affect the numbers. (How much more overhead could we absorb by running this drill an extra hour per shift? What happens if we try to conserve cash by reusing some of these polishing disks? Can we squeeze a little more out of salvage if we rework these parts on a different machine?) This is a vital part of the process. There is no education and no improvement without it. Make sure it happens. We have one factory where it didn't happen for a long time. The plant manager lied to us. When we found out, we fired him, but the experience taught us a lesson. Now we run spot audits throughout the company once a week to make sure that everybody has been brought up to date.

* **Insist That People Write It Down.**
At first we thought it was enough to tell people the latest financial results on a weekly basis. We did a lot of talking, explaining, and coaching in our Chalk Talks, but that was about it. Then we discovered one of our factories hadn't been playing the Game at all, and I began to have nightmares. I worried that we were victims of our own PR—that we weren't really teaching people to understand the financial statements, we just thought we were because so much had been written about it. We talked it over and decided to start distributing blank scorecards to everybody in the company. Not only would people *hear* the numbers in their Chalk Talks, they would write the numbers down.

This is actually an important step in the whole educational process, one we should have taken early on. When you report to people every week about the condition of the company, you establish credibility. When you get them to write the information down, you teach. Education comes by repetition. It's like learning the multiplication tables. If you do it often enough, it becomes second nature. That's what we want. We want to be sure that we are really teaching people what they need to know—that we are taking ignorance out of the workplace, that we are educating people to understand what needs to be done.

THE WEEKLY SCORECARD

In the early years after the buyout, we did the projected monthly Income Statement on a blackboard in our conference room. (See Springfield Remanufacturing Corp. Projected Income Statement on page 237.) I'd stand by the board and write down the numbers as people gave them to me. Then we'd total them up and see how we were doing on our pretax profit goal. We still take the same basic approach, but now we have printed scorecards, which we modify from time to time as the company changes and as we get ideas for improvements.

1. SALES PROJECTIONS—This is an innovation designed to serve as an early-warning system. Every week, someone from the sales department estimates what our sales will be for the next six months, both in the United States and Canada. If the projections change unexpectedly, we can go to work on the problems while there's still time to do something about them.

2. PLAN—This column comes straight out of the annual game plan (Chapter 8). These are the numbers that we forecasted we would be generating in each category for this month.

SPRINGFIELD REMANUFACTURING CORP.
PROJECTED INCOME STATEMENT, U. S. DIVISIONS
(000) Omitted

Date_____

① SALES PROJECTIONS

	②PLAN	**CURRENT**	**NEXT**	**③MONTH 2**	**③MONTH 3**	**MONTH 4**	**MONTH 5**
UNITED STATES							
CANADA							

SALES:

	③PLAN	**③MAPLE**	**③WILLOW**	**MARSH-FIELD**	**NEW STREAM**	**TOTAL**	**PERCENT**
④ GROSS SALES — CANADA							
GROSS SALES US							
BEHIND SCHEDULE							
AVAILABLE-TO-SHIP							
PROJ. END BEHIND SCHEDULE							
RETURNS/DISC/ALLOWANCES							
NET SALES SHIPMENTS							
⑤ STD COST-OF-GOODS-SOLD							
⑥ GROSS STD. INCOME							
⑦ MEMO: INVENTORY RECEIPTS							

MANUFACTURING VARIANCES:

⑧ PUR. PRICE/RECLASS/FREIGHT							
MAT'L USAGE/SCRAP							
INV. ADJUSTMENT							
LABOR PERFORMANCE							
O/H SPENDING							
OVERHEAD ABSORPTION							
OVERHEAD VARIANCE							
TOTAL MFG. VARIANCES							
⑨ CONTRIBUTION MARGIN							

EXPENSES:

⑩ ENGINEERING							
SALES & MANUFACTURING							
GEN'L ADMIN.							
ESOP CONTRIBUTION							
WARRANTY–CLAIMS PAID							
WARRANTY–ALLOWED							
VARIANCE							
WARRANTY ACCRUAL							
TOTAL WARRANTY EXPENSE							
⑪ TOTAL EXPENSES							
⑫ OPERATING INCOME							

NON-OPERATING INCOME/EXP.

OTHER INCOME/EXPENSE							
INCOME FROM SUBSIDIARIES							
INTEREST EXPENSE							
⑬ TOTAL NON-OPER. EXPENSE							
INCOME FROM CONTINUING OPER.							
⑭ INVENTORY DISPOSAL PROGRAM							
⑮ INCOME (LOSS) BEFORE TAXES							
⑯ PBT % MONTH							
⑰ PBT % CUM.							

3. MAPLE/WILLOW/MARSHFIELD/NEWSTREAM—These are four different businesses owned and operated by SRC. Maple Street is our original plant, now specializing in heavy-duty engines. Willow Springs is where we rebuild automotive engines. Marshfield is a wholly owned subsidiary that remanufactures components called torque amplifiers. Newstream, a joint venture with one of our customers, assembles repair kits for truck engines.

4. SALES—We don't record a sale until the order is shipped, and we deduct orders that come back. So we calculate our net sales by subtracting our behind-schedule orders and our returns from gross sales.

5. STANDARD COST-OF-GOODS-SOLD—Our standard cost system allows us to figure out immediately how much it should cost us to produce the goods we ship. We simply multiply Net Sales Shipments by the standard from the annual game plan.

6. GROSS STANDARD INCOME—When we deduct Standard COGS from Net Sales Shipments, we get Gross Standard Income. This is the gross income we would make if we were able to manufacture all our products at the standard rate. "Gross income" is simply the difference between sales and the cost of producing the goods or services that customers buy. It has to be high enough to cover all the nonproduction expenses and still leave a profit. If it isn't, you're in trouble.

7. MEMO: INVENTORY RECEIPTS—Inventory is a Balance-Sheet item, but we note it here partly because we want to keep an eye on it, and also because we need it to do the Cash-Flow Statement later in the meeting.

8. MANUFACTURING VARIANCES—In the real world, you seldom hit your standards on the nose. When you miss, you create a "variance," that is, the difference between the actual cost and the standard cost. If your actual costs are higher, there is an unfavorable variance that must be deducted from Gross Standard Income. If you come in below standard, the variance is favorable and increases the Gross Standard Income. We track the variances on every aspect of manufacturing costs, and then we total them up. A favorable variance is noted in brackets ([ ]).

9. CONTRIBUTION MARGIN—This tells us the actual gross profit we made on these products. We calculate it by deducting the Total Manufacturing Variances from the Gross Standard Income. (If the total variance figure is enclosed in brackets, it is favorable, and so we add it to, rather than subtract it from, Gross Standard Income.)

10. EXPENSES—These are all the operating expenses not directly associated with actually manufacturing products.

11. OPERATING INCOME—Operating income tells you how much you are making from the actual operations of the company. You calculate it by subtracting Expenses from the Contribution Margin.

12. NONOPERATING INCOME/EXPENSES—In our case, we are talking mainly about income from our subsidiaries and interest paid on debt.

13. INCOME FROM CONTINUING OPERATIONS—When you deduct Nonoperating Expenses from Operating Income, you get Income from Continuing Operations. That would be the same as pretax income, except that we have a program to dispose of excess inventory.

14. INVENTORY DISPOSAL PROGRAM—Just what the name implies.

15. INCOME (LOSS) BEFORE TAXES—Ditto.

16. PBT % MONTH—That's our pretax profit margin for the month.

17. PBT % CUM—Our cumulative profit before taxes for the year to date. Remember, a margin above 5 percent pushes us into bonus territory.

HOW TO LEAD WITH AN OPEN BOOK

At the beginning of May 1991, I faced a perplexing problem. The economy was in a recession, but we had just finished the strongest first quarter in our history. The trouble was that we had left a lot of money on the table, and we were heading into a period that looked as though it was going to be very tough. As we sat down for our weekly staff meeting, I had to decide what sort of message I wanted to send out to the organization. Did I want to praise people for a great quarter? Cajole them for letting opportunities get away? Warn them about the dark clouds on the horizon? It was, I admit, the kind of problem most CEOs would love to have. In the end, I did what I usually do—I let the numbers do the talking. And people got the message loud and clear.

There's a natural tendency to talk about a system like ours as a boon to the people on the shop floor, a way to make their lives more meaningful and rewarding, and to give them hope for the future. I think that's all very true. But those of us who run open-book companies have a little secret: the biggest beneficiary may well be the person at the top.

KNOW WHEN TO PUSH, WHEN TO HUG, WHEN TO CHEER, WHEN TO BOO, AND WHEN TO KICK PEOPLE IN THE BUTT.

That can be very difficult. It's easy to get distracted, to blow little problems way out of proportion, to miss the big ones. If you don't have some means of maintaining perspective, you may run around like a raving maniac, sending the wrong signals. You may demoralize people when you should be building them up. You may meddle when you should be standing back. You may teach them to cover their asses when they should be taking risks. So you need something to guide you. That's where the numbers come in.

The numbers tell you what's really going on in the organization. They tell you who is doing well and who is in trouble, who is improving and who is slowing down, who pulled off a brilliant coup and who made a dumb mistake, who needs a new challenge and who needs a vacation. A CEO's job is to be on top of the organization's numbers. Our system makes that job very easy. People produce the numbers on a daily basis. I can get them instantaneously. And they're good numbers, real numbers. We can give them right to our lenders. We're so current with our numbers, outsiders are shocked. In most businesses, it takes weeks to come up with numbers like ours, and even then they aren't as accurate because they aren't being collected by the people who do the work. They are being put together by the accounting department, and there are no checks to make sure the numbers reflect reality.

So I can use those numbers to guide me. I can see trends emerging before they become crises. That allows me to take action while things are still going well. I don't mean tell people what to do. I mean point out to them that a problem could be developing, and give them the opportunity to head it off.

THE FINANCIALS GIVE YOU A DIFFERENT PERSPECTIVE ON PROBLEMS; THEY ALLOW YOU TO LET THEM DEVELOP, OR EVEN WORSEN, IN ORDER TO GET A THOROUGH SENSE OF WHAT'S GOING WRONG.

It doesn't bother me to see that we have problems. The important thing is whether or not people are working toward solutions. We're always going to have problems. The question is, what are we doing to fix the problems? The numbers give me perspective. They tell me what's really important and what isn't. Missing a target for one month isn't important. Missing it for three months running is important.

The numbers also provide me with the security I need to let people take risks. They show me how far I can let people go before I have to step in and pull them back. That's very important. If you want people to grow, you have to let them take risks, and you have to let them fail. The tricky part is knowing how much to let people fail, where to draw the line. The numbers are my guide. They tell me when one person's failure, or one department's failure, is endangering others.

THE NUMBERS PROTECT
ME FROM PARANOIA.

When you are the head of a company, paranoia is an occupational hazard. You hear all the problems and the complaints, all the criticisms. You see people being disloyal. You may find out that some of them are stealing. Under the circumstances, it's not unusual for the boss to become paranoid, and that paranoia can undermine a business. The boss thinks he (or she) is going to get ripped off if he's not careful—which may happen. What he doesn't see is that he's painting himself into a corner with a sign that says, "Protect yourself from getting screwed." Some people will protect themselves to the point of not being able to win, not being able to grow, not being able to profit. They just can't stand the idea of getting screwed. So they set up a lot of barriers. When you knock down the barriers, you find that most people weren't out to screw you in the first place. You've designed a system to protect you from the 10 or 20 percent of the population with bad intentions, and you've discounted the 80 or 90 percent with good intentions. This happens all the time. We constantly set up rules for the people who break them. In the process, we penalize the contributors. I happen to think that's not fair. I know that it's a big mistake. If we had run SRC that way, we would never have been able to take $100,000 in equity in 1983 and turn it into $20 million in 1991.

chapter 10

A COMPANY OF OWNERS

Most companies pay their people $8 an hour or whatever and let it go at that. At SRC, we give people equity as well because we're in business to achieve our dreams and we want them to achieve theirs, and all of us have a better shot at succeeding if everyone is a stockholder. The fact is you can accumulate more wealth by sharing equity than by keeping it all yourself. SRC's stock is worth what it is today because of everything the people here have accomplished. No way could we have accomplished as much if I and the other members of the buyout group had held on to all the stock for ourselves.

That's because a company of owners will outperform a company of employees any day of the week. We do everything we can to instill the habits of ownership in people, and to encourage them to think and act like owners. When you think like an owner, you do all the little things necessary to win. You make the extra phone call to be sure the customer is happy. You figure out how to slice an additional 25 cents from the cost of a part. You spend money on the sales presentation, not on the hotel room or the rented car. You wipe the grease spot off the product before you put it in the box and ship it.

But people will only think like owners if they have a larger purpose, if they are not just working for a paycheck. You can't turn employees into owners simply by letting them choose their hours or paint their work areas, as some management gurus seem to think. That's a start, but it's not nearly enough. People have to see the Big Picture. They have to know what they are doing, why it's important, where they are going, and how business is helping them get there. Only then will they have the desire to go out and use the tools you provide and play the Great Game of Business to win.

Equity is the fifth tool in our Great Game kit. It is the means by which the company delivers on the promise of the other four—the standards, the bonus program, the annual game plan, and the communications process centered around the Great Huddle. With those four tools, people can steadily increase the value of the company and have fun in the process. They can win every day by beating their standards. They can win every week by improving the overall score. They can win every quarter and earn cash rewards under the bonus program. They can win every year and protect their jobs by hitting the targets in the annual plan.

But the big win comes from playing the equity game.

For every dollar we make in after-tax profits, our stock value goes up by about $10. That's real money. When people leave, we repurchase any SRC stock they own, and they cash in their shares in the ESOP. From time to time, we also create special "trading windows," during which people who work here can buy or sell stock in SRC. One way or another, employees and former employees have sold back equity worth a total of $6 million since 1983.

The ones who've done best, however, are those who've held on to their stock or bought in during one of the trading windows. A share of SRC stock worth 10 cents at the time of the buyout in 1983, was worth $4.05 on January 1, 1986; $13.02 on January 1, 1989; and $18.30 on January 1, 1991. That's an increase of 18,200 percent in nine years, and these values are probably understated. Our net worth is determined annually by an independent valuation firm, which conducts an extensive audit after the close of each fiscal year and sets the official stock price used in all transactions. Like most such firms, the one we use tends to be conservative in its valuations, since inflated prices would be devastating to its clients. So it is altogether conceivable that, if we were ever to go public, the market value of our securities would turn out to be considerably higher.

Such is the magic of the multiple. Indeed, there are many companies right now trading publicly at twenty-five or thirty times their annual earnings. That's amazing when you think about it. If you go out and generate after-tax profits of X dollars, the public will pay you thirty times X to own your company. So every dollar in your hand is suddenly worth $30 in the public equity market. An extra $100,000 on the bottom line gets you an additional $3 million from investors. This is the kind of money you win by gambling, except here it's a lot less risky, and you can control the spin of the wheel.

Equity can provide the greatest expansion of wealth most people will ever see. It's like hitting an oil field. I can't think of any other game that offers the same odds and a comparable payoff, and I've played a lot of games. I've put money on just about every event you can bet on. This is the best deal around, hands down, because you can influence the results. You can pretty much determine whether or not you win.

Who invented this game of capitalism? I sure didn't. It was here long before I came along. I'm just teaching other people how to play it, showing them what an incredible game this really is. When you hit the equity jackpot, you can do more than pay your bills. You can actually achieve some of your dreams. The opportunity is there. If you take it, you can create a better life for yourself and your family. That's the best reason I know for playing the Great Game of Business. It's the message we are constantly sending out to the people who work at SRC.

Equity makes the message real.

THIS IS THE POINT IN THE STORY AT WHICH I LOSE MANY BUSINESS OWNERS.

They like everything about the Great Game of Business up to the part about sharing equity. It's also a problem for people who run companies they don't own, or work in divisions of larger companies, and who simply don't have access to equity as a tool. They ask me:

✓ Can you play the Great Game of Business without equity participation?

✓ Will the other techniques work if people don't
own stock?

✓ Can you get people to think and act like owners
even though they are not owners in fact?

The answers are all yes. You can set standards, put together a bonus program, come up with a game plan, and
get the chatter going through something like our Huddle
system. People will respond. They will learn. They will get
caught up in the action and start figuring out ways to make
money and generate cash. I know of companies where all
that happens. Most of them have done extremely well,
even though employees don't own any stock. But unless
you bring people in as real owners, you will never complete
their education. You will stop short of the most important
lesson. You will show them the rainbow but not how to get
to the end of it.

Equity is the basis for all long-term thinking. It is the
best reason for staying the course, for sacrificing instant
gratification, and for going after the big payoff down the
road. If you have equity and understand it, you know why
it's important to build for the future. You can make the
long-term decisions. You still pay attention to the day-to-
day details, but you're doing it for the right reason: because
it's the best way to achieve *lasting* success.

Companies that don't share equity are making a mistake. They are leaving up a barrier that should be taken
down. They are setting limits on how far people can go.
When you come right down to it, they are shortchanging

their employees. But they are also shortchanging themselves, because equity just happens to be one of the biggest management bargains around.

▐▐▐▶ the walmart effect: how to get the equity markets to compensate and motivate your people

There is a great opportunity available to most businesses in this country, one that all but a handful pass up. It's the opportunity for owners to offer bonuses for which they don't have to pay. In return for the contributions people make to your company, you can give them pieces of paper called *shares*. It's just paper to you, but—if you have a well-managed business—somebody out there will want to buy that paper. Sooner or later, your employees will be able to take all those pieces of paper and cash them in.

Nobody used this tool more effectively than Sam Walton, the founder and chairman of Walmart. Say what you will about Walmart's buying, its merchandising, its pricing, and its strategy in locating stores, the real secret to its success is having one of the most highly motivated workforces on the face of the earth. Walton kept his people motivated with stock, which he gave them every opportunity to earn. He did that knowing full well there were investors around who craved every share of Walmart stock they could lay their hands on. So what happened? The public started paying his people, giving them regular bonuses for doing the little things required to make Walmart successful. With the appreciation in the value of the stock, a woman who worked at the checkout counter wasn't making $5 an hour anymore. She was making two, three, four times that amount.

So Walton just kept looking for ways to put more stock in employees' hands. For example, if the stock split, going from, say, 1 billion shares at $35 per share to 2 billion at $17.50. Suddenly Walton had a lot more stock he could make available to his people. And within a short time the public bid the price of the stock right back up to $35. In this way, Walton kept the stock price low enough to be affordable to employees. Later, when the price rose, they got what amounts to a bonus, and the public footed the bill.

Of course, the public was not stupid. The public was getting its money's worth, and so was Walton, because there's a message attached to those bonuses. Just to make sure people saw the message, Walton put up notices in stores and electronic tickers in his headquarters to keep employees posted on the current stock price. He'd tell them: "Here is your pot at the end of the rainbow. Now it's up to you to make it bigger. You can make it as big as you like if you just go out and do the right things."

People got the message, and Walmart got outstanding performance. It got clean stores, friendly employees, fast service, and good prices. It got a workforce that was motivated to concentrate on the basics—sell, smile, love the customer. And it got rid of the distractions that often kept people from concentrating on the basics. If an employee wanted to buy a home, or send a kid to college, or take care of a sick parent, she didn't spend time at work fretting about how she was going to pay for it. She didn't have to take on a second or third job. She just sold some of that stock.

It was a terrific deal all around. There were people on the cash registers at Walmart who were virtually millionaires, and somebody else was picking up the tab. So Walmart kept its operating costs phenomenally low and its morale phenomenally high—all of which helped to make the stock a good buy for the public. The public could clearly see the benefits of investing in a company of owners, and it did so happily. And the cycle went on.

That's what you can do with equity. It allows you to compensate people in a way that doesn't go into the basic cost structure of the product or the business. As a result, you can keep your labor costs below those of your competitors, which means you protect jobs, but you can still offer people the opportunity to earn big rewards in return for outstanding performance. In that sense, equity is similar to the bonuses we pay under the Stop-Gooter program, only better. With equity, you can harness the power of the multiple. You can offer bigger rewards; you can provide a higher level of education. You can show a person who's making $8 an hour how to get her compensation up to $20 an hour—by investing in herself.

So why doesn't every company make stock available to employees? If the benefits are so great and the costs so small,

you'd think all but the most hidebound company owners would be passing out equity. Instead, as we all know,
companies with equity participation are still the exception
rather than the rule.

Greed undoubtedly plays a role, although only if combined with ignorance. Sharing equity does not make you
poor, after all—just ask Sam Walton, one of the richest
men in America. A bigger factor than greed, I suspect, is
fear. Many owners and top executives don't want to share
stock because they are afraid of sharing information, for
the reasons discussed in Chapter 5 on open-book management. This is not altogether illogical. There is no point
in giving people stock if they can't see the numbers that
determine its value. Open-book management is the best
way to make equity participation work. If you're afraid of
opening the books, keep the stock to yourself. You're going
to encounter enough problems as it is without having a lot
of ignorant, angry shareholders working for you.

But fear and greed aside, there are three common argu-
ments against equity participation. I often hear them from
people who have given stock to employees and lived to re-
gret it. For that reason alone, they deserve to be addressed.

The Case Against Equity Sharing #1:
People Don't Appreciate It.

This is the complaint I hear most often from company
owners who have had bad experiences with equity participation. They're right. *Employees don't appreciate stock—if
you don't educate them about business.* You can't get people
to think and act like owners by putting pieces of paper

in their hands. Your employees may say they want stock. They may even demand it. A lot of people confuse equity with gold, thanks to some of the myths that grew up in the 1980s. But equity won't serve as a motivator if people don't know how they can affect its value. They may even get angry and cynical when it doesn't miraculously make them rich. Then you will rue the day you let them have it. Ownership comes with responsibilities. People have to know what they are.

The Case Against Equity Sharing #2: Let People Invest the Money for Themselves.

Some people argue against equity participation by proposing an alternative. An Employee Stock Ownership Plan (ESOP) is basically an investment vehicle, they say. So why not give employees the money you would put in the ESOP and let them invest it as they please? Pay them bigger bonuses. Set up a 401(k) plan, which allows them to put off paying taxes on the money until it's withdrawn. If they're hot on equity, they can buy the stock of other companies— Walmart, for example. They can diversify. They can invest in other kinds of securities. When you give people money instead of stock, you give them independence, control, and safety. You let them follow the first rule of prudent investing: don't put all your eggs in one basket.

It's an interesting argument, but it misses the point. The real question, after all, is whether or not people can invest in the stock of the company *where they work*. An ESOP is not just an investment vehicle, any more than a home is just a place to stay. When people invest in other companies, they are looking for a good return. When they invest in themselves, they are making a commitment. They are changing their relationship to their work. They are going for the pot at the end of the rainbow. Besides, you probably can't afford to give them as much money as they stand to make on the equity in the company. You would be paying them in ordinary dollars, after all, drawn out of the company's earnings. Equity dollars are considerably more potent, thanks to the power of the multiplier. If you try to pay that kind of money out of earnings, you'll bankrupt the company in no time.

The Case Against Equity Sharing #3: It Divides the Company.

Finally, there's an argument that equity promotes factionalism. Those who want to go public line up against those who want to be acquired, and both groups are against those who would maintain the status quo. Conflicts of interest arise. People get confused about their responsibilities. Managers don't make good owners, and owners don't make good managers, or so the argument goes.

There's a kernel of truth to it. Equity occasionally does go to somebody's head. We had one manager with a lot of stock who acted as though this was his plantation, and the employees were his slaves. Eventually, he pushed it too far and had to leave. But the problems almost always come down to the individuals involved. Equity isn't the issue; it's the excuse.

In fact, I've generally found that equity has the opposite effect, allowing people to put pettiness aside and see the

Big Picture. It helps you take the anger out of the conflicts that arise in any business. Without equity, it's easy to get caught up in petty disagreements. With equity, you can say, "Hey, wake up and smell the roses. These conflicts are really pretty insignificant. Let's look at the whole. Look at what you're giving up if you don't work this out."

⏸️▶ how to share equity

If you do decide to share equity, there are only so many ways to go about it, and each of them is highly regulated. When we started out, we thought we'd give shares to everybody who came to work at SRC. Then we discovered we could only do that if we went through the process of going public, which would have cost more money than we had at the time and might have opened us up to challenges we weren't prepared to handle. (For example, what if a competitor decided to acquire us in a hostile takeover at some point?) So we stayed private and looked for other ways to let people acquire an ownership stake. Eventually we came up with three:

* The ESOP

After a year of full-time employment at SRC, people become participants in the Employee Stock Ownership Plan (ESOP). The ESOP, in turn, is the single largest shareholder in SRC, with 31 percent of the stock as of January 1, 1992. (It started out with 3 percent of the stock and continues to grow every year.) There is a vesting period of about seven years, as required by law. That's how long you must remain in the ESOP before you are entitled to receive 100 percent of the value of your shares when you leave.

The role of an ESOP can vary significantly from company to company. At SRC, the ESOP is primarily a way to let people share in the financial risks and rewards of ownership: the value of an ESOP share rises or falls just as if it were a share held directly in SRC. Although the ESOP has no voting stock in the company, it has all the legal rights of a shareholder, which are considerable. It is managed by a committee of five people, three of whom are appointed by SRC's board of directors. The other two are elected, one by the hourly people, the other by the salaried people.

* Special Offerings

From time to time, we also give people the chance to buy shares in a special type of offering that some states allow as a way of encouraging employee ownership. Under Missouri and federal law, you can get exemptions from registering an offering to employees as long as all of them (or almost all of them) live in the state. Those exemptions allow you to sell shares directly to your people without taking the company public. There is no limit to the number of people who can buy in, provided they are full-time employees of the company and full-time residents of the state, or have special exemptions.

We put together our first such offering in 1986, issuing 177,000 shares (valued at $500,000). To allow for maximum participation, we divided the offering into stages. In the first stage, people could buy from 200 to 450 shares. If the offering didn't sell out, we moved to the second stage, in which people could buy up to 9,550 shares. There was also a third stage, but we didn't get that far. All the shares went in the first and second stages. We even had some hourly people buy in. One guy invested his life savings. He bet on himself, and he did very well. In the next five years, the value of his stock increased 216 percent, from $8.45 to $18.30 per share.

* Internal Trading

We had thirteen shareholders when we started out in 1983, all of us managers and supervisors at SRC. Today we have forty-five shareholders (not including the ESOP), and they come from all parts of the company. Since we aren't ready to go public, we restrict direct ownership of SRC stock to employees and directors, but—within those parameters—we encourage a certain amount of internal trading. It gives new people a chance to buy in, and old shareholders a chance to realize some gains, and it promotes a general awareness of equity within the company.

We do, however, regulate the trading to make sure it doesn't get out of hand and hurt the company. Under the original shareholders' agreement, we have the option to buy back the stock of any shareholder who dies, quits, or leaves the company under any circumstances, and we can pay over a long period of time. In addition, we give present shareholders an opportunity to sell back their stock in trading windows that we open every two or three years, as our financial resources permit. We also issue stock options to employees who take on extraordinary responsibility and risk. Existing shareholders can buy and sell nonvoting stock among ourselves without approval from the company.

As a result, we control who can and can't own stock. We set it up that way to protect the whole. We didn't want stock getting outside the company. We were worried about outside investors bringing a perspective we didn't share and forcing us to do things we didn't want to do. In addition, we wanted to preserve opportunities for people inside the company to buy in.

THE YEAR WE VOTED NOT TO PAY OURSELVES A CHRISTMAS BONUS

The test of an education comes when you have to make real-life choices based on what you've learned. We faced one of those moments at the beginning of November 1989, when people had to decide between protecting their equity and paying themselves a Christmas bonus.

We had already missed the first-quarter and second-quarter bonuses, which wasn't all that unusual. If you choose good targets, it often takes six months to start hitting them. Then, at the end of October, it became clear that we were going to miss the third-quarter bonus as well—for the first time ever. The third-quarter bonus is paid at the end of November, just in time for Christmas shopping, so people were understandably upset about losing it. What made the situation even hairier is that we were off by only .01 on the current ratio.

The supervisors got together and requested a meeting with me. There was grumbling on the shop floor. People had been working very hard all year, coping with some new business that had come in unexpectedly. The supervisors had been cheering them on, encouraging them to go for the bonus. Now there wasn't any bonus. What were the supervisors supposed to do? How could they keep people pumped up for the rest of the year?

I heard them out. I said, "I understand what you're saying, and I'm as interested in morale and motivation as you are. We can go ahead and pay the bonus if you want to. There's a real good chance we're going to hit it in the fourth quarter anyway, so we can just advance the payout from February to November, and let people have the money in time for Christmas.

"But you and your people should think carefully before you accept this offer. If we don't hit our targets in the fourth quarter for some reason, we're going to be out the money we've already paid. That money has to come from somewhere. In fact, it will come out of profits. If that happens, our stock value won't go up as much as it should this year. And remember, every dollar in after-tax profits is worth about $10 in stock value. So it's your choice. We can pay the bonus now, or we can wait until we've earned it. You decide."

For the next week, there was an intense debate throughout the company. It took the production chief half an hour to make the five-minute walk across the shop floor to his office every day. People kept stopping him to ask what he thought and to get his help in evaluating the numbers. Everybody was trying to calculate the likelihood of hitting the targets in the fourth quarter.

When I got back together with supervisors a week later, I asked them what they'd decided. They told me they had conducted a straw poll. About 40 percent of the people wanted to get the bonus; they were mainly the younger workers who had not been in the company long enough to acquire much equity. The other 60 percent preferred to wait until the bonus was earned. "So what's your decision?" I asked. They wanted me to decide. I said, "No way. You're the ones who are going to have to live with the consequences." They voted overwhelmingly against the bonus.

As it turned out, we missed the bonus again in the fourth quarter by .01 percent. So I had another morale problem. I went back to the staff and said, "Okay, I know you're good, and I can't walk away from the fact you've put in four solid quarters without getting a bonus. So what we'll do is keep the old bonus program." That was the first time in seven years that we'd kept the goals from one year to the next, but this one had a higher level. People needed a win. We had to let them prove how good they were. And they pulled away in the first quarter of 1990.

Our main purpose in sharing equity is to spread the financial benefits and responsibilities of ownership as widely as possible through the company. The ultimate legal authority on most issues remains in the hands of the people who own SRC's voting stock. That's me and five managers from the original buyout group. Two more managers had voting stock to begin with. One left, and the other sold it during one of the trading windows. In both cases, the company purchased the stock and retired it. Those of us who still own voting stock have used it for only one purpose: to elect the board of directors.

Sharing equity does not, in fact, force you to give up control of the business, as some company owners fear. If it doesn't change the way you run the company, however, you're doing something wrong. There is a great benefit in having an educated workforce that understands all aspects of the business: you have a lot of people you can turn to for help in making the tough decisions.

letting the people decide when the boss can't

I go for a consensus in the following circumstances:

> I'm not sure what the right decision is.
> I can see both sides of the story.
> The issue seems really gray to me.

Then the only fair way to make a decision is to let the majority rule. I don't know everything. When I can't answer a question, I'll give it back to the people in the company. I'll rely on their creativity to come up with a better idea than I've got. I do that whenever I think that I may be getting out of bounds, that I'm not looking at the issue clearly. For example, the question came up at one point as to whether we should have a new cafeteria. When I raised it during my meetings with employees, they said, "There's a lot we want before a cafeteria." They wanted more machine tools and other things to make them more productive.

But I rely most on the employees when a decision comes up that just tears me apart. No matter how many ways I look at it, I can't figure out the right thing to do. I faced one of those in December 1986, when General Motors abruptly canceled an order for 5,000 engines, representing 40 percent of our business for the coming year.

The numbers said we had to cut a hundred people from the payroll or risk losing the company. But that kind of layoff would have been a tremendous failure of management. There was nobody else to blame. I had to take responsibility even though there was no way I could have seen this disaster coming. I had to decide whether to take somebody's job away. I knew my own ass was protected, as least for the moment. That just made it worse. I'd sit in my office and stare at the ceiling and think about all these people depending on us to feed their families. We'd told them they had jobs. If they were going to leave, it should be their choice, not mine.

I spent weeks going over the numbers with the other managers, looking for a way out. We talked to customers and salespeople, followed up leads, tried to get GM to reconsider—without luck. Finally I went to the people. We held a series of employee meetings throughout the company in the middle of March 1987. I painted the picture as bleak as it was. I told them that if we kept everyone around, we would have to go out and generate approximately 55,000 man-hours of new business, and if that turned out to be the wrong decision, there was no contingency. Instead of having to lay off a hundred people, we might have to lay off two hundred. We'd need a new infusion of outside capital, and that could affect the whole thinking of the company. It's possible there would have to be a change in management as well.

I got a mixed response. There was a group of senior employees who didn't want to take the chance. They weren't close to the new group, the ones who would be laid off. They said, "Hell, if it's between me and them, let it be them." And they had a very good point. In order to get by without a layoff, we would have to get one hundred new product lines up and running in three months. You just can't introduce products that fast. I agreed: it looked impossible.

So we got ready to order the layoff. But then those senior people, the hard-core guys, came back to me. They'd obviously been talking it over among themselves, figuring out exactly what it would take to get the new lines up. They said, "Geez, we've been thinking about it, and we can weather it. We'll have to train these kids, but we'll make it. We can do it." They didn't want to lay people off any more than I did, but I don't think they were going with their emotions. I think they'd figured it out statistically. They could break down the elements of the job in more detail than I could, and they decided they could meet the challenge.

WHAT IS DEMOCRACY IN BUSINESS?

We run SRC with a lot of participation, but it is not a democracy in the political sense of the word. A political democracy derives its authority from the consent of the governed. A company derives its authority from the consent of the marketplace. The people who work for a company may think it's just terrific, but they'll have to work somewhere else if the company doesn't make money or runs out of cash. So the market tells us what a lot of our decisions have to be. Often the trick is to recognize what it's saying.

Nevertheless, there are more possibilities for democracy in business than people realize. Instead, they allow themselves to be manipulated. I mean, people who own stock in public companies have power they never use. Why they don't use it, I have no idea. There is a tremendous gap between the power they have and what they do. Why do so few shareholders exercise that power?

There has never been a really important decision in this company that hasn't been by acclamation, if not unanimous. Every major decision is talked through in advance. People are asked to contribute, to say whatever they think. Do we want to bring everyone in as shareholders? Do we want to grow? Do we want to decentralize? When we began thinking about decentralization, we talked to everybody in the company. I have folders of notes from the meetings we held. First I went to the supervisors. Then we went to the entire workforce to find out what they wanted. We took their wants to the management team, and we tried to figure out how we could afford them. Out of all those discussions came the plan to decentralize.

In business, it's the head of the company who decides how the company is going to be run, and I have decided to use a democratic process. I ask people to contribute, to vote, to participate, to have input. I have a lot of trust in that process. I'm trying to find a system that is simple, that people can understand, and that they can follow. I want to give them a game plan that allows them to make their own decisions. I want them to see how their decisions fit into the overall puzzle. So you have to educate them first. Without education, you don't have democracy. All you have is manipulation. There is no democratic process if people don't have any idea what you're talking about. The better educated people are, the more democratic you can be, and the better it will work.

At a certain point, growth becomes an obstacle to democracy, because you have to keep bringing new people up to speed. That may involve keeping the others on hold—saying, "Wait a while till these guys catch up." That's a problem we struggled with. It was one reason we began to set up subsidiaries. If we created smaller businesses, we could let them take the message to people. Small businesses can communicate quicker and better. And when you're operating on a small scale, you have more time. Whereas when you're operating on a large scale, the problems all get magnified.

Back at the time of the American Revolution,

Thomas Paine called his pamphlet *Common Sense* because he thought democracy was a matter of common sense. I feel the same way. The way I run this company is just plain common sense. It's the fairest way of doing things. There are so many unfair things in the world, why not create an environment where at least you try to make things fair?

This system works. That's why I use it. I don't know of any way to have a more successful company. It works because it gets people to contribute, to participate, to learn, and to grow. Democracy doesn't work well if people don't participate. The only problem with the political democracy we have in the United States is that not enough of us contribute. At SRC, we get people to contribute by telling them the truth about business. We try to appeal to their brains, to show that if they contribute, they'll get something back. That's where equity is an important tool.

It was a case of the system taking care of itself. If I'd heard something else from the organization, I might have had to react differently. But when those guys said, "Let's try it," that was all I needed. I really wanted to go that way. When you can see compassion in your fellow workers, that's a big reward. It motivates you even more, because you see what a good group you're working with.

But I have to admit, it was pure hell introducing those new product lines. We told people that the pressures would be overwhelming, but I don't think we had any idea how overwhelming they were really going to be. We cried in

July, it was so rough. We couldn't get our quality up. We couldn't get our routines together. We had severe start-up problems. It was like recovering from a stroke—very slow and very painful. It hurt. It really hurt. I'm talking about long-term pain. But we dodged the bullet. We avoided the layoff. In fact, we wound up adding one hundred people to the payroll that year.

chapter **11**

THE HIGHEST LEVEL OF THINKING

Let me tell you about something that terrifies every person who runs a company—or at least it should. It has been sneaking up on us for years, while no one was paying attention. Now it's here, and it's big, and everybody is aware of it and scared by it. In an instant, it can leave you destitute. It can steal your job. It can destroy your company. It can devastate your family. It can ruin your life.

I am talking about the cost of health care.

This is the toughest problem we face in business today. I don't have the answers. I don't know who does. For decades, we ignored health care as a business issue, with the result that costs rose 24 to 40 percent a year. We assumed that we were protected by insurance. We didn't face up to the fact that health-care costs are all passed along to the policyholders in the form of premiums. Now the problem is out of control. I spent four years looking into this one line on the income statement. I broke it down into fifty-six categories. I can quote numbers and statistics. The whole thing became an obsession for me. When my youngest daughter was being delivered, I stood there and watched the doctor use gloves that cost $2.22 a pair. I knew we could buy them at our factory for 19 cents. I got so distracted watching him throw those gloves away that I almost forgot about my baby being born.

The health-care issue will do that to you. The costs are staggering, and somebody has to pick up the tab. The longer I looked at the problem, the more consumed I was by it. I lost all my perspective. Then something happened that reminded me just how frightening this issue can be.

The son of an employee had a heart attack. By the time the ambulance came, he was in a coma. It was a terrible tragedy. He was an active, vigorous boy, seventeen years old, with a great future ahead of him. I had known his mother for years. She'd worked for our lawyer before she came to SRC. She is one of the finest people I know. And yet, when I heard the news, my first thought was, *How are we going to pay the hospital bills?*

I was scared to death that we might have to wind up paying for long-term medical treatment. That could cost us $400,000 a year in additional premiums, and it would come straight out of earnings. We might be forced to cancel the bonus program. Everyone would take a hit on the stock. I didn't know what we would do, or how I should feel. Should I just be concerned about his illness? Shouldn't I be concerned about the effect it might have on the other people in the company and their families? What if we had two or three more like him?

The questions tore me apart. I didn't know what to pray for. The truth is I didn't know whether I wanted him to live or die, and that scared me most of all. What kind of a person was I becoming? I had always told myself I was in business to improve people's lives, and here I was half hoping that one would be ended. Of course, I wanted him to get better—that was easy. But what if he had to go into rehabilitation? How would we pay for it? No matter what we did, everyone in the company would be affected. Everyone would make sacrifices. Everyone would go without something. Was that fair? I honestly didn't know what to think.

In the end, we didn't have to deal with those tough, tough questions. Another company did. It turned out the boy was covered under his father's insurance at the place where he worked. So somebody else paid the bills for the boy's hospitalization and, later, his rehabilitation. But the episode left me badly shaken. It almost broke me. I had been serving on a local coalition of business and medical people who were trying to come to grips with the health-care crisis. Shortly thereafter, I resigned. I felt that I couldn't face this issue anymore, that it was turning me into a monster.

Unfortunately, it's an issue we all have to face, and it's not the only one. We are surrounded by problems that are having a major impact on business, not to mention the rest of society. I am not talking about anything vague or abstract here. It's not just the quality of life that is suffering. These problems are hitting us where we can see them, feel them, measure them: in the income statement. We get hit by decaying highways in rising transportation costs. We get hit by poor education in inferior product quality and higher warranty claims. We get hit by environmental neglect in soaring compliance costs, insurance rates, and liability claims. We get hit by poverty and crime in increasing taxes. And as more companies find it harder to operate profitably, we get hit by business failures in a higher bad-debt allowance.

What we're looking at here is overhead. Call it "social overhead" if you want to, but it's overhead just the same. It's measurable. It's quantifiable. It shows up on the income statement of every business in the country. Whether or not you break it out as a line item, whether you even know it's there, you are already paying for that social overhead. It's part of the total overhead you have to absorb.

And there's nothing you can do to avoid it. Health insurance is a line item that affects all of us directly. As long as you offer it, you're pretty much helpless. The costs are going to keep rising no matter what you do. You can cushion the effect by getting people to change their habits. You can put pressure on them to stop smoking, lose weight, exercise, or whatever. But that's tough. It's an invasion of privacy. It may not keep them from getting sick anyway. It wouldn't have prevented that boy's heart attack. And it won't put you in control of your health-insurance costs. They will continue to go up and up, because somebody has to pay for all the people who *don't have* health insurance, and that group is getting larger and larger every day.

Yes, there is one temporary alternative available: you could just drop health insurance altogether, assuming you can live with yourself afterward. But the costs will just come back to you in another form—lost productivity, employee turnover, or inability to attract good people. What's more, you'll pay whenever you buy a product or a service from a company that does have health insurance.

You can run, but you can't hide. Sooner or later, the health-insurance beast will catch you. And when it does, it may well take away your business. It will drive up your costs until you can't make money anymore, or it will destroy your company from within, by undermining morale. I really don't like this issue. I've broken it down into the smallest increments, and I still can't find any answers. Sometimes I think that, instead of health insurance, we should give each person $4,000 a year to do with as he or she pleases. If people want to invest it in being healthy, fine, because that's your only hope of beating the odds. Otherwise, you'd better find a way to earn a 25 percent annual return, or you won't have the money you need to take care of yourself when you eventually get sick. But where is anybody going to get a guaranteed annual return of 25 percent?

In the past, there were two ways of responding to problems like this one. One was benign neglect: maybe if we ignore it, it will go away. Sometimes it did, sometimes it didn't. The other response was to get the government to deal with it. We can't afford either approach anymore. We've already tried the first one, and it didn't work. As a result, we're in worse shape than ever. On the other hand, the government alternative is out of our price range. There is no more expensive way to solve a problem than by means of bureaucracy, regulation, and mandate. Who will pay for another Social Security system or Medicare program? We would just be *increasing* the overhead at a time when we're struggling to absorb what we have.

We're at the end of innocence. There is no one who can solve these problems for us. We've run out of cheap sources of funds. We can't pay for solutions by taxing the rich: they don't have enough money. If we tax business, we're just buying a new, worse set of problems and aggravating the ones we already have. We can't borrow: the Japanese and the Europeans have tightened up on credit. Besides, even governments have to pay their debts sooner or later. To do that, you need cash, and there are only three ways to get it: (1) you can print money—and further undermine the economy through inflation; (2) you can sell off assets—and give up ownership of your national resources to foreigners; and (3) you can get the country focused on making money and generating cash.

Which brings us right back to the Great Game of Business and those two principles I talked about in Chapter 1. They are not just the basis for a sensible approach to managing a company. In fact, they offer the only real hope we have of solving the problems we face as a society. The alternatives are not solutions at all. They are just ways of managing the decline of our economy, our standard of living, and the opportunities for our children, our grandchildren, and generations beyond.

What's required is a new way of thinking and a vast program of education. By and large, that education has to be carried out in the businesses of America—on the shop floors, in the warehouses, behind the retail counters, over the water coolers and the copying machines, at the desks, in the meeting rooms and the cafeterias. We have to change the entire mentality of the country, a mentality we have created by the way we have run companies in the past. We have to get rid of the excuses. We have to uproot the idea that you can always blame somebody else for your problems and always look to somebody else to take care of you. All of us have to take responsibility for ourselves. We have to become *self-reliant*. We have to get into bench-marking, meeting the standards, watching costs, being held accountable, establishing goals, compensating with bonus programs, using the multiple, and teaching people to think and act like owners—we have to do it all, because it's the only chance we have of getting our economy and our society back on track. But it won't happen unless management leads the way.

///

THE TENTH HIGHER LAW IS:
Change Begins at the Top, or—as We Say in Missouri—Shit Rolls Downhill.

///

Like it or not, the responsibility for the future rests squarely on the shoulders of the people who run America's businesses. We are the only ones left with the credibility and the clout to bring about real change. This is nothing to cheer about. We all need balance in our lives, and our society would benefit from more balance as well. I wish that churches had greater influence, government were noted for its wisdom and efficiency, and the schools were a source of national pride. As it is, the leadership has to come from business. If you want to see one of the people we're counting on to turn things around, look in the mirror.

As businesspeople, we need to get back to basics. We need to refocus on our primary social mission: creating jobs. When you create jobs, you are creating the means for absorbing overhead, including all that social overhead we have accumulated. The fewer jobs we create, the more people there are on unemployment or welfare, without health insurance, getting caught up in poverty and crime. The consequence: higher overhead for each of us to absorb internally. Because it all comes back to us. We pay, no matter what.

||||▶ where jobs come from

Thirty years ago, I took up bass fishing for my health. It was near the end of 1983, the first year after the buyout, and the pressures were getting to me. My hair was falling out in clumps. I couldn't eat or sleep. I missed steps when I walked. I called a doctor, who told me it was either Lou Gehrig's disease or multiple sclerosis. The next doctor was more encouraging. He said it was stress.

I thought fishing might help me relax. So I bought some equipment, got some pointers from my friends at SRC, and started practicing. I was terrible. I read instruction books and took lessons. The fish just ignored me. I watched the pros. I studied articles in fishing magazines. I worked and worked on my technique. Nothing helped. I couldn't catch fish to save my soul. When I competed in the SRC bass fishing tournaments, I came in dead last.

One day, I was standing on the dock at the end of another losing effort, and I noticed a guy nearby who was obviously one of the old-timers on the lake. He was sunburned and weather-beaten, with deep creases in his hands and face, and not a tooth in sight. He looked like the Old Man from *The Old Man and the Sea*. I ambled over to him and struck up a conversation. I wanted him to check me out, tell me what I was doing wrong. He looked my equipment over and didn't say anything. I made a few casts. He just watched. "So what am I doing wrong?" I finally asked him.

"Nothin'," he said.

"Nothing?" I said. "Then how come I don't catch fish?"

"Let me tell you somethin', son," he said. "Everyone who comes fishin' here gits the same number of bites. The only difference between thems that catch the fish and thems that don't is preparation and concentration. You gotta make sure your hook is sharp and your line don't have no nicks. Then you gotta *watch that line*. You pay attention to them little things, and you'll catch all the fish you kin handle."

I think of that story whenever I run into people who don't know what to do with their lives because there just aren't enough good opportunities around. I also think of it when I hear about companies laying people off because their services aren't needed, because there isn't enough work for them, because the opportunities have all dried up. What a waste. There are opportunities everywhere— opportunities to grow, opportunities to start new businesses, opportunities to create jobs and absorb overhead. Everybody gets the same number of bites. You catch the fish when you're prepared and ready to respond.

At the beginning of the 1990s, we started new businesses at SRC as fast as we could get them up and running. At the same time, we decentralized our existing business, breaking it into smaller units that could be run as separate companies. It was all part of a plan to transform SRC into a diversified collection of enterprises and an ongoing business incubator. By and large, the new companies were run by people who had received their business education at SRC. Most of them had come up through the ranks—as hourly workers, salaried professionals, and middle managers; they rode the roller coaster with us in the 1980s, learning all about the Great Game of Business in the process. By the 1990s, they were ready to apply what they'd learned to enterprises of their own. They were given the opportunity to acquire the businesses in the future, whenever they chose to. Meanwhile, SRC kept on spinning off new ones.

Frankly, we had more opportunities than we could handle. Everywhere we turned we found another business waiting to be launched. We started one to remanufacture a troublesome engine component, thereby turning a $500,000-per-year problem into a company with annual revenues of $2.5 million. We started two others to help solve problems for a couple of our customers, Navistar and J. I. Case. We discovered a turbocharger business operating right under our noses in one of the factories, all set to be spun off. We even began a seminar business in response to people from other companies who wanted to see how we play the Game.

||||||➡ downsizing for opportunities

There is no magic in starting these companies. You need two components. I call them overhead absorbers and cash-flow generators. An *overhead absorber* is a product or a service. It is a way people can spend their time producing something for which a customer will want to pay, and thereby absorb the overhead that's required to operate any business. A *cash-flow generator* is simply a customer or a market, preferably guaranteed. It is a way people can be reasonably sure they'll be generating the cash they need to get the business off the ground. Whenever we can put an overhead absorber (a product) together with a cash-flow generator (a customer who will make a commitment to buy the product), we have a business. Then it's just a matter of working out the details. Sometimes you have to haggle with the customer to get an acceptable deal. Sometimes you have to do some marketing. Sometimes you have to tinker with the product to get the quality you want at a cost you can afford. But those are the normal challenges of business. Once you've figured out the solutions, you can get on with the process of creating jobs.

In a sense, we downsized, but not the way other companies do it. Instead of laying people off, we took our best and brightest and created opportunities for them. We continue to show people that we want to see them get ahead, that there are no dead ends in this organization, that they can go as far as they want to, and that we mean it when we say we want to help them achieve their dreams. At the same time, we are all moving to the next level in the education process. We've always liked the idea of equity. Now we are getting a new lesson in the power of multiple. While our people are out starting businesses for themselves, they are also generating additional earnings for the parent company, which boosts our stock value. Some of these businesses could eventually be sold for twenty, thirty, forty times earnings. Who gets the proceeds? The employee-stockholders of SRC.

This deal is so good I sometimes wonder if it's completely legal. It's easy. It's fun. It's challenging but not very risky. It's a way to make a ton of money. And everybody benefits. Not only that, but we are putting more and more people to work. We are helping them to be self-reliant. We are starting them on the educational process, teaching them about making money and generating cash. And we are absorbing more overhead, including some of the social overhead that's becoming such a burden to us all.

So why don't more companies do it? Why don't they set their people up in freestanding subsidiaries? For the same reasons, I suspect, that they don't share equity or open up the books: fear, greed, paranoia, ignorance. When you don't trust your people, you're not likely to help them start businesses that might break off and become more successful, and might even become competitors. Of course, that kind of thinking often boomerangs. People may become so angry and frustrated that they go out anyway and compete against you as hard as they can. That's too bad for you, but it's all right for the rest of us. The new companies, after all, are doing their part to create jobs and absorb overhead, which takes some of the pressure off everybody else.

What I find much more baffling and troubling is the way big companies have gone about downsizing. I am no fan of their efforts to slim down and get "lean and mean." I might be if I thought they were really getting back to basics, introducing a new style of management. I see very few signs of that. Granted, there's a lot of talk about employee involvement, participatory management, self-directed work teams, empowerment. In nine cases out of ten, it's a crock. It's just a way of eliminating middle management.

What's really happening is that the world has become more competitive and these companies have stood still. So now they have to cut costs. There are basically three types of cost: labor, material, and overhead. They can't do much about labor and material, so they attack the overhead by eliminating supervisors and middle managers. Sure enough, they bring their unit costs down, but they don't become more competitive because productivity is as low as ever.

We had a classic case in Springfield—Zenith Electronics Corp., which had the last television plant in the United States. It was getting beaten to death by third-world competitors. The Koreans were selling TVs in the United States at less than Zenith's material cost, which suggested some dumping might be going on. It was unfair, but it was a fact of life. Somehow Zenith had to get its unit costs down so that it could be competitive on price. There are only two ways to do that: increase productivity or reduce standard

costs. Zenith, like most other big companies, chose to reduce standards by downsizing, by eliminating good minds,
and by taking the brains out of the organization. The attitude was, "We need money, and we can't make money
through people." In the end, they couldn't make money at
all. The plant was all but shut down, and 1,500 jobs were
moved to Mexico.

That's typical. It all goes back to the basic proposition
that, to stay in business, you have to be the least-cost producer or have something nobody else has. These companies don't have anything unique anymore, so they try to be
least-cost. They see empowerment as a way to get there—
empowerment meaning that people supervise themselves,
that you don't have managers on the shop floor. But it's an
illusion. The managers aren't being laid off because they
can't contribute. In many cases, they've done good work for
fifteen, twenty, twenty-five years. They are the field managers and coaches. You need those people to improve productivity, or even just to maintain it. You can reduce overhead
by letting them go, no question about it. But if empowerment doesn't help you increase productivity, it's a failure.
All you're doing is lowering the standard of living outside
the four walls of your company. In effect, you're taking the
overhead of the business and putting it out on the streets.
It comes back in social overhead—rising health-insurance
costs, for example.

I'm not saying downsizing is bad per se. When we spin
off companies, we are downsizing. We are taking overhead
off the shop floor. We are keeping our unit costs down. But
instead of dumping loyal employees who have done a good
job for years and years, we are financing them. We are of-

fering them a chance to own and run a business. We are creating jobs rather than eliminating them.

Too many businesses have forgotten that they are here to create jobs. That's how they add value to an economy, a society, a nation. When management is forced to lay people off, it is conceding that it has failed in one of its primary roles. This might be reason to consider replacing management, but I can't understand why anybody would want to celebrate it for being "lean and mean."

the hunger for ownership

When we first came up with the plan to set people up in their own businesses, I got very excited. I could hardly wait to present it. The idea had grown out of several months of discussions, during which we'd talked to people about what they wanted over the long term, where we all wanted to go. The decentralization strategy seemed like just the ticket to get there, and it also addressed a number of other challenges we were facing—how to cope with the pressures of growth; how to give people a rest without passing up opportunities; how to keep up with our customers, who were coming to us with more and more ideas; how to grow without getting big and bureaucratic.

So we held a series of meetings at which I laid out the strategy to people. I talked about ownership. I told them we wanted to make it possible for anybody who was interested to have a business. We would help people with the financing and the business plan, and provide ongoing advice and support. In time, they could buy us out if they wanted. The decision would be theirs. Everybody would have a shot at the brass ring. I told people I wanted to hear from anybody who was up for the challenge and felt ready to go. If some people preferred first to get more experience and training in SRC itself, we could arrange that, too. For that matter, they were also free to sit back and let the opportunity go by. But I wanted them to know we were serious. We were actively looking for new businesses to start. I said I'd be grateful if people would pass along any ideas they might have. The response bowled me over.

The first proposal came from a guy who wanted to buy a liquor store. Then someone else showed up with a plan to start a bar. Next came a Laundromat, and a beauty salon, and a gas station with multiple bays for repairing several automobiles at the same time. We even had one person propose an Amway distributorship in Mexico. We received dozens of ideas. Most of them, like these, were not very feasible. Not that I took them lightly. As much as possible, I worked through the numbers with people to help them see the pitfalls. Eventually, I just said, "Look, we want to start businesses, but they have to be somewhat related to what we do now." But the response showed me how much desire people had to be in business for themselves.

That desire is pretty much universal these days. Throughout the world, there is a growing hunger for ownership. You can see it wherever you look. It's in Argentina and Singapore, in Czechoslovakia and Mozambique, in Morocco and Taiwan, and the Baltic Republics. It has been one of the driving forces behind the transformation of Eastern Europe. Today we read in the newspapers about people with a passion to own a tractor, a plow, a piece of land, a street vending cart, an apartment. Tomorrow we will read about their passion for owning companies.

This should be a source of pride and concern to Americans. Pride, because we were the pioneers, and we are still a source of inspiration to all these people. Concern, because every one of them is a potential competitor, and they all have a tremendous advantage. They can study the way other people practice capitalism—the Americans, the Germans, the Japanese, the British, the Swedes—and they only have to take the best. They don't have to saddle themselves with a compensation system that gives executives outrageous salaries and perks no matter how they perform on the job. Or management practices that pit people against one another and divide companies into warring factions. Or corporate bureaucracies that block change. Or traditions of secrecy that promote ignorance. Or ridiculous, antiquated shop rules left over from a bygone era.

The new capitalists can look around and see what works and use it, leaving the rest behind. By that fact alone, they will get a jump on us. They'll be playing smarter games, quicker games. While we sit here trying to decide what to do, they'll be out there satisfying the hunger for ownership. They know that hunger. They can feel it. They can taste it. They realize what a powerful motivator it can be. They have been focusing on it while we have been ignoring it. As soon as they figure out how to harness it, they can hitch their wagons to it and rocket right by us. That is the real challenge of global competition.

It is a challenge that we can meet, that we have to meet. We don't have much choice. This is not a new technology or a clever strategy we are talking about. This is a force of history. The drive for ownership will shape the world well into the next century. We can choose to join it, or we can let it pass us by, but make no mistake about the consequences. We will be overwhelmed by the social overhead that will just keep growing until it crushes us, if we:

- Don't meet the challenge.
- Don't feed the hunger for ownership in our own people.
- Don't use it to educate them and motivate them, and get them to take responsibility for themselves.
- Don't all become self-reliant and accountable.
- Don't accept certain basic standards of fairness and justice and, yes, equity.
- In short, if we don't start playing the Game by a set of rules that make sense.

There's no reason to let that happen. We have the only resource we need to solve the problems facing us and to create a stunning future for our children: ourselves. You can turn the Game around right now. If enough of us do, we will all be winners.

//

chapter 12

THE ULTIMATE HIGHER LAW:
A MESSAGE TO MIDDLE MANAGERS

There is one additional higher law.

//

THE ULTIMATE HIGHER LAW IS:
When You Appeal to the Highest Level of
Thinking, You Get the Highest Level of
Performance.

//

That's really the whole point. It's what all the other
higher laws lead up to. It's also the main reason for playing
the Great Game of Business. The Game allows you to create an environment in which you can constantly appeal to
people's best instincts, in which you can ask them to rise

above the day-to-day frustrations and think at the highest level—that is, use all their intelligence and ingenuity and resourcefulness to help each other achieve the common goals.

But what if you work in a company that doesn't care about playing the Game? What if your boss isn't interested in getting you or anybody else to think at the highest level? What if you are a manager who believes passionately in everything we've talked about here, who wants nothing more than to live by the higher laws of business, but who has none of the tools we use to break down barriers, eliminate ignorance, and show people the Big Picture? What if you don't even know the numbers used to measure your performance?

Go ahead without them. The truth is you don't need them to play the Game in a single department or office. It's different when you're trying to get a whole company involved. Then it's essential to provide tools that can be used by departments with totally different functions to stay focused on the goals. But if you are a middle manager who wants to start the Game in one discrete area of a business, you can get by without a bonus program, or an equity participation plan, or an elaborate communications system, or access to the company books. You don't even need the approval of your boss. What you need, above all, is personal commitment. For middle managers, the first step in the Game is to take a clear-eyed look at the way you operate and to ask yourself the tough questions—without using your boss as an excuse:

- What are you *personally* giving to the people you manage?

- Do you spend as much time thinking about them as you spend thinking about customers, or other departments, or people higher up in the organization?
- Do you share your problems, or do you keep them to yourself? Have you asked your people for help in carrying your load? Do they even know what your load is? Have you told them your Critical Number?
- Do you yourself operate with an open book? Do you let your people know everything that you know?
- Are you getting the benefit of their intelligence, or do you still think you're responsible for coming up with the answers on your own?
- Do your people know what to do without being told, or do they wait to get a list from you? Is everybody working toward the same goal? Does everybody know what it is? Do you let people figure out the best way to get there?
- Do you know what gets your people angriest? Have you ever asked them about their frustrations and their fears? What keeps *them* awake at night? Have they told you their Critical Numbers?
- Have you talked to your people about your own fears and frustrations? Can you let down your guard enough to do that? Are you willing to make yourself vulnerable? Do you have enough self-confidence to take the chance that you might get screwed?

- Most important, if the answers to such questions are no, do you really want to change?

I don't mean to let top management off the hook here. I firmly believe that if we don't have a revolution in American business, we will do serious long-term damage to our way of life. But this is one revolution that will have to come a person at a time. It all goes back to the fifth higher law: You gotta wanna. The motivation has to come from inside. That applies to bosses as well as workers. Whether you're the president of General Motors, or the operator of a fast-food franchise, or a middle manager in a multinational company with a traditional approach to business, *you gotta wanna change.* The biggest obstacle does not lie in the boardroom or in the corner office, but in ourselves.

By the same token, you can start playing your own version of the Game even if you have no support from executives further up in the organization. Bring your people together, sit them down and talk to them, get at the root of their problems and concerns. Try to put aside your own natural defensiveness. Let each person talk freely and frankly, without interruption. Then go back and look for a pattern and a consensus. How do your people view their position in the company? How do they view their environment? What do they like about the company? What don't they like? What do they think is the biggest problem? What scares them the most? What gets them angriest? From that, you will be able to figure out their Critical Numbers, and you can set up a game to go after it.

But don't stop there. Tell them *your* Critical Number. That is absolutely essential. You can't ask people to think at the highest level if they don't know what your real goals are. Tell them what scares you the most, what gets you the angriest, what keeps you awake at night. Explain how things look from your perspective. In every job I've had, I've always found it fascinating to talk to people about what I've discovered as I moved up the ladder. They have all kinds of notions and speculations, and they're very curious to know the reality. Paint the picture for them. Unlock the secrets. Think of yourself as an explorer on their behalf. To be a happy manager, you have to enjoy sharing the things you've learned. When you keep them to yourself, you can't enjoy them. Even if you are successful, you will never feel comfortable with the wins. When you share your knowledge, you have people with whom you can celebrate every victory. As a manager, you will have a ball.

Having a ball is important, for you and your people. It's one of the major rewards of playing the Game. But you can have a ball only if you are working together as a team, if everybody is going after the same Critical Number and the same goal. When people have different numbers and different goals, it's like having a crooked spine. The organization is constantly in pain. The fundamental purpose behind the Great Game of Business is to eliminate that pain by making sure the various parts of the organization are in alignment. To do that in an entire company, you need tools like the ones we've developed at SRC. To do it in a department, or an office, you mainly have to be willing to open up, to share.

Of course, playing the Game in your own area of the business won't alleviate the pain resulting from misalignment in the company as a whole. You will still have to contend with mixed messages, interdepartmental rivalry, corporate politics, nonsensical decisions, hidden agendas, and all the other frustrations endemic to companies in which the leaders don't take responsibility for getting everyone to pull in the same direction. In the end, you may not be able to save the company. You will, however, save yourself and your people. You will create an island of sanity in a sea of confusion. You will also gain some measure of control over your destiny, thanks to that ultimate higher law. By getting people to think at the highest level, you make it possible for them to perform up to the peak of their abilities, and performance is the only control any of us really have. As long as we perform, as long as we are productive, as long as we deliver what we promise, and contribute, and add value, our services will always be in demand. The Game helps you to do all that and have a little bit of fun in the process. That's reason enough for playing it—even if you're all alone.

GET IN THE GAME:

THE "INTERACTIVE" GUIDE

part **2** **OVERVIEW OF THE PRINCIPLES AND PRACTICES OF THE GREAT GAME OF BUSINESS**

KNOW AND TEACH THE RULES
Financial Transparency and Education
High-Involvement Planning
The Critical Number

FOLLOW THE ACTION AND KEEP SCORE
Keep Score—Scoreboards
Follow the Action—Huddles
Forward Forecasting

PROVIDE A STAKE IN THE OUTCOME
Rewards and Recognition
MiniGames
Ownership

INTRODUCTION TO THE GUIDE

When practicing the Great Game of Business (GGOB), the breakthrough comes when companies shift from focusing on an *event* (bonus plan, financial literacy program, etc.) to using the GGOB as an *operating system* to run their organization. The GGOB is a system, a pattern, a strategy, a way of thinking. If you want to fully leverage the power of the Game, you must treat it as a system and persistently work it.

The purpose of this guide is to help you learn and implement the system. Think of it as summing up the concepts in the book you've just read and arranging them in a specific, practical "working" methodology.

The guide is organized in two sections. Part One, "Get in the Game: A Practitioner's Story," is the tale of one "factitional" entrepreneur's journey (a fictional story based upon scores of firsthand, factual accounts—of real implementations). We've learned through the years that the best way to teach the Game is by sharing stories—our own, as well as thousands of practitioners who've been there before. The guide provides tips on getting started with the GGOB as well as insights on how to sustain it and make it stick.

Part Two, "Overview of the Principles and Practices of the Great Game of Business," provides an overview of the system by outlining the principles and practices that make up the GGOB.

The goal is to share with you all the tools, resources, tips, stories, stumbling blocks, potential pitfalls, solutions, and understanding necessary to successfully implement the GGOB. We want to share everything we've learned. The challenge, of course, is putting more than thirty years of lessons in one book. That's where the "interactive" part comes in. Throughout this guide you will find links to the GGOB's *online* Resource Site, where you can access additional resources and downloadable tools. Each will be indicated by a globe (●). In this way, the resources will always remain fresh and relevant, no matter when you choose to read this book.

You can use the following link to access the resource site:

(●) www.greatgame.com/gigguide using the log-in code "GGOB20."

Get in the Game:
A PRACTITIONER'S STORY

He was staring at the dog-eared, tattered paperback poking out of his carry-on. He'd read *The Great Game of Business* years ago and told himself that if he ever had the chance to run his own company, he would run it this way . . . "open book." He thought about this as he jostled around in a minivan cab from the St. Louis airport to his hotel. The van was crammed with his entire management team; they were chattering with excitement. It was the first time they had ever all traveled somewhere together. The fall Annual Gathering of Games Conference started in an hour.

Randy's company had been started thirty years ago. It consisted of three divisions: On-Location Services, Dry Cleaning, and Emergency Restoration Services. His father had built it up from nothing and had run it for decades in the classic style: command and control. Last year, when Randy finally bought him out, he did so with a mixed bag of emotions: excitement, opportunity, freedom, and the "oh hell" moments when he thought about how the buyout left the business so leveraged financially.

Now that it was *his*, Randy often felt a rush of realization as to why his father ran the business with an iron fist. Surely his dad was somewhere in his bass boat laughing . . .

Randy knew it was time to do something, and today was the day.

He was excited about the Gathering. He'd heard that practitioners had been meeting at this conference for over two decades, sharing best practices, talking about their experiences, discussing what worked, and what didn't. They had even created an All-Star Award to recognize "the best of the best." That was all well and good, Randy thought, but all he wanted was a chance to really see how it worked in the real world—to see how someone had actually applied it. How somebody had taken the ideas from *The Great Game of Business* book and adapted them into his or her own business and culture.

He'd heard a lot about open-book management and just knew it was the answer. He'd read articles in the *Economist, Inc.* magazine, the *Wall Street Journal*, and the *New York Times* that lauded the benefits of financial transparency. As Randy was soon to learn, he was in for quite an eye-opener at the conference. He was about to learn that people who practice the Great Game of Business and really leverage the idea go far beyond just opening a company's books.

▐▐▐▶ experience the game

The Gathering of Games

The Gathering Conference gave Randy and his management team a vision of what was possible. As it had all those years ago when he first read *The Great Game of Business*, his enthusiasm took over. He met hundreds of people from all over the world, from every industry and from every level in business. The conference and the people proved to him that he really *could* have an impact on his business. He really *could* change people's lives at the same time. It was unbelievable to Randy to see that regular people were doing extraordinary things and sharing in the rewards. His whole team realized that if *those* folks could do it, *they* could do it too. Afterward, they felt those three days away from work were the best investment they could have made.

It was at that conference that Randy met Tom, a business owner from upstate who used the Great Game of Business to run his business. Randy made arrangements for his whole team to travel to Tom's enterprise to see the GGOB in action for themselves. A conference is one thing, but seeing it in action in a business is something else.

A Practitioner Visit

A week after the conference adjourned, Randy and his team drove up to see Tom. Tom had invited Randy's entire implementation team (the employees and managers who volunteered to be a part of starting the GGOB) to his weekly Huddle.

Tom was in the IT business; he described himself to prospective clients as "your outsourced IT department." His people were computer geeks who didn't go to school to become businesspeople. In fact, they couldn't give a hoot about learning business. They wanted to write code, crunch data, and be left alone. With the high demand for these kinds of knowledge workers, Tom used to have a problem with employees jumping ship. Since implementing the Game he'd seen a real change.

Randy and his team were greeted warmly and hustled into the break room. When everyone was seated for the Huddle, what they saw astounded them.

Tom's people talked about their business like seasoned entrepreneurs. In a half hour, they built a complete financial picture of their business—a forecast of how this month was going to end. It wasn't Tom standing in the front of the room reading last quarter's numbers to a room full of half-asleep employees. It was *his team* building a forward-looking profit and loss statement from scratch. Everyone walked out of the room with a clear focus on what needed to happen in the coming week to improve the "score." It was so clearly communicated, even *Randy's* team walked out of the break room understanding how Tom's business was doing, how the month would end, and how each employee could "move the needle."

One of Randy's teammates, Meredith, observed, "It's as if they were making promises to each other, one department to the next—*promises in writing!*"

"Hell, they even forecasted their *bonus*! And they do it every single week!" Dan declared in disbelief.

Before Randy's team left, they took Tom to lunch so they could ask him the really tough questions without his employees there to back him up.

"Three years ago, if someone had told me we'd be doing this, I'd have told them they were crazy," Tom confessed.

"What changed your mind?" asked Randy.

"For the past fifteen years, I ran the company as a benevolent dictator. You know, we were one big, happy family, and I was the patriarch; we had great morale, and it was a great place to work. But it was not their job to worry about the business. That was *my* job. All they had to do was come in and punch the clock. Hard part of it to admit is that I was just dumbing down my people. They didn't have the education, competence, *or* the authority to do anything 'real' in the business. *I finally realized that I couldn't do it alone anymore.* I want to retire in a few years, and I realized that the business would have to be sold off or shut down . . . either way, the people were going to lose the great thing they had helped to build."

Randy confessed that while he completely bought in to the GGOB, his father thought Randy was nuts to want to "open the books." "My dad's warning me that if I open the books in lean years, people might run for the hills and lose confidence in me as a leader. And in good years, they'll see that the company's doing well and want a piece of the action. How do you deal with that?"

Tom leaned back and grinned. "I've been there, believe me. So you're worried that when your people finally see your bottom line, they'll want a raise, right? Guess what, Randy—they *already want one*! Here's the reality. Your people already think you make a ton of money. They're making decisions and taking actions based on that assumption, *right now*. Probably wasteful ones, because they simply think you can afford it. Transparency is great. It builds trust when you teach your people the realities of business. But 'opening the books' is just one part of the Game."

"Fair enough, Tom. So why'd *you* finally do it?"

"Peer pressure. I'd been going to the conference for a couple of years. In fact, it was over beers with a friend at my second Gathering when he put me on the spot and asked me 'When are you going to pull the trigger? Don't you care about your people? Do you believe they're capable of learning this stuff? What are you afraid of Tom? You don't share salary information. Your people won't run out and tell the world how much money the company is making. So you gotta get over it. You should've done this ten years ago and you know it. You've got the values, the soul for this thing. Now show the courage to forget your fears and think of the benefits to *you*, Tom! What if you weren't the only one losing sleep over cash, costs, and competition. What if everybody was worried about making payroll and getting that shipment out? How would that feel? Now go do it! Call me if I can help, and by God, PAY IT FORWARD!'"

Tom paused. "He was pretty tough on me, but it got me off square one, and so I packed up my management team and we drove down to Springfield, Missouri, to attend the SRC Experience, to see it all firsthand. It was amazing to see what was possible—and come away with real proof that it worked, plus tangible and usable knowledge. That's what really got me going."

Randy excused himself and pulled Tom to the side. "I don't know if you've picked up on it, but what about Gerald? He's head of my Dry Cleaning division and quite a cynic. I think he's going to be a problem. He feeds off the power of his job, and he always has strong objections to doing things differently."

Tom replied, "Look, Randy, there's always going to be some who either resist it actively, or just don't jump on board at first. Some will see the light in time, while others won't like the transparency and accountability and will self-select out. It's like cultural Darwinism. Just be clear that this is not the 'bestseller-of-the-month program'—that you intend to run the business this way. Plain and simple. Focus your efforts on the 80 percent of people who will get behind this, rather than on the 20 percent who won't."

"There is one more thing . . . a pretty big one . . ." Randy went on, looking ashamed. "I feel like I'm a good leader, but I don't know that I really consider myself a 'numbers' person. I feel like the creative, entrepreneurial 'flywheel' in my brain is running at 10,000 rpm, but the financial wheel is barely turning. I'm not sure I understand the financials all that well myself."

Tom smiled and patted him on the shoulder. "Randy, you and most every other entrepreneur." He chuckled. "I'm one of 'em. When I started out, I just trusted my bookkeepers to take care of the money side of things, and it was a mess. Since I'd never run a business before, I just thought that was that way it was supposed to be. It finally got so bad I had to fire 'em, and it took weeks to unravel the rats' nest they left behind. After having to go through that, I *did* learn about the financials; heck, I'm still learning. So don't worry so much. You'll all learn together."

Randy looked doubtful and turned back toward the table, processing what Tom had said.

"And don't forget you've got an ace in the hole," Tom called after him, "You're really smart to have hired Sam. With his experience with the GGOB, it'll be like having a coach on the payroll! Leverage that!"

Tom was referring to Sam, head of operations. Randy had hired Sam six months ago to help him make the transition to taking over for his father. Randy was understandably a bit shy about making Sam too "high profile," as they had been friends for many years. In fact, it was Sam's enthusiasm for the GGOB that led to Randy going to the Gathering of Games in the first place. Sam's previous employer had seen tremendous growth and profitability, year after year, by using the GGOB.

As they finished their lunch, Gerald asked a good question. "So how long is this going to take?"

Tom replied, "Set realistic goals. It will probably take six months to get your feet under you and really get going with the GGOB. You'll see amazing results all along the way—real, measurable results, because your people are that amazing. Then you'll need another six months to deeply embed the practices and stay true to the discipline. To get really good, and start to see long-term sustainable results, give it a good, disciplined eighteen to twenty-four months."

Tom went on. "When I first met Jack Stack, he told the story of how he made a promise. That if he could save those jobs at SRC back in 1983, he'd teach *everybody* he met to understand business. What started as a way to save jobs became a way to create jobs. It then evolved into creating wealth and finally led to sharing wealth with the folks who helped create it."

The afternoon went far too quickly, and it was time to head home. The team thanked Tom and his staff as they left.

The next Monday, Randy called an "All Hands on Deck" meeting and passed out copies of *The Great Game of Business*.

He began by asking a simple question. "How much do you think we make out of every dollar we sell?"

Though hesitant at first, the answers started to come. "60 cents!" "25 cents!" "50 cents!"

"Those are all good guesses, but I think you'll be surprised to learn that we actually make about a nickel on any dollar we sell around here," Randy stated, looking at a room full of silent people, their heads cocked in disbelief.

"Only 5 cents? Why even bother?" came a half-serious comment from the back of the room.

Randy laughed. "Great question!" He quoted one of his favorite authors. "Emerson once wrote: 'The man who always knows "how" will always have a job; The man who also knows "why" will always be his boss.' I want to teach you not only the *how*, but the *why* we are in business."

He went on, "This business has been running pretty evenly for nearly thirty years, just kind of bumping along. I want to grow it. I want you all to have more opportunities; more chances to grow, to earn, to make something for yourselves. And I want more too."

Randy continued, "I can't do it alone. This is the way I want to run our business. If we're going do this, we're going all in. Now you know me; I go away to a seminar or workshop, and come down from the mountain with the tablets, all excited by the latest bestseller or scheme. But guys, this is different. The GGOB wasn't dreamed up in some New York think tank or in some fancy boardroom at a consulting firm. It was created by people just like you, in a factory down in Springfield, Missouri, thirty years ago; now those same people have built sixty companies, and thousands of companies like ours have been proving the success of this method ever since."

Randy went on. "Just give me ninety days. I promise to teach you the rules of business—to teach you how our company makes money. When that happens, I'll expect you to do something with that knowledge, to help us do better. And when we do all that, I'll share a stake in the outcome with you. *We are going to win or lose as a team.*"

"Now look around you. To your left and to your right. Not everybody in this room will be here in six months. Not because of layoffs, but because this culture, to build a business of businesspeople, is not for everybody. In a culture of performance, there's transparency and accountability not everyone can handle."

"We're in!" exclaimed Meredith, one of the most enthusiastic assistant managers. "But how's this gonna work?"

"Here's how it plays out," Randy began.

IIII▶ design the game

The Business Appraisal

"It's pretty straightforward. Here's why we call it a game," Randy read aloud from Stack's second book, *A Stake in the Outcome*:

> *The Great Game of Business was originally a phrase I used in an effort to make business a little less intimidating to people. I wanted them to see business the way I saw business. I wanted them to realize that it didn't have to be*

an instrument of exploitation, or a tool of greed, and you didn't need an MBA to understand it.

Some people outside the company later took offense at the phrase. They thought we were trivializing business by referring to it as a game. Well, there's a grain of truth to that objection. While I didn't mean to trivialize business, I was certainly trying to demystify it, knock it off its pedestal. I wanted to break down the walls of hype and nonsense that make business an elite sport for the select few and keep everybody else in the dark and out of the money.

And I wasn't telling people anything that wasn't true. Business is a game, after all. I'm not saying that it's like a game. I mean it's a game as a form of human activity. It's not an art or a science. It's a competitive undertaking, with rules, ways of keeping score, elements of luck and talent, winners and losers, and all of the other characteristics of games. What's more, it can be as exciting, as challenging, as interesting, and as much fun as any game you can think of—provided, that is, you understand what's going on.

The difference, of course, is that the stakes are higher. You're playing for your livelihood, for your family's welfare, for the future. You play for the jobs of the people you work with. You play for your customers and your customers' customers, and for the health of both your community and theirs.

And you play for money—potentially lots of money. As we all know, people who play the business game well can make a fortune at it. Okay, so some of them get greedy and keep the winnings to themselves. But I wanted people to understand that business doesn't have to work that way. There was no reason you couldn't set up a company so that everybody could play the game together and share the rewards. Then the game of business would truly be great, in the full meaning of the word.

As Randy set down the book, he said, "Before we can play a game, we need to understand what game we're in, so I need your input! I need your opinions and observations about the business. If I'm going to ask you all to think and act like owners, we have to *treat* you like owners and ask you what you think. We'll grab this information through a couple of surveys. One is a 'practice assessment' and the other is an 'input survey.' ● It'll give us the perspective we need on how we are doing on the GGOB practices now, sort of a baseline. We need to know what we do well and not so well. We also need to know what you see as the opportunities for the business, and what issues we are facing. We want to know what you think are the key issues facing the company in the next 6 to 12 months."

"This is about defining the rules of *our* game. Understanding the rules of *our* business. Not only that, but you'll need to understand the *language* of our business, too."

"Language?" asked Lee, a team leader in the On-Location Services cleaning division.

"Yes, language. There's a secret language of business, you know. Every successful businessperson understands it. It's the language of the financial statements. The Income Statement, the Balance Sheet, and the Cash-Flow Statement. Do you want to know something incredible? These financials were created more than 500 years ago. Yet nobody ever taught you this stuff—even me!"

"Don't worry, guys, " Randy said as he registered terror in the eyes of half his employees. "That will happen in time. For now, we need to get your input on the realities in our business. There are other places we have to look for key issues, like doing some benchmarking."

"What's benchmarking?"

"Good!" Randy laughed as he realized he was using jargon his people didn't know. "That's understanding how we stack up against the 'best of the best' in our marketplace. We'll do this by reaching out to our industry associations, researching our competitors, and talking to our customers. We'll also need to look at what our financial history is telling us. Think of all this as a '360 degree' performance appraisal for our business."

● Practice Assessment and Input Survey: www.greatgame.com/gigguide

"It's going to take several weeks for us to conduct this 'appraisal work' on the business, get the data collected and analyzed, and then get the results back to you. That'll give us time to collect the financial info, talk to our associates and our peer groups, and dig into our customer and competitive intelligence."

After fielding dozens of questions, including a number concerning, *We've been down this road before; how's this different?*, Randy addressed the elephant in the room.

"We're actually gonna *do* something with this. This initial appraisal process will help us get to a Critical Number we can all focus on, and the system of the GGOB will give us the understanding, communication, and execution that will help us reach that goal—together."

"A Critical Number?" This question came from around the room, verbally and nonverbally.

"Sorry, I got ahead of myself. The Critical Number is at the heart of the Great Game of Business. It's the overarching goal of the Game. If you're going to play a game, you must first understand what it means to win. When you define the Critical Number, you define winning. Look, business doesn't need to be any more complicated than a good game of Monopoly, provided you understand the rules, you have a way to follow the action and keep score, and you know your stake in the outcome. In a nutshell, those are key elements of any game and are the principles behind the Great Game of Business."

Randy pointed to a poster of the GGOB process.

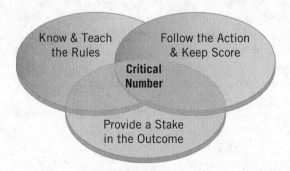

"Winning is a process, and it all starts with your input. Can I count on your candid responses?" It wasn't a resounding yes, but it would do. Randy knew it would take time for people to embrace the idea.

"Great. So let's get started!" said Randy.

Focus on the Critical Number

Thursday, employees received a group text before the meeting. Gerald, as usual, was running fifteen minutes late, signaling his continued passive-aggressive campaign against the GGOB. He seemed to be fighting it, subtly, at every turn.

When everybody got together, somebody finally asked: "What do we do with all this information?"

"We're lucky to have Sam with us now, to help walk us through the GGOB process. He's been through this Critical Number exercise a dozen times at his previous company and we think he'll add a lot to seeing us through it." The agenda ● was laid out and the coffee was served.

Sam began, "Guys, we're going to get some clarity on what our goals are for the next six to twelve months, and we'll get it by considering our financial trends, the input from our people, and of course our marketplace. Each area gives us a different perspective on our business. Again, think of it as a 360-degree performance appraisal on our business. We'll walk out of this room with one or at most two Critical Numbers for the business."

"So what the hell is a Critical Number?" puzzled Gerald, as if he wasn't even present for the recent company-wide meeting.

Randy answered, "Gerald, it's the one thing that defines winning for our business in the coming year. Some people we talked to think of it as a weakness that needs to be driven out of the company. What we're looking for is that number which at any given time will have *the greatest impact on our business*."

The discussion rolled around the room as the team came to grips with what Critical Number means. From around the room, comments and questions arose.

● Path to Critical Number: www.greatgame.com/gigguide

"But won't our Critical Number always be the bottom line? Profit? I read the book you gave me. Stack says in the book that the objective of a business is to make money and generate cash. Why aren't those our Critical Numbers, Randy?" said Deborah, the CFO.

Randy smiled and answered, "Look, guys, there's no wrong answer here. We need to come to grips with what our issues are in the business, and focus on the most important. We could just pick a number, sure. But if we don't go through this process, and really explore all the different perspectives and get our people's input, we could end up being *dead right*."

"Dead right? Don't you mean dead wrong?" asked Kevin, head of Emergency Restoration Services.

"No—dead right. We'd be right, but we'd be dead, because our team didn't buy into the Critical Number we came up with in the 'ivory tower.' Remember, people support what they help to create."

"Good point," added Dan. "It'll be hard for everybody to say 'Oh, that's management's number' if they have a hand in creating it."

Sam added, "Look, profit will always be important. The team's always got to be thinking about making money and generating cash. But we also need our people focused on what will make our company stronger by addressing our key issues and eliminating our weaknesses. In fact, profit will undoubtedly be impacted by our Critical Number. It's *how* we go about generating profit that's so important. Here's an example. If we made all our profit from one big customer, would profit still be our Critical Number?"

The room was quiet while people thought about it. Sam continued. "What would happen if the customer went out of business? What if they 'fired' us?"

The entire room seemed to answer, "We'd be out of business!"

Sam was ecstatic with the quick response. "Exactly! So what would our Critical Number be then?"

"Obviously to get away from just one customer—get all our eggs out of one basket!" Kevin declared. Everyone nodded in agreement.

"Bingo!" Sam shouted.

The meeting continued, the team got all the data out, discussed it, and put it on big flip-chart paper. The writing was literally on the wall, and everybody was beginning to see what the information was telling them.

The whole company had been built around the Emergency Restoration Services division's response to fires, floods, and the damage that natural disasters cause. It's what they called their emergency "Code Blue" work. But everybody in the room knew how scary that was. The numbers showed that they'd experienced a couple of years with major drops in the number of emergencies and natural disasters—conditions they had absolutely no control over.

Everybody knew that counting on natural disasters to pay for all their overhead was *no way* to grow a business. They had to face reality. When they compared themselves to their industry, they quickly saw that the other parts of their business were not up to par either. The Dry Cleaning plant's margins and expenses were out of line with their peers in the industry. They were getting their butts kicked. They were using a lot more resources to produce the same output as similar dry cleaning operations.

Someone muttered, somewhat jokingly, "We're being taken to the cleaners!," to which Gerald shot a pointed glance, as the Dry Cleaning operation was his responsibility.

Sam began to further organize the discussion on large flip-chart paper, "Financial Issues," and started to capture the issues that the financial trends and their industry benchmark data were pointing out. He wrote:

> Financial Issues
>> Operating expenses as compared to the industry
>>> are too high
>> Dry Cleaning ops underperforming, Gross
>>> Margin almost 5 percentage points below
>>> the industry
>> We're undercapitalized (due to the loan
>>> taken out to buy out Randy's father)

After combing through the employee and management input, other issues surfaced and the picture became even clearer.

Marketplace Issues
    The company is heavily reliant on Code Blue
        business
    Lack of focus on large accounts
    Lack of efforts toward cross-selling services

Operational Issues
    Costs in the Dry Cleaning plant are not being
        controlled, particularly in labor and supplies
    We need a better control on expenses to help
        manage through the downturn

People Issues
    More accountability, implement the GGOB
    Leverage the Code Blue technical expertise in
        other areas

Sam directed, "You've seen how we stack up against the marketplace and what our people have to say about the business. Now we'll prioritize the issues. Let's take a break, and when we return, based on what you see on the flip chart, come back with what you believe are the top three issues we need to focus on for the next six to twelve months."

During the break, the conversations ranged from excitement to anxiousness to hesitancy, but everybody seemed to be on board.

When they reconvened, Sam had everyone call out what they saw as the top three issues of the company. As they were collected, repeated items were given hash marks to indicate multiple people had seen it as an issue. The result was one flip chart with the teams' top issues.

> Top Issues
>   Poor financial performance in the Dry Cleaning
>   operations
>   Opportunity to improve cross selling to existing
>   customers
>   The company too reliant on Code Blue business
>   Operating expenses as a % of sales high
>   compared to our industry peers
>   Undercapitalized, due to the additional debt for
>   the purchase of the business

Randy took over. "So which of these issues will have the biggest impact on the business? What is the *one thing* that if we don't address it, nothing else will matter?" The discussions ensued, trying to nail down the "one big thing."

He summarized: "We've been relying on the big dollars coming in from Emergency Restoration for too long, guys. The data shows that, doesn't it? Bottom line: one bad year in the restoration business puts us at risk."

You could've heard a pin drop. Everybody in the room knew it was true, but didn't want to admit it or perhaps lacked the courage to deal with it.

The team knew they couldn't count on fires, floods, and tornadoes. But they could really see now through the flip chart that most of the issues identified were symptoms of their unhealthy dependency on emergency "Code Blue" business. The much bigger issue in the business, they realized, was *how to diversify away from Code Blue business*.

With Sam's experience leading these discussions, he pressed further. "So if diversifying away from Code Blue business is our biggest issue, how do we define or quantify that?"

Dan, the head of the On-Location Services division, suggested, "More sales outside of Code Blue business."

From across the room, Deborah, the CFO added, "Is it sales or is it margin? If Dry Cleaning performed like its industry shows it could, we'd have more margin."

Gerald bristled at the comment. "Oh, okay, I get it. You're gonna put all this on *me*!"

Randy interjected immediately, knowing Gerald's mind-set. "No! We are all in this together. We win or lose as a team, re-member?"

The discussion continued with a volley of questions, an-swers, and suggestions. The beauty of it was in the interaction. Unlike Randy's father, who would simply dictate the goals of the business, Randy was pulling the answers from his people. They were an integral part of the process.

"What if we could generate enough Non-Code-Blue busi-ness to cover all our overhead? Then all the Code Blue we *did* get would be gravy, wouldn't it?" Everybody looked at Meredith as if she was a genius.

"That's right, as long as we think of our target as Non-Code-Blue Margin, rather than revenue."

"So, it's settled. Non-Code-Blue Gross Margin is our Criti-cal Number. Agreed?" asked Randy. Nearly everybody nodded in agreement.

Before Randy could continue, Gerald challenged. "There's no *way* we could cover our overhead like that this year."

Sam countered, "No, but could we reduce our dependency on Code Blue Margin by half this year, and maybe more next year?"

"Can we do that?" seemed to be the sentiment of the entire room.

Sam said, "Look, guys, we don't have to solve this Critical Number 100 percent the first year. Any improvement at all is still a win, in my book. So what's *possible*?"

Dan looked around. "I don't know, maybe reduce it by a quarter?"

Meredith asked, "Okay, so let me ask a dumb question. Where would the other money come from, you know, if we're going to focus outside our Code Blue business. Where will the additional Non-Code-Blue Margin come from?"

Randy suggested, "Maybe that's for the whole team to answer."

Act on the Right Drivers

That evening, Randy was reflecting on the Critical Number meeting. Seeing his team piling on the company's issues was inspiring. Who would have thought that they would come up with something as sophisticated sounding as Non-Code-Blue Gross Margin? So simple, and easy to understand but also really powerful in changing the company . . .

He thought to himself, *We've always talked about going after more dry cleaning business and cross selling, but every time a tornado siren or fire alarm goes off, everyone mobilizes to get the job done and those ideas go out the window. Now we have a rallying cry that everybody can see, understand, and connect to. It's like a big central theme for the whole team to link back to, no matter how busy they are. What incredible focus we'll have!*

Something unexpected was happening too. Randy started to feel less stressed out. Usually, it was this time of night when he would quietly fret about the business. His heart would pound in his chest as he lay awake in bed feeling completely alone and isolated. Now he felt like his people were starting to "get it" and he knew there were six other people across town lying awake tonight as well. *What a great feeling . . .* he thought, as he drifted off.

The next morning, the management team was already there when Randy pulled in—everyone but Gerald. They couldn't wait to get started.

"You know what's really cool about this Critical Number stuff, Randy? What I like about it is that we're always being pulled in a million directions. Now at least we know the 'one thing' we've just *gotta* do," declared Dan. It was clear he'd been up late into the night thinking about it. "Sure makes it a heck of a lot easier to know what we really need to focus on."

This was huge. Randy had been very good at setting goals and making sure everyone knew their jobs, but he had never really set the agenda for the business, shared the strategy, or set expectations on a big scale. Randy was anxious to see what others thought about what they'd come up with. Even more important, he was excited to see what each of the manager's teams would come up with to tackle the issues. After all, this is what the GGOB was all about.

He thought to himself, *We went through the process of collecting data, opinions, information, and intelligence. The team got really smart about their business and were able to reach a consensus on what they should focus on. Now they are going to get their whole teams' creative input on how to achieve their goals.* Randy felt he was tapping the intellectual capacity that was right under his nose . . . for the first time.

"So what do we do today?" seemed to be the sentiment from the team.

"Well, we start by teaching everybody what our Critical Number is, what it means, and why it's so very important to the business. Then we need to ask each and every one of our employees what *they* think they could do to help us reach the goal."

That week, the managers started by getting their departments together and going through an exercise to figure out what they could do, both individually and as a team, to influence the Critical Number and bottom-line financial results.

In the On-Location Services division, Dan explained to his team the entire Critical Number process. He started by sharing with his team the results of the survey they took and the issues that were identified. He went on to explain how the management team had worked through the issues and selected a Critical Number—a company-wide goal that everyone would have a stake in—and how On-Location Services could help achieve the goal that was the Critical Number, Non-Code-Blue Gross Margin.

"Non-Code-Blue what?" laughed Lee, one of the lead carpet cleaners. Lee had said what most of the employees in the room were thinking.

Dan laughed, too, and explained the idea behind building Gross Margin outside of Emergency Services.

"Soooooo, what's Gross Margin?" asked June, an outspoken associate.

"'Gross Margin' is the money we have left from a sale, after we pay labor and materials (our Cost of Goods Sold, or COGS for short). So if we clean a carpet for a customer for $150, and it costs us $75 by the time we're done with the time it takes, the chemicals it takes, and whatnot, how much do we have left?"

"Easy, Dan; it's $75." replied June. Everybody nodded.

"*That's* Gross Margin. Pretty simple isn't it? Sales minus our Direct Costs is Gross Margin. How do you think we could improve that margin?"

"Charge more!" cried Sandy, the janitor.

"Reuse the chemicals?" queried Lee.

"Do stuff right the first time. You know, make sure we don't make mistakes."

"Wait a minute. Do we make half on everything we do?" came back June.

"No, different services produce different margins. Why?" answered Dan.

"Well, why don't we just sell more of the stuff we do that are the highest margins? You know, the stuff we make the most money on?"

Dan was impressed. "Wow, June. That's pretty good."

June went on. "What are our highest margin services?"

In a heartbeat, Dan's assistant manager, Bill, piped up, "That's easy. Scotchgard."

"Scotchgard?" everyone asked.

Bill replied, "Yes, hands down. We make 75 percent on every Scotchgard application we do. I've been bitchin' at you guys for years to upsell every customer—but you never listen."

"Well, we didn't know we made 75 percent on it either!" laughed Lee.

And so it went. All through the organization, meetings were producing amazingly simple but impactful ideas, "drivers" that could really affect the Critical Number. They were collected on a sheet ● that showed everybody their direct line of

● Line of Sight Tool: www.greatgame.com/gigguide

sight to the Critical Number: how each department and each employee connected to Non-Code-Blue Gross Margin. For the On-Location Services division, it was "upsell more Scotchgard." For Emergency Restoration ops, it was "cross-sell our restoration clients our other services." And for Dry Cleaning, it was, "Get a handle on our cost of supplies." Once posted, these "drivers" were fleshed out by having the teams nail down how they'd measure their activities.

People were getting excited. But it wasn't long before somebody asked, "So if we help the company make more money, what's in it for us?"

Sam answered, "Great question. There's a lot in it for all of us. First is job security. As you saw in the industry data, we are not performing up to snuff with our peers. Eventually, we'd have to change or our competitors will eat our lunch. Second, if we create a plan and go after it together, we should be able to beat the market. And if we beat the market, we deserve better than market compensation. Randy is willing to give us all a stake in the outcome. A share, a part of that additional money in the form of a bonus plan. We're starting to work on that next.

"It's gonna take us a while, as a management team, to get the GGOB together since we've got to finish the budget/annual plan, work on the company scoreboards, and of course, design that bonus plan. But we'll get it done."

"I'll believe it when I see it, but okay. How long is 'a while'?" snapped Gerald.

"We're talking about thirty days or so. But bear with us, we're new at this, too. There is something we're going to do right away, though, right here in our own department. In fact, all the departments will have their own 'MiniGame.'"

Create an Early Win with MiniGames

The managers were excited about the Great Game, but they were terrified about what would happen if people didn't get engaged around the Critical Number. The team realized that it was going to take some time to finish the bonus plan, create the scoreboards, and then start to run Huddles, learn how to forecast, and so on. They were concerned that they could lose employees along the way while the team was designing the big Game. They knew they were going to need some way to keep people interested. So why not play a series of smaller games while management worked on the big Game?

That is where MiniGames came in. As Tom had explained when the team visited his IT company, MiniGames were just like the big Game, with all the same elements, but in microcosm. The MiniGames had a goal, rules, scorecards, and a reward for winning. They were usually set around an operational or financial number that were "drivers" of the company-wide Critical Number and played out at the departmental or workgroup level. Randy liked them because MiniGames were short term in length, generally sixty to ninety days; employees could start playing these right away and give the management team a chance to design and refine the rest of the GGOB.

In the On-Location Services division, since they realized Scotchgard applications had high margins and customers liked the service, they realized it was a great opportunity to *create an early win.*

Dan and Bill had pulled together some numbers on how many Scotchgard upsells their team had done in the past year. They were embarrassed when they discovered that only one in ten customers actually bought Scotchgard historically.

"Why don't we sell more? I mean, it's as easy as saying, 'Do you want fries with that.'" Dan asked.

Lee, one of the field leaders, said, "Dan, I didn't even know it was that important. It's not that hard to do. I mean the carpet cleaning itself is the labor-intensive part. Had I known we made so much money on Scotchgard, I would have suggested it to everyone. I'm sure that half our customers would say yes if we just asked them the right way. It's really good stuff."

Dan asked, "Are you saying we could go from upsales of 10 percent to 50 percent of every job we do?"

"Absolutely," Lee said, getting buy-in from the other field leaders.

"So there's our improvement goal—our 'x to y by when' for

this MiniGame. We want to go from 10 percent to 50 percent. In other words, instead of one in ten customers taking Scotchgard, we think up to five may take it, right?"

"Okay, I think we should play it for ninety days so we can get really good at upselling, and drive the Critical Number," Dan declared.

The carpet team began to work through the MiniGame process. After only ten minutes of brainstorming, they dubbed the game "Scotch on the Rocks" and sketched out a scoreboard. It took the shape of a giant tumbler that would be filled with ice cubes, each one representing a new Scotchgard customer. Every time a customer bought the upsell, the name would go on an ice cube that would then be placed in the glass. Lee offered to make the scoreboard and ice cubes out of posterboard. They decided to add a section at the bottom that would display the total Non-Code-Blue Gross Margin dollars that new customers would bring in. They made three levels of "scotch" to represent thirty, sixty, and ninety days. The team could easily see if they were winning the game by how many "rocks" were in the glass.

Everybody was excited by the idea. The team decided the best place for the scoreboard was in the break room, where it could be seen by every employee every day. In fact, they could have a short, ten-minute standup Huddle around it each day, updating it with new customers and dollars and sharing what was working and what wasn't. The best part was that it was so simple that anybody could see, at a glance, if they were winning or losing.

In three months, they knew they'd service about 150 customers, and their goal was to upsell 50 percent of them. That meant they needed 75 customer upsells, or "rocks" in the glass. Seventy-five customers times the average Scotchgard price of $200 equaled $15,000 in additional revenue, or $11,250 in Gross Margin. And all of it was Non-Code-Blue Gross Margin.

"There's our goal!" Dan exclaimed. Everybody "got it" immediately and could visualize how simple it would be to drop another rock in the glass each time they made an upsell.

SCOTCH ON THE ROCKS

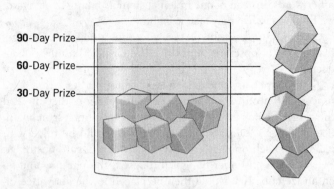

"Holy cow!" cried Beth, one of the carpet team leaders. "Are you saying our MiniGame prize is $11,000?"

Dan clarified, smiling, "That'd be great, Beth, but no. The $11,250 goes toward funding our Critical Number and our bonus pool. The management team is working on it now, though it may take us a while to get the plan finished. But we'll make sure all this gets counted. It'll be retroactive. There's still going to be a reward for winning this MiniGame and that's what our team will decide.

"The way MiniGames work best is to create prize 'levels' of rewards that we can win along the way, with each incrementally better than the last. Sam showed me an example of one that started with a ball cap, went to a T-shirt and then to a jacket, and ended in everybody going to a ball game together. What do you think the rewards ought to be?"

Sam had given them a copy of the MiniGame design checklist ● and they quickly completed it.

1. **Name the game.**
    The improvement objective.
    "Scotch on the Rocks": Upsell Scotchgard Treatment to Customers.

● MiniGame Checklist: www.greatgame.com/gigguide

2. **Set the goal.**
   X to y by when.
   From 15 customers to 75 in 90 days.
3. **Estimate the benefit.**
   The potential impact/return.
   $11,250 in Non-Code-Blue Gross Margin
4. **Identify the players.**
   Those who can impact the goal.
   On-Location Services Team
5. **Determine the time frame.**
   Long enough to change behavior.
   90 days
6. **Create a theme and build a scoreboard.**
   Be creative!
   Huge scotch tumbler that we fill with customer "rocks." Scotch will fill the glass at 30-, 60-, and 90-day intervals. If the rocks exceed the scotch, we win that level prize.
7. **Decide on the reward.**
   Think low on cash, high on fun. And make it memorable.
   30 Days: Mocktail party on Friday of the first month
   60 Days: Rocks on the House—10 of your favorite rock songs (iTunes Card)
   90 Days: Giant party at Dave and Buster's to celebrate winning the MiniGame

The entire team was getting excited now. They had a goal, a scoreboard, a Huddle schedule, and fun prizes they all agreed on. Because the team who would play the game helped to design it, buy-in was high, success seemed attainable, and the prizes cost very little in the scheme of things.

Dan reminded everybody, "Small wins add up to big wins. If we hit these goals, we'll have fun, learn a good habit, and add to our annual bonus pool at the same time."

Provide a Stake in the Outcome—Rewards and Recognition

The Great Game of Business was already working. MiniGames like "Scotch on the Rocks" were running in almost every department in the company, and energy was high. Scotchgard upsells had doubled in one week! That got the employees' attention, but the managers were amped up to do even more. Dry Cleaning's MiniGame was "Taking It to the Cleaners" and the Emergency Restoration team's MiniGame was "Scrolling for Dollars," a game that involved reaching out to their database for cross-selling opportunities in their downtime.

After a week of working with the employees on understanding the Critical Number and how they could each influence it, momentum was building. Some really solid ideas were emerging, and people were becoming engaged. Since MiniGames were in place, Randy knew he had to press forward and reassemble the management team around designing the rest of the Game, the scoreboards, Huddling, forecasting, and especially the rewards and recognition.

I can't wait to change my bonus plan, Randy thought to himself. Theirs had never worked—it hadn't changed behavior or made any impact on the business. His dad had been giving discretionary bonuses for years, and of course people felt entitled to them, regardless of whether the company was doing well or poorly. Randy simply hadn't had a better way, or the courage, to make a change. The old bonus system was disconnected from the performance of the business. He wondered how many years he'd paid bonuses when he was in the hole.

It was time to bring out the big guns and design an effective bonus plan. It was important to him that he didn't screw up this part of his Game. He was grateful to have Sam on his team. Sam had helped to design numerous GGOB bonus plans at his previous company. Even better, Sam had been instrumental in teaching employees to understand the process, too. He'd also incorporated the GGOB budget and bonus tools he'd used in the past.

At the next management meeting, Randy told everyone, "Bonus programs are big concepts to get your head wrapped around. I want you to really understand how ours works, because you'll be responsible for teaching all our people."

Sam jumped in to emphasize a very important lesson he learned at his previous company. "Guys, people's understanding of their bonus plan is the biggest reason bonus plans succeed . . . or fail. The success of this bonus plan will have everything to do with how well we communicate it and teach it. If they don't 'get it' or can't follow what's happening, *or don't believe they can impact it*, we may as well give 'em a jelly of the month club and hope for the best." Everyone chuckled, catching the reference to the classic scene in *National Lampoon's Christmas Vacation*.

Randy added, "You saw the results of this during our visit to Tom's company. All employees knew exactly how they were progressing on the Critical Number and could calculate their potential bonus every week. They had a clear understanding of where the opportunities were and how they could directly impact the score and their rewards. Wasn't that impressive?"

The team nodded in agreement.

"For this bonus plan to work, you will all need to feel very confident in your ability to understand and to teach it to your people. If *you* don't believe in it, nobody will. Sam and I are going to put together the first draft of our bonus plan, based on the concepts in the book. I want each of you to go back into *The Great Game of Business* and read the chapter entitled "Skip the Praise—Give Us the Raise." It does a great job in explaining the general philosophy of how rewards should be provided, while ensuring that jobs and the security of the business don't suffer. You'll see that creating a good, solid bonus plan isn't as simple as 'make a dollar, share a dollar.'"

The next day, the management team reconvened. They were all excited to talk about what their bonus plan would look like. Randy began by asking, "What did you get out of the book?"

Meredith said, "Well, the obvious concept is that we use the bonus to rally people around a common goal; in our case, Non-Code-Blue Gross Margin. It needs to be a team effort. Everybody has the same big goals tied to the same big rewards, and we have to work together to achieve them. We either win together, or don't win at all."

Dan continued, "Our bonus plan needs to ensure the long-term financial security of the company, *then* share a significant portion of the gain. To me that's job security first, then bonus."

Gerald added, "Give people a chance to earn a bonus early and often!"

Kevin said, "Always celebrate the win and be sure to recognize the players. And communicate, communicate, communicate!"

"Fantastic, everybody! Great job. We're going to be touching on each of these concepts. Let's start with what Sam and I have been developing. We first took the annual financial plan that all of us have been working on for the past couple of months.● As you know, this year we're projecting to end the year with a top line revenue of $7.7 million and a profit of $590,000. We've all agreed growth of 10 percent is achievable, for a top line target of $8.5 million in revenue. Based on what you say we need to support that growth, we came up with $650,000 in bottom line profit before tax."

Randy added, "Our focus this year is to meet, or better, *beat* that $650,000 profit number, while increasing our Non-Code-Blue work. So the bonus program that Sam and I have drafted is designed around achieving those two Critical Numbers.

"We'd like to provide our people an opportunity to earn up to 20 percent of their wages in a bonus. Half the bonus, or 10 percent of their wages, will be tied to the company's overall profit. The other half will be tied to us improving our Non-Code-Blue Gross Margin. This way we're keeping people focused on how this business makes money, and what they can do to impact that, as well as eliminating a weakness in our business.

"There's a big difference in how bonuses work in the Game and the way we used to do things. In the past, we gave out discretionary bonuses as a percentage of profit . . . a profit-sharing program. You know, make a dollar, share a dollar."

Sam said, "In the Game, we must first set a minimum threshold of profit before any bonus can be paid."

●Annual Plan/Budget Tool: www.greatgame.com/gigguide

Gerald shot back, "Hold on a second, Sam. If all the expenses are being covered, and we're showing a profit, aren't we entitled to a share of it?"

Randy leaned forward. "Gerald, where do you think all that profit goes?"

"Huh?" Gerald stammered. "Well, you know, like . . ." He almost blurted out "your two vacations and your wife's new car," but instead finished with, ". . . like additional income for you."

"This is what 'open book' is all about," Sam with a smile. "First of all, almost half the profit will go to pay the tax man."

Randy stepped in and said, "Look, Gerald, it took a long time for me to really put the pieces together on this. *There are investments this business needs to make that are beyond expenses on the P & L.* There's equipment, facilities, inventories, and, yes, a return on investment for shareholders. All these things need to be addressed for the long-term growth and security of the business before we are in a position to fund a bonus plan."

"Think of it as setting a threshold, a baseline. If we understand 'the nut' we have to cover, we know where a bonus plan can safely start," Sam stated. "Now you can see what we mean by 'self-funding' the bonus. We don't pay a penny out until all our obligations are met, safeguarding the long-term financial security of the company, first. It goes back to save jobs, create jobs, create wealth, share wealth."

"Okay, I get it. What is our threshold?" asked Dan.

"Sam and I worked through the plan and determined what cash 'buckets' need to be filled next year. Aside from tax, there's *accounts receivable*, or money we've earned, but customers haven't sent us the check. Another bucket is *debt*. In our case, we have to pay off some of the loan I took out to buy the company from my dad. We also have some investments in inventories and *capital expenditures*. Things like new trucks, equipment, computers, and such. The final bucket to be filled is a *fair return for the owners*. After adding it all up, our threshold totaled $550,000." ●

"I cannot believe how much profit we have to generate *just*

● Bonus Threshold Tool: www.greatgame.com/gigguide

to *maintain* this business. That's incredible! This is going to be a *big* idea for us to get our employees to understand," Meredith said, shaking her head. "I know it is for me . . ."

Sam looked serious as he said, "Yes, it is, and they won't understand it tomorrow, but in time, and with some teaching, they will learn it. If we don't do it now, entitlement will creep in and haunt us forever. We'll battle the misconception that Randy's walking out of here with half a million bucks a year."

"Got it, Sam, but I'd really like to get back to that 20 percent bonus thing. How do we get that?" Kevin asked.

"We want to make our bonus significant enough to keep people in the Game . . . maybe 10 percent of wages; or if we really blow it out of the water, up to 20 percent of wages. That could be as much as an additional month or two of pay.

"For example, if 10 percent of wages is the top end of our bonus pool for our Non-Code-Blue Gross Margin Critical Number, and payroll is $1,100,000, that gives us a potential maximum bonus pool of $110,000. That means we'd have to generate $220,000 in additional Gross Margin, since 50 percent goes to the team and 50 percent goes to the company. Now we know our 'stretch' target for a maximum bonus payout. Now divide that into ten levels, each worth 1 percent of wages. That's a lot of potential wins!"

Sam went on to say that they should translate the percentages into how many additional hours' or days' pay each level represented rather than just as a percentage of wages. "Folks on the floor think in different terms, so why not put it in their language?"

Kevin wondered, "How do we determine the payout?"

"Randy and I are proposing an SRC-style quarterly payout," said Sam.

"This is what I like most about the GGOB," Randy said. "Typically in the past, we'd wait till the end of the year, after the books were closed to see if there was anything left . . . then we might pay a discretionary bonus. See how removed all that is from behaviors that funded the bonus?"

"We want to reward our folks close to the time frame in which their behaviors created the results. For example, if our team can drive improvements in the first quarter, I want to reward them as soon as possible, so they can see how their performance directly impacted their reward. We accomplish this in two ways. First, we'll structure the plan in incremental wins or levels, so it's not all or nothing. *All* improvements are wins."

"Second, we'll make payouts progressive, so people will stay engaged. We'll start with 10 percent of the pool first quarter, and progressively ramp it up . . . 20 percent second quarter, 30 percent third quarter, 40 percent fourth quarter. Plus, it's cumulative. In other words, if you miss a bonus one quarter, you can make it up the next."

Period	Period Payout	YTD Payout	% of Salary
1st Qtr.	10%	10%	1% to 20%
2nd Qtr.	20%	30%	1% to 20%
3rd Qtr.	30%	60%	1% to 20%
4th Qtr.	40%	100%	1% to 20%

Randy handed out the draft bonus plan he'd been working on with Sam. It showed all the levels and payouts possible.● What was especially exciting was that the team really got energized thinking about how their people were going to get into this.

The looks around the room varied from excitement to concern. Sam saw Meredith struggling with the concept and asked what she was concerned about.

"Doesn't it still come back to reasonable and achievable? I'm not sure if our people will see this as achievable. Can we really add $220,000 in profit on top of an already big profit goal?" she asked.

Sam replied, "So let's find out . . . add it all up. You guys have been talking with your teams about how they can help drive Non-Code-Blue Gross Margin. How much can we get

● Bonus Plan Tool: www.greatgame.com/gigguide

⬤ Bonus Plan Tool

| Salary | CRITICAL NUMBER: PROFIT BEFORE TAXES | | | | BONUS POOL | BONUS PLAN | | |
LEVEL	Q1 TARGET	Q2 TARGET	Q3 TARGET	Q4 TARGET		ADDITIONAL % OF PAY	ADDITIONAL DAYS PAY	ADDITIONAL HOURS PAY
Prior Yr.	—	—	—	590,000	—	—	—	—
Plan	162,500	325,000	487,500	650,000	—	—	—	—
1	152,200	306,600	463,200	622,000	11,000	1.00%	2.6	20.8
2	154,400	313,200	476,400	644,000	22,000	2.00%	5.2	41.6
3	156,600	319,800	489,600	666,000	33,000	3.00%	7.8	62.4
4	158,800	326,400	502,800	688,000	44,000	4.00%	10.4	83.2
5	161,000	333,000	516,000	710,000	55,000	5.00%	13.0	104.0
6	163,200	339,600	529,200	732,000	66,000	6.00%	15.6	124.8
7	165,400	346,200	542,400	754,000	77,000	7.00%	18.2	145.6
8	167,600	352,800	555,600	776,000	88,000	8.00%	20.8	166.4
9	169,800	359,400	568,800	798,000	99,000	9.00%	23.4	187.2
10	172,000	366,000	582,000	820,000	110,000	10.00%	16.0	208.0

Quarterly Payout %	10%	20%	30%	40%
Progressive Payout %	10%	30%	60%	100%

(Base Pay × Level % × Progressive Payout %) − (Previous Payout)

Example:

(Base pay= $30,000 × Level % = 10%) × (Progressive Payout % = 30%) − (Previous Payout = $300) = $600 2nd Quarter Bonus Payout

⬤ For a copy of this tool, visit www.greatgame.com/gigguide.

SALARY LEVEL	CRITICAL NUMBER: NON-CODE-BLUE GM				BONUS PLAN			
	Q1 TARGET	Q2 TARGET	Q3 TARGET	Q4 TARGET	BONUS POOL	ADDITIONAL % OF PAY	ADDITIONAL DAYS PAY	ADDITIONAL HOURS PAY
Prior Yr.	—	—	—	1,100,000	—	—	—	—
Plan	300,000	600,000	900,000	1,200,000	—	—	—	—
1	277,200	556,600	838,200	1,122,000	11,000	1.00%	2.6	20.8
2	279,400	563,200	851,400	1,144,000	22,000	2.00%	5.2	41.6
3	281,600	569,800	864,600	1,166,000	33,000	3.00%	7.8	62.4
4	283,800	576,400	877,800	1,188,000	44,000	4.00%	10.4	83.2
5	286,000	583,000	891,000	1,210,000	55,000	5.00%	13.0	104.0
6	288,200	589,600	904,200	1,232,000	66,000	6.00%	15.6	124.8
7	290,400	596,200	917,400	1,254,000	77,000	7.00%	18.2	145.6
8	292,600	602,800	930,600	1,276,000	88,000	8.00%	20.8	166.4
9	294,800	609,400	943,800	1,298,000	99,000	9.00%	23.4	187.2
10	297,000	616,000	957,000	1,320,000	110,000	10.00%	26.0	208.0

● For a copy of this tool, visit www.greatgame.com/gigguide.

from the Scotchgard idea? How much margin is in On-Location Services if we could get the hospital account? What about cross-selling opportunities? There's another $50,000 in potential gross margin there. Hey, remember the benchmarking data? It indicated we were several points higher than the industry on operating expenses . . . there's a real opportunity to pick up another $20,000 there by cutting costs. Gerald, I know that you might think it's a little optimistic, but your people came up with $25,000 in efficiencies in the Dry Cleaning plant as well."

Randy added, "One thing Tom pointed out about playing the Game is that when they tracked and measured their expenses every week, they were able to find opportunities they never would have ever thought were there."

"You just gave me enough in five minutes to fund 50 percent of the bonus pool. I think there's much more possible than what we've listed here. It's now up to all of us to identify what those opportunities are and help our people understand how their efforts and ideas can fund their own bonus," Sam stated.

Randy asked, "What do you think, Meredith? Is it achievable? Is it reasonable?"

Meredith replied, "I think so. . . . It seems reasonable considering that the first few payout levels are well within what we have achieved before. And now that we have identified a few of the opportunities to get us there, I'm more confident that it's achievable."

Sam said, "This is great, guys. Everybody loves a good bonus. But let's remember that many times cash isn't the only motivator."

Kevin smiled as he said, "It isn't? You need to tell that to my wife." Everybody laughed.

Sam replied, "There's the money side of providing a stake in the outcome, sure. But there are other components that are just as important. Three things we simply cannot overlook are understanding, involvement, and recognition."

Dan said, "Sam, I gotta say, we're pretty good at recognition . . . letting people know we appreciate them. It's part of our culture."

"I get that Dan. But let me explain. We just figured out a

pretty awesome bonus plan, right? Well if our people don't get it, if they can't really understand it, and can't keep up with it as we play, we're sunk. We must be vigilant about teaching and communicating this plan . . . and to keep encouraging folks to keep reaching for the goal. The teaching and the learning never ends. That's 'understanding.'"

He went on, "The next thing to pay attention to is 'involvement.' Being involved and informed is a huge part of keeping people engaged. Everybody wants to know their opinion matters. Being valued and involved shows employees that the company respects them and trusts them to make the right decisions. And that's empowering and motivating."

People were nodding their heads as Sam continued. "The third motivator beyond a cash bonus is 'recognition.' Dan, you said it best . . . it's part of the culture Randy's created here. We need to be sure we identify and acknowledge people's efforts in reaching our collective goals, by celebrating our wins and recognizing the players. For people to pitch in and really give their full and immediate attention, they must know, without question, that they will be recognized and appreciated for the contributions they make. We have got to make sure we make it a big deal . . . you know, really celebrate when we win. Let's make sure people feel like winners. That's what people will want to replicate . . . they'll know exactly what behaviors got them their rewards . . . their recognition. And they'll be proud and want to do it again."

The entire management team had a lot to think about. Dan summed up their feelings with, "Now I get it. This really explains why Jack Stack calls it 'a stake in the outcome.' This is *way* bigger than just a simple bonus plan."

Keep Score—Design the Scoreboard

It was hard to believe they were already thirty days into the process, and they were just starting to work on the scoreboard. It was exciting, though, to see how much progress the employees were making on the MiniGames they had created . . . they were already "getting" the Critical Number and were moving the needle. Now that the bonus plan was hammered out, the management team had reconvened to discuss how they would keep score.

Sam began to recount his previous experience with the Game.

"When you visited the company I used to work for, you couldn't help but see scoreboards. The walls and halls were plastered with them! We probably should've owned stock in a whiteboard company." Everyone smiled as they pictured it. He went on, "We were fanatics about keeping score. Everybody wanted to know if we were winning or losing. It was as if we flipped the idea of scorekeeping on its head. It wasn't management scoring teams, it was the teams scoring themselves. The employees *owned* it. They kept score, made the scoreboards, and man, the scoreboards were everywhere."

"What all did you score?" asked Kevin.

Sam recalled, "Well, of course there was the big, company-wide financial scoreboard that told us if we were making money. That was in the cafeteria, where we could all 'live' with it every day. Right next to it was a scoreboard highlighting our Critical Number. You know, it was really visual, to communicate our progress. I remember one year we painted different colors on the cinder-block wall, block by block as we gained on our Critical Number, like a giant Tetris wall."

Randy added, "As you'd walk out into that business, you'd see how the scoreboards out in the 'shop' were cascaded through every department. In fact, it was like reverse cascading. Is 're-verse cascading' even a word? Anyway, I mean that numbers were flowing *up* instead of *down*, because they fed information from each team and department up to the company-wide scoreboard."

Dan was animated. "Yeah, I could see that at Tom's IT company. It was really cool to see individual scorecards; they called them 'playbooks,' I think, which led to the team forecast and to the departmental scoreboard. And then we saw it all come together at the Huddle on the financial scoreboard!"

Gerald joined in. "My people already have dashboards on their computers, but I'm not sure anyone is using them. Nobody sees them. It seems like having them be really visible is important."

"That's exactly right, Gerald. It's a lot about visibility," answered Randy. "Make it where people can't help but see the score, and you'll get accountability. Winners are fanatics about keeping score. My college football coach would say, 'if you're not keeping score, it's just practice; people play differently when they're keeping score.'"

Sam continued, "There's one more type of scoreboard. Speaking of Tom's company, you know you're at a real GGOB company when you can't turn the corner without running into a MiniGame scoreboard."

Meredith laughed out loud. "No kidding . . . *literally* run into a scoreboard! At Tom's place, I bumped into a deer! One of his IT groups was 'Hunting for Customers' and used a full-size deer decoy on a pullcart, with a target painted on the side. It was awesome!"

Randy refocused the team. "Okay, Sam, we get it. Scoreboards are important, . . . where do we start?"

"There are three steps in designing a good scoreboard. First, what do we think is important to score? Second, who's going to 'own' the score? And third, how do we make the scoreboards forward looking?

"First, let's give some thought to our financial scoreboard. This will show our people if we are winning or losing as a company. In other words, are all our efforts making us money? This scoreboard will be a simplified version of our financial statements, starting with the Income Statement. Simplified meaning we won't fill it with every general ledger item, just the major line items or categories that represent the important results or outcomes that have the biggest impact on our company. The aim is to make clear 'where' and 'how' financial outcomes are created. We'll teach everyone how money comes into the business and goes out of the business . . . and what's left afterward."

Sam added, "Having company scoreboards that only track operational numbers or key performance indicators is like going to a baseball game and the scoreboard only shows errors and the number of outs but doesn't report runs scored."

Sam brought out the GGOB scoreboard template to begin the process. The group took the financial statements and began to group line items into categories, looking for ways to simplify and to focus on the 20 percent of line items that drove 80 percent of the results. After thirty minutes of work, the scoreboard was taking shape.

"Sam, this is starting to look a lot like our end-of-the-month financial statements; what makes this different?" asked Gerald.

Sam said, "There's one *big* difference; these are forward-looking financials. Our end-of-the-month numbers are historical. You know what the problem is with history, don't you?"

Meredith blurted out, "Yeah! You can't change it."

Randy jumped in."*Exactly*. Now you know the difference. With our financial scoreboard, we'll be forecasting how the month will end . . . and we'll do it every single week. That's how the Great Game of Business helps us control our destiny. If something's going right, we can leverage it. And if something's going wrong, we have time to fix it."

Sam addressed some puzzled looks in the room. "We'll be spending a lot of time learning 'forecasting,' guys, don't worry. For now, let's finish our scoreboard."

They had built a simplified Income Statement from top line to bottom line. Now they had to bring it to life.

The team established "line item ownership," or who was going to be responsible for tracking and forecasting that number. "Gerald, you're Dry Cleaning. Dan is On-Location Services, and Kevin is Restoration." They continued down the entire sheet, establishing a name for each line item, including all the direct cost and operating expenses.

"Seems like Deborah ought to have most of these lines, because the CFO's the only one who has all these numbers," quipped Kevin, only half joking.

Deborah spoke up and with a smirk said, "I *knew* this was going to make more work for me!"

"It's not about who can *access* the numbers, guys, it's about who can *influence* the numbers. That's why we call it 'line item ownership' . . . *you* own it; *you're* accountable for it. I'm sure that Deborah can support us on gathering and understanding the numbers, but they will be generated by all of *you*." Sam was pointing at each of the team as he spoke. Deborah sighed with relief.

From left to right, the next column was the "plan." This number came from the month-by-month budget Randy and Sam had worked out earlier. Sam stated, "The plan represents our goal, the target, we're shooting for all year. The plan is fixed. It won't change through the year. Every week we'll be forecasting against the plan, looking for the variances, good or bad."

Sam continued. "Now it gets fun! The next five columns are how we use the scoreboard to encourage everybody to be looking forward. This is what makes the GGOB so different. This is the third step in designing a good scoreboard."

Randy added, "Most companies steer their businesses while facing backward. They tend to measure the past, telling them only what's happened. They can't see what's coming at 'em . . . only what's already hit 'em."

Dan asked, "So we'll put up our weekly results each week, right?

"Wrong! But great guess." Sam went on, "No, we want you to come up each week and give us your forecast of how the *month* will end. That way we have time to make moves during the month as the score changes. We'll forecast the month every week and put it in its own column. The GGOB calls it 'forward forecasting.' The practice is so nice, they named it twice."

Gerald protested, "What, so you want us to be fortune-tellers? How can Kevin predict a fire or tornado?"

"Look, don't get hung up on the word 'forecast.' If 'forecast' bothers you, forget it. What I want from you is your *opinion* of what's going to happen . . . and Gerald, I *know* you have an opinion." Randy stood on what he had said.

It took a moment, but Gerald had to laugh, as he knew it was true. "Yeah, I can give you *that*."

"We'll get into that when we start Huddling. Let's finish the scoreboard." With that, Sam wrapped up with a column for "actual" and a column to the far right for "variance." This is where the team would see how they varied from the plan, and their last forecast, good or bad.

⊕ Scoreboard Design Tool

FINANCIAL SCOREBOARD Nov 12	Calc.	PRIOR YR.	PLAN	OWNER	WEEK 1	WEEK 2	WEEK 3	WEEK 4	WEEK 5	Nov-12 ACTUAL	ACTUAL YTD	PLAN YTD	VARIANCE
REVENUE													
1a Restoration—CODE BLUE													0
1b Dry Cleaning Plant													0
1c On-Location Services													0
1d Other													0
1e													0
1 Total Revenue	1a:1e	0	0	0	0	0	0	0	0	0	0	0	0
COST OF GOODS SOLD													
2a Restoration—Labor													0
2b Restoration—Supplies													0
2c Dry Cleaning Plant—Labor													0
2d Dry Cleaning Plant—Supplies													0
2e On-Location—Labor													0
2f On-Location—Supplies													0
2g Other		0	0										0
2h		0	0										0
2 Cost of Goods Sold		0	0	0	0	0	0	0	0	0	0	0	0
Code Blue GM	1a-(2a + 2b)	0	0	0	0	0	0	0	0	0	0	0	0
Non-Code-Blue GM	1b-1d]-[2a-2g	0	0	0	0	0	0	0	0	0	0	0	0
3 Total GROSS MARGIN	1-2	0	0	0	0	0	0	0	0	0	0	0	0
4 GP %	3/1	#DIVID	#DIVID	#DIVID	#DIVID	#DIVID	#DIVID	#DIVID	#DIVID	#DIVID	#DIVID	#DIVID	0
EXPENSES													
5a Salaries & Benefits													0
5b Sales & Marketing													0
5c General & Administration													0
5d Other													0
5 Total Expenses		0	0	0	0	0	0	0	0	0	0	0	0
6 PROFIT BEFORE TAX (PBT)	3-5	0	0	0	0	0	0	0	0	0	0	0	0
7 PBT %	6/1	#DIVID	#DIVID	#DIVID	#DIVID	#DIVID	#DIVID	#DIVID	#DIVID	#DIVID	#DIVID	#DIVID	0

⊕ For a copy of this tool, visit www.greatgame.com/gigguide.

🌐 Critical Number Scoreboard

CRITICAL NUMBER #1

Target	PBT	JAN	FEB	MAR	APR	MAY	JUN	JUL	AUG	SEP	OCT	NOV	DEC	TOTAL
	PLAN													-
	Actual / Forecast													
	PLAN YTD	-	-	-	-	-	-					-	-	
	Actual / Forecast YTD	-	-	-	-	-	-					-	-	
	LEVEL ONE BONUS TARGET													

CRITICAL NUMBER #2

Target	PBT	JAN	FEB	MAR	APR	MAY	JUN	JUL	AUG	SEP	OCT	NOV	DEC	TOTAL
	PLAN													
	Actual / Forecast													
	PLAN YTD	-	-	-	-	-	-	-	-	-	-	-	-	
	Actual / Forecast YTD	-	-	-	-	-	-	-	-	-	-	-	-	
	LEVEL ONE BONUS TARGET													

DRIVERS

Target	PBT	Owner	JAN	FEB	MAR	APR	MAY	JUN	JUL	AUG	SEP	OCT	NOV	DEC
80	Net Promotor Score													

🌐 For a copy of this tool, visit www.greatgame.com/gigguide.

"Aren't we forgetting something?" asked Deborah.

"What?" replied Kevin.

"Our Critical Number?" came Deborah's response.

Sam smiled. "I was wondering when somebody would mention that. We made it through every line item without calling our Critical Number. Since it's based on Gross Margin, we could put it right here on our scoreboard. We can break the margin into two lines: Code Blue Gross Margin and Non-Code-Blue Gross Margin. We can also include a few drivers that directly influence NCBGM in our Cost of Goods Sold. Make sense?" By now, the entire management team was very comfortable with NCBGM and nodded in agreement.

"As we Huddle each week, it will really help us to know how we are tracking on our Critical Number 'year to date.' We'll add a few lines at the bottom to capture this. One thing is for sure, if we measure it, we'll move it! With this line everyone can track how we're progressing toward the bonus. Next we'll call it out even more by building a 'themed' Critical Number scoreboard. You know, sort of 'thermometer' board, where we can see how we're progressing at a glance."

Randy thanked the team for the time they had put in to drafting the scoreboard. (See scoreboards on pages 338 and 339.)

Sam pointed out, as the team stood to leave for the day, "Our final step in designing the Game will be to structure the way in which we'll communicate around the scoreboard. A scoreboard is only as good as the communications and actions you create around them. If we don't keep up the discipline of Huddling around these scoreboards, it will all be for naught."

▐▐▐▶ play the game

Follow the Action—The Huddle Cycle

The management team gathered, as had become their recent custom, in the cafeteria. They were surrounded by the scoreboards they'd created the week before. They watched the Great

Game Huddle video,⬤ which reminded them of what they saw in person at Tom's IT company. The entire management team felt the same way about what they had seen. The "Huddle" was no ordinary staff meeting.

Randy started by saying, "I liked how they define the Huddle in the video." Reading from his notes, he went on, "If the Critical Number is the heart of the Game, the Huddle is the heartbeat. It's a rhythm, a communication rhythm, where everybody is kept informed and involved in the progress of the Game.

"After watching the video, the 'aha' moment for me was the Huddle *cycle*. At Tom's place, I just assumed that was the only Huddle. It's actually a series of Huddles that make the whole system work. The numbers are created and shared at a series of meetings from daily departmental check-ins or 'pre-Huddles,' to weekly company-wide gatherings. It was pretty impressive to watch how the information came from every corner of the business into an accurate, up-to-the-minute Big Picture view of the company's overall financial performance."

"And this happens every week?" asked Kevin. "Boy, we have some work to do . . ."

Sam added, "I know, it looks like a lot to take on. Don't worry, though." He passed around an illustration of the Huddle Cycle, and then he continued. "It's the discipline of the Game. It will become our weekly ritual for calculating and communicating the score. It'll take time to make it stick, but we'll get there . . . been there, done that." Sam smiled confidently, hoping to set the team at ease.

Randy said, "Okay, team, you heard my take. You've been to a live Huddle, you've seen the video, and you've been holding MiniGame Huddles. You're getting the feel for what a Huddle needs to be. When you were all at Tom's Huddle, what made it different? What did you see?"

Gerald began, saying, "It didn't last long! Everything was fast paced and to the point. I couldn't believe the amount of information that was processed in what . . . forty-five minutes?"

Kevin added, "Yeah, part of that was that everybody was on

⬤The Great Game Huddle Video: www.greatgame.com/gigguide

The Huddle Cycle

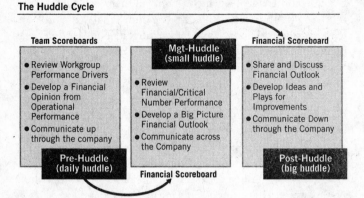

time and prepared for it," looking directly at Gerald. "I also liked that the meeting was structured and focused," continued Kevin. "Everybody knew the agenda *and* what their role was in it."

Meredith commented, "Communication revolved around their Critical Numbers and the stories behind those numbers . . ."

"I remember that the majority of the discussions were forward looking," said Dan. "They were sharing emerging issues and concerns, rather than dwelling on the past."

Sam liked their responses. "Very good. What else? Where did the numbers come from . . . the CFO?"

"No!" replied Deborah. "It was the people doing the work who were calling out their forecasts. That was pretty cool."

Randy agreed. "And there was very clear accountability for the numbers . . . they *owned* 'em. You could really see the follow-through as well, couldn't you?"

Sam quickly jumped in. "It's the repetition, Randy . . . the frequent engagement with your peers that drives the accountability and follow-through. It took me a while to make that connection. Knowing others are counting on us tends to raise our level of commitment."

Meredith added, "I thought a lot of the accountability was the result of the commitments they made to each other. I remember calling them 'promises in writing.' First they gave a brief update on the commitment they made the previous week, then followed up with a new 'commit,' as they called it, for the coming week. That gave the meeting a real feeling of getting things done."

"And people seemed to have no problem challenging each other," added Gerald.

Bill, Dan's assistant manager, had been pretty quiet but had really gotten a lot out of the visit to Tom's company. "Everybody in that Huddle had a clear understanding of problems and opportunities and how they could impact the outcome." He went on, "And if they were struggling, they weren't afraid to share it. They weren't afraid to ask the team for help. I liked that."

Meredith added, "Yeah, Bill, they openly discussed both their wins and losses . . . and because they all were working from a common scoreboard and a common 'bottom-line' goal, they couldn't help but team up and focus on the issues rather than who's to blame. The overall objective, improving the bottom line, was right there for all to see."

Deborah pointed out, "They seemed to take time to make sure everybody understood things. Questions were encouraged and even rewarded. Tom even gave dollar bills out in the Huddle to people who answered questions. That was different."

"People were leaving more informed and educated about the business, that's for sure," Kevin added.

Deborah added more. "And at the same time, they were *sure* to not close the meeting without recognizing contributions and successes. People left the Huddle pretty fired up and energized, knowing exactly what needed to be done next."

"Fantastic, guys," Randy said proudly. "You are really getting this. All right, let's do this. Tom said the best way to get started is to jump right in. Next Tuesday at 9 A.M. we're going to have our first Huddle. Remember, this is the management Huddle, just one step in the cycle. We'll do it for a few weeks, maybe more, to get really comfortable with our scoreboard and the process; then we'll roll it out to the whole organization. Sound good?"

Heads nodded in agreement.

"Here's the agenda," Sam said. "Randy, you need to chair this Huddle. You'll set the tone. You'll give brief comments about the Big Picture, where the company is now, where it's headed. That will give everyone context of the 'state of the Game'; then it's time to check the score. We'll forecast our numbers and create a financial outlook for the company. We'll keep it tight, stick to the scoreboard, share the stories behind the numbers, and focus on the variances. Then we'll make our commitments."

Meredith perked up. "These are the 'promises in writing' we saw at Tom's place. Right?"

Sam replied, "Exactly, Meredith. It's not four things. Or ten things. A commit is *one* thing that you can do this week to improve the score. It is so simple, but powerful."

Randy stated, "We'll track and report progress, commit to results, and continually think about how we can improve those results. All along we keep learning and getting better."

Sam went on, "We'll wrap up each meeting by going around the room, so each of you can give an update on what's happening in your area of the business. Highlight the wins, recognize folks, and touch on important nonfinancial things." ●

"Guys, this is one of the most important steps we'll take to make sure the Game works for us," Randy said earnestly. "We have to take it seriously. We have to stay disciplined to it, and you have to come prepared to really make it work."

Sam agreed and gave the team some perspective. "The first month of these Huddles is gonna be awkward. A little long, maybe unorganized . . . in all reality, just plain ugly. But we'll keep going, and we'll figure it out along the way. Once we get comfortable, then we'll roll it out. But I want to make sure all of us in leadership are confident in becoming the teachers and coaches for all the other employees on the numbers and the process."

Randy ended the meeting with, "It begins and ends with our leadership."

● The Huddle Checklist: www.greatgame.com/gigguide

Over the weekend, Sam decided to send the team an e-mail. He had been noticing anxiety among management about coming to their first Huddle on Tuesday. He knew a lot of that angst was driven by the fact that each of them would be required to make their first forecast and their first commitment to the rest of the team. His e-mail read:

> From: Sam
> To: Kevin, Dan, Bill, Gerald, Meredith, Deborah
> Cc: Randy
> Subject: Forecasting
>
> Attachments: Forecasting Tool 4.jpg; Forecasting Tool 3.jpg; Forecasting Tool 2.jpg; Forecasting Tool 1.jpg
>
> Team:
> As we approach our first Huddle and the first forecast I'm sensing some anxiety from some of the communications I've received. Based on that I thought I'd take a few minutes to give you some forecasting tips that might be of help.
> Based on my experience regarding forecasting you can approach it in at least four ways:
>
> 1. Use complex Excel spreadsheets drawing upon models such as linear regression, multiple regression analysis, or some modeling theory like the Monte Carlo method.
> 2. You can use one of the four tried and true forecasting tools that are included in the attached files.
> 3. You can hire someone with an MBA (which will probably produce results similar to the tools outlined in #2).

346 / the Great Game of Business

    4. You can draw upon your knowledge of the
       business, a little historical information,
       your experience and intuition, and apply
       all that to the numbers.

My advice—relax a bit and use #4. ☺

Sam

Ironically, the attachments were not "tools," but photographs. Attachment one was a "Magic Eight Ball"; number two was a coin flip; number three was a crystal ball; and number four was a roll of the dice. Everyone on the team got the joke *and the point*. Sam just wanted them to use their knowledge, experience, and "gut" to give their best opinion of how the month was going to end.

The e-mail worked. By the time Tuesday rolled around, everybody was actually looking forward to their first real Huddle. And each of them had been putting together their first forecast, knowing that they would not be thrown to the wolves if it wasn't spot on.

As the team walked into the cafeteria, they noticed that Randy had posted a new sign next to the big financial scoreboard. The quote printed on the sign gave everybody perspective on what they were about to do, and it set them at ease.

Randy took a deep breath and started the meeting. "Hello, everybody! Good morning! Welcome to our first official Huddle. A great way to begin is to go back to the book; that's why I posted the sign behind me." He pointed to the new sign. It read:

> *When we come out of our Huddle, we see the whole field before us. We know who is where, and how the game is unfolding, and what each of us has to do to make sure we keep moving closer to the goal line.*
> JACK STACK, *The Great Game of Business*

"Our objective today is to make that happen. We have our financial scoreboard, on the wall, bigger than life," which he pointed out, "and you each have a printout of the scoreboard as well. We're going to build a forward-looking financial picture of our business this morning. Sam, why don't you kick this thing off!"

Sam began to lead the team down each line on the scoreboard. "Sales! What is your forecast for Restoration?" As each line item was called, its "owner" called out the month-end forecast, which was then written on the big board. As the number was written down, each manager provided a brief story behind the number, something that reflected the risk or opportunities in the number. At the same time, each manager wrote the numbers on the scoreboard in front of them.

Sam continued, "COGS! What's labor looking like for Dry Cleaning?"

Gerald looked over the top of his glasses at the board, then at Sam. "I'm going with plan."

Sam looked puzzled. "Gerald, do you think that forecast will hold up by the end of the month? It looks like sales are up quite a bit," he said, pointing at top line Dry Cleaning sales. "I thought you were going to be working weekends to get everything out . . ."

Meredith nearly came out of her seat. "Labor's going to go up $2,100 because of the overtime, Sam!"

"There you go!" responded Sam enthusiastically. "Now *that's* a forecast! You take the realities of your situation, use your experience to make the best estimate of what will happen by the end of the month, and put it on the board. Great job, Meredith!" Gerald was not amused.

"As we get better at this, you guys will be watching and building your own departmental, team, and individual scorecards. Your own operational numbers will help you get a better sense of what your forecast should be. This will allow you to get more of your people involved, because operational numbers come from where?"

"Our people!" was the chorus from around the room. "Exactly!" Sam said smiling, pointing around the room.

"So when you come in and provide your forecast, it will have the full buy-in and support of your people. *If people don't partici-pate, they don't buy in. If they don't buy in, they don't commit. If they don't commit, they don't deliver!"*

Randy added, "That's right. That's what you'll do in your 'pre-Huddles' with your teams. It's about creating line of sight. They'll all know where they fit in all these numbers, and they'll understand their actions and decisions really do make a differ-ence."

The Huddle continued down through the bottom line, and it was time for everybody to commit to something each of them could do to personally improve the score.

Meredith knew exactly what to do. "My 'commit' . . . my 'one thing' is that I'm really going to focus this weekend to get as much done as possible. My commitment is to cut that overtime in half."

Following the agenda Randy had laid out, the team contin-ued around the room. Near the end, each manager gave a brief update on his or her division. During his turn, Kevin recognized his "Scrolling for Dollars" team for what a good job they were doing with their new MiniGame. He asked that kudos be given next time anyone saw them in the hallways.

They had done it. The management team had successfully built a picture, lumpy as it was, of how the business was going to perform by the end of the month. Like Randy had promised, and the sign said, they could see the whole playing field, they knew who was where, how the game was unfolding, and what each of them had to do to keep moving closer to the goal.

It would take several weeks before they began to feel more comfortable . . . not only with the numbers, the forecasts . . . but also with the idea of becoming the coaches and teachers that would bring this understanding and discipline to the troops.

Drive Results from MiniGames

The divisions had been playing MiniGames for ninety days and had driven both awareness and results. It was clear that the "reg-ular" folks, the hourly employees, understood more about the business than anyone had thought possible. They were tracking, measuring, and forecasting metrics about their jobs . . . and it was making a difference. "Scotch on the Rocks" had more than doubled upsells, and the team at On-Location Services had enjoyed monthly celebrations as they exceeded each goal. Energy had never been higher among the employees, and people were even starting to ask if they could begin working on their next MiniGame.

The Emergency Restoration division had a great success with their MiniGame, "Scrolling for Dollars." Their goal was to increase cross selling of other "nonemergency" services by mining their database in their downtime, in an effort to drive Non-Code-Blue Gross Margin. They'd planned to do it for ninety days.

They created targets for each month. Level 1 was 250 calls/touches; Level 2, 275 calls/touches; and Level 3, 300 calls/touches. Kevin, the head of Restoration, and Randy both thought their goals were too low, but Sam suggested they let the team give it a shot so they could "own" their game. He suggested that if management set the goals, it would be *their* Game and not the team's. They agreed to let it play out, though it was clear that Randy and Kevin were a little skeptical. Deborah, the CFO, was concerned that there were no "measurables" linked to the game beyond the number of calls. She suggested they should have an actual dollar figure attached to the MiniGame; still, Sam persisted. He guaranteed that if they made the calls and touches and put themselves out there, there would be an ROI, measurables, and the MiniGame would be self-funding.

They called it "Scrolling for Dollars" because they would scroll through names in their database to make the cross-selling calls. They could quickly tell their previous Code Blue customers about Dry Cleaning and On-Location Services. It was a great use of their time, as they discovered there were so many services they could offer. They offered numerous "on-location cleaning" services such as air duct cleaning, mold remediation, tile and grout cleaning, and upholstery cleaning. All were services their customers could use. And all were services that contributed to improving the Critical Number.

It was a play on the old TV show *Bowling for Dollars*, so the

Restoration team themed it accordingly. The rewards matched the three levels they'd created. If they reached their Level 1 goal, the team would receive a mouse pad themed with their bowling motif. Level 2 would get them a cool, retro bowling shirt, with the MiniGame and company logos on the back. If they achieved Level 3, the entire team would have a bowling party at the end of the ninety days, including pizza and the works. Sam pointed out that because they chose their own rewards, the cost was negligible compared to the potential financial impact of the MiniGame. Their scoreboard was a computer mouse moving down a bowling lane toward the pins as they completed calls/touches.

The MiniGame was only halfway through and was a huge success. Not only did they reach their goals of making the calls, but the impact was remarkable. The first month they had made 102 calls, of which 25 people they spoke to had interest and wanted more information; three made appointments. One customer even called back and asked for an On-Location Services quote on an entire office building. The real topper was in the third month, when one of the face-to-face meetings they had with the local hospital resulted in a callback, asking for a proposal.

After hearing the fabulous news, the team from On-Location Services came by during one of Emergency Restoration's MiniGame Huddles and gave them a standing ovation. This clearly moved the Restoration people. Better yet, the team had their confidence and self-esteem raised enormously. They felt that everyone in the company was behind them. Kevin, Deborah, and Randy looked at Sam during the celebration. Randy simply said, "Priceless. I can't wait to see what happens by the end of this MiniGame."

With the energy and momentum so high, the associates wanted to learn more. It was the perfect time to "roll out" the company-wide Game. People could see the results of their daily decisions. They were experiencing cause and effect firsthand: how they were directly impacting the business, and how the numbers all added up into the Big Picture. The employees were taking responsibility for the financial performance of the business. They were starting to think and act like owners. And the big Game hadn't even started, or had it?

Randy and Sam had talked for a long time about how the rollout might be handled. They finally decided to do something that Tom had described when he launched the Game at his IT company.

Launch the Big Game

Everybody had gathered in a neighborhood gymnasium that Randy had rented for the afternoon. As they shuffled in, there was a sense of excitement, an energy as people anticipated the event. They were told it was going to be fun, that they'd learn something, but they'd also be introduced to the "bonus plan," which certainly got their attention. Everybody had been waiting to learn about it, and now that the MiniGames were paying off, they knew that this GGOB thing just might work.

As employees walked in, they were each handed a T-shirt. The shirts were color coded for each division: red for On-Location Services, green for Dry Cleaning, and "code" blue for Emergency Restoration. The office and admin folks were wearing white. Randy had invited some other advisers and friends to attend as well. Off in the corner were seated the banker, in his three-piece suit, Randy's insurance agent in a polo shirt, and another man in a black suit.

Over the PA system, an announcement came to take a seat, as the meeting was about to start. When things settled down, people began looking around to figure out where Randy was. Sam stepped onto the wooden floor, stopping at center court. He welcomed everybody and got them to give themselves a round of applause for the great job they had done on the MiniGames. Still, Randy was nowhere to be seen.

"Since we began the Game almost three months ago, I know you are all dying to know more about how the big Game will work, and of course the WIIFM: the 'What's in It for Me' . . . our annual bonus plan. Well, we've been working hard at it at the same time that you all have been working hard at improving business at your divisional levels with MiniGames. What we've come up with is pretty exciting. To better understand the Big Picture, we wanted to have everybody be a part of building our first financial scoreboard. This will be our company-wide score-board that we'll Huddle around every week. You already can feel a difference in the way things are working, can't you?"

The crowd gave out a holler. They were excited.

"You bet there's a difference. Now imagine taking that to the next level and aligning the entire company around our Critical Numbers; just think of what's possible!" Sam knew it was time for the "reveal." "Ladies and gentlemen" he announced, like a ringmaster, "please welcome the sales team and our president and CEO . . . Randy!" A fanfare blasted over the PA, and people cheered as Randy burst through the side doors, followed by the sales team, who were pushing a wheelbarrow that appeared to be stacked full of cash. They did a victory lap around Sam and landed the wheelbarrow at center court.

"Hey, everybody! Are you ready to play the Great Game of Business?" Randy yelled.

Another cheer went up as people responded to the theatrics.

"What you see here is a wheelbarrow filled with $7,700,000, the exact amount of services we sold last year," Randy pointed to the cash, which was play money the management team had put together into bundles representing ten thousand dollars each. "Each of you is going to help us move these dollars around, so we can all understand how money flows through our company. When we're done, we'll see what's left and talk about the bonus program for the coming year. How's that sound?"

More applause came, but it died down quickly. People wanted to get moving.

Two of the white shirts from the office team came out onto the court carrying a big roll of what looked like butcher paper. As it was unfurled, the crowd could see a gigantic version of what looked like an Income Statement, now revealed on the floor of the gym. They had written in big letters "Sales/Revenue, COGS, Gross Margin, Expenses, & PBT." Under Sales and COGS, there were lines for each division; Emergency Restoration, Dry Cleaning, and On-Location Services; exactly the same line items the management team had agreed earlier to include on the company-wide scoreboard. The huge banner spanned no less than twenty feet in length.

Randy continued, "Okay, so here's how the company brings in money. Blue shirts . . . get down here! Kevin, you call out your revenue number for Emergency Restoration. The office team will write your number on the big board, and your team will take money from the wheelbarrow representing the revenue they brought in last year . . ."—which they did with pride. They were, after all, the biggest revenue producers last year. As the blue shirts parted, the crowd could see the scoreboard was now updated with the number representing revenue for their division. The other divisions followed suit, each placing their pile of money on the scoreboard in the spot representing their sales line. The wheelbarrow was now empty.

Randy was grinning from ear to ear as he said, "Now let's run through Cost of Goods Sold, COGS! Materials Department! Purchasing! Come on down!" and they did. Each department called out their number, which was then neatly written on the big scoreboard. "These numbers represent the materials we needed to deliver on the sales we just went through above . . ." Randy explained. Then the materials and purchasing people went to the scoreboard and moved money from the sales lines to the COGS lines as their numbers were called out and recorded on the scoreboard. Randy called out, "Now I need people from each division to come down and account for labor!" Blue, red, and green shirts stepped onto the floor as Randy directed each to move labor dollars from Sales to COGS. Again, each number was recorded on the scoreboard while the money was moved. Everybody in the bleachers could see the "sales" piles dwindling. It was a great visual to see all the employees working together to count, move, and flow the money through the business. What was left was moved by the admin team from "Sales" down to "Gross Margin."

It took time to go through the exercise of explaining in detail how the Income Statement was being built, but no one in that gymnasium would ever forget the powerful visual.

"So are we all following how money is moving through the business so far?" Randy asked, to which every head nodded. It was impossible not to see what was happening on the floor. Now it was time to run through Expenses. Randy had the team turn to General Administration expenses: things like Salaries, Sales and Marketing expenses, and Rent. Each person responsible for a line item, and the team, came up and moved money from Gross Margin to the expense lines, until only a small pile was left.

Sam pointed out the remainder and asked, "So what do we do with this?"

"Bonus!" Cried some, while others yelled, "Bottom line!" Everybody was yelling and smiling. Randy couldn't help but feel they were getting it.

Sam stepped over, picked up the remaining stacks, and began to walk down to "Profit Before Tax." As he laid the money down, people noticed the man in the black suit had donned sunglasses and was walking from the corner to the scoreboard. As he turned his back to the crowd, they could see "IRS" taped to his back. The crowd took to their feet, and the stands let out a rousing "BOOOOO!" as the IRS man took what seemed like half of the PBT and placed it on the tax line.

As things settled down, Sam took the last remaining dollars and waved them overhead at the crowd.

"So now we can see how hard it is to make money. We just watched all last year's numbers come to life, and how little was left over. How could we do better this year?"

"Sell more!" "Cut expenses!" All the same responses he had heard three months ago were coming back, but this time people were almost a little mad . . . they wanted to get into the middle of *this* Game.

"What do you say we run through this again, only we'll do it with the numbers we have been working on for the coming year." And they did. The white shirts flipped the paper to reveal their new plan and the people swarmed onto the floor to watch the flow of money through the business. This time, there was much more left at the bottom.

During this run-through, there was one big difference. Instead of one line for Gross Margin, there were now three. Code

Blue Gross Margin, Non-Code-Blue Gross Margin, and Total Gross Margin. Every soul in the room now knew that the Critical Numbers of the business were going to be focused on . . . every single week of the coming year.

The meeting continued, with the pace and energy of a pep rally. The bonus plan was revealed, and the promise was made that each member of the management team could answer questions about it anytime. The connection between the bonus and the Critical Numbers of bottom-line Profit and Non-Code-Blue Gross Margin was discussed The team had gone so far as to theme the yearlong bonus campaign "Code Green." The idea was easy to grasp and very well received. The annual bonus scoreboard was stunning. It was a secret agent "mission possible"–style board, in which the Code Green mission was to cover overhead with NCBGM. For every thousand dollars of NCBGM the team generated, a large dollar bill was plastered onto the scoreboard, covering part of the evil "overhead" graphic. You could tell in a glance at the scoreboard if you were winning or losing.

Randy felt this was a great first step toward the "insurance policy" he'd always wanted: moving the culture of the business toward building a diversified, sustainable, growing company.

As the launch came to a close, Randy said, "We're going to be meeting every single week at the same time, to have our Big Huddle like this. We'll do the same thing, only in our cafeteria, on our big financial scoreboard. The management team has been practicing Huddling and the forecasting process for several weeks as you know. You will all get more exposure to that now. In fact, each of you has been doing these things with MiniGames for the past couple of months. You've been Huddling with your teams weekly, forecasting, tracking, measuring and reporting . . . and winning! Now, you'll be able to apply those skills to the bigger Game. The management team will be counting on you for support in the 'pre-Huddles' that will help us build our team and work group numbers, all of which roll up into our company-wide financial picture and Critical Numbers. Then you can see how your departmental forecasts add up to the company's overall financial forecast." He paused for effect. "The idea is for everybody to have clear line of sight; to understand how your decisions and actions every day make or break the business."

Sam added, "Remember, everybody, the objective of the Huddle is posted right on the wall of the cafeteria. When we leave the weekly Huddle, you should be able to see the whole playing field, know where everybody is, see how the game is unfolding, and what each of us must do to keep moving closer to the goal."

As they left the gym, everybody was handed a Code Green folder, spelling out the details of their mission. It included the annual plan, the Critical Numbers, the bonus scoreboard, and a glossary of terms. As Randy and Sam handed them out, they said, "Here's your mission, should you choose to accept it. Be sure to bring your folder to the Huddle next week." Though some eyes rolled, every person left with a feeling of enthusiasm, pride, and a clear feeling of involvement and respect.

▶ elevate the game

Fall was in the air and Randy thought about the last time he was in St. Louis. It was this time last year when he experienced the Great Game of Business at the Annual Gathering of Games Conference, and today he was back again. This time, instead of just attending, he was also presenting. Sam had suggested it months ago, reminding Randy of Tom's "pay it forward" story. Telling his story at the Gathering brought with it a mix of feelings: nervousness, excitement, anticipation. He was set at ease a bit when Tom and Sam agreed to present as a panel, to talk about the challenges and rewards of implementing the Game for the first time.

The room was packed. Every seat was filled and there were people lining the walls. *Wow, standing room only. Hope I don't let them down*, he thought. It was humbling. The session began on time, and Randy told the group about his father, the company, his trip to St. Louis last year. He told of Tom and told the story of their visit to his Huddle, and how instrumental Sam's experience was in their success.

Ongoing Business and Financial Training

"Once we established our Huddle rhythm, it was a steady diet of business and financial literacy. Although we didn't call it financial literacy training. We called it 'Path to Achieving Your Stake in the Outcome,' PAYSIO for short. We did it through formal 'classroom' training ● and backed it up with constant literacy 'bites' in the Huddles . . . small, 'bite-sized' lessons we could teach in fifteen to twenty minutes. Doesn't seem like much at the time, but if you do one or two a month, you can easily get twelve to twenty-four lessons into a year without thinking about it. And the lessons seem to stick, because they were short enough for people to grasp. One of our first 'bites' was called 'The Biggest Bang for the Buck.' ● The purpose was to show how anybody in the company can make a significant impact to the bottom line. We explored the relationship between the effects of a percentage increase in sales versus a percentage reduction in expenses. What will give us the biggest bang for the buck? Pretty simple, but really impactful."

"And because we're growing, that means we're hiring. We have to be diligent about assessing, onboarding, training our new people so we don't dilute our own culture," Sam added.

They shared photos of the big financial scoreboard, the "themed" Critical Number scoreboard, and their team scorecards that each department used. Sam explained how the "cascading" of scorecards made such a big difference in visibility and accountability. "It's really great when everybody on the team knows which way the goal is!" he said at one point, and the audience laughed out loud.

"One of the most foreign things for everybody was forward forecasting. In fact, Sam called it 'poorcasting' at first," which

●YoYo Company Formal Training and Literacy Bites: www.great game.com/gigguide

raised another round of laughter." Randy went on, "But we got it in time. And now, our people couldn't . . . and wouldn't . . . live without it. It's their chance to control their own destiny." The audience was feverishly taking notes.

The three speakers had set aside time for Q & A, and hands flew up without asking twice.

A young woman standing against the wall called out, "So did you hit your Critical Numbers?"

Sam answered, "We had a number of wins! We paid out a bonus for both the first and second quarters. Our Profit Before Tax Critical Number paid out on level 7 in the second quarter! Everybody enjoyed five and half days of additional pay, and they're forecasting to do better in the third quarter. It has been great to see everybody driving efficiencies around the company."

"But did you diversify your company? Did you hit your other Critical Number?" came a challenge from another row. People leaned forward to hear the answer.

Randy took this one. "I didn't think we were going to do it, honestly. First quarter we really struggled with it. It took a lot of communication to keep people focused. They were rock stars on the profit side, but changing behaviors around the importance of Non-Code-Blue Gross Margin was a challenge. Fortunately we've had a good year so far in our Code Blue Restoration business. But the threat is still there. What if the Code Blue business isn't so good? I want us to eliminate that weakness."

Sam added, "Yeah. Imagine hitting level 7 on Profit Before Taxes, and zero on Non-Code-Blue Gross Margin. People wondered why we even had a second Critical Number."

Randy continued. "You bet they did. It's human nature. But we persisted and kept up the Huddles and the education. It was the MiniGames, though, that really cracked the code. They were an incredible source of innovation, engagement, and problem solving. They kept people in the Game and lent focus to the importance of Non-Code-Blue work. Second quarter is when they really started to see the light. We ended up doing very well on diversifying, or as we call it, our Code Green efforts. Not as well as PBT, but well. Our people have added $88,000 in Non-Code-Blue Gross Margin and hit level 4, which paid another three days of additional pay! Boy, did we have fun celebrating that win!"

Tom added, "Combined with the PBT bonus, everybody came out of the second quarter on track to receive 11 percent of their annual wages in bonuses if they keep up the momentum. They all know exactly what's at stake."

The crowd spontaneously burst into applause. These stories were a big reason people came to the Gathering. From the front row, a man in a navy blazer calmly asked, "So what's next, Randy?"

High-Involvement Planning

"Good question," Randy answered, "I've been thinking a lot about that lately. It's been a year since we started getting into the Game, and almost nine months since we started playing. Our people are really understanding the business, so much so that they are not only asking the right questions, but they are coming up with the answers. I think we're ready to involve them more in planning the business for next year."

Tom spoke up, "A year ago, you'd never believe that this man would be standing up here telling his story, much less talking about including his people in high-involvement planning." Tom carried a lot of weight with this crowd, as he had received the All-Star Award for his own practice of the Game. "Incorporating a high-involvement planning process was how we took the Game to the next level at my company. It made a huge difference in ensuring everybody understood and accepted the company's goals, because the plan was a direct result of their input."

Randy continued, "Tom's absolutely right. I'd never have believed it possible. But when we get back, we'll be conducting the 360 degree appraisal process again. From the GGOB practice assessment, to the employee surveys, financial trend analysis, the works. The difference this time around is all of it will be part of the company's planning process. Developing our plan will be a company-wide effort."

Randy added, "Our planning process has traditionally consisted of me and our managers, the supposedly 'smartest people in the room' heading out on a retreat to plan the coming year. But we would come down from the mountaintop, with our sacred tablets in hand, and without fail be sorely disappointed with the lack of enthusiasm shared by the employees about our grand plans. I want to change the mind-set from 'that's your plan' to 'this is our plan.' There should be agreement and buy-in at all levels. Granted, the management team will continue to work closely to bring the plan together, but the process should include input from all the stakeholders of the company. As Tom pointed out to me, 'To get real ownership in the plan, we have to focus on how people are involved in the process. If people don't participate, they don't buy in. If they don't buy in, they don't commit. If they don't commit, they don't deliver.'"

Tom added, "We've found that our people became more and more curious about the company's market, its strategy, its competitive advantages, and where the company is headed and how we plan to get there. They want to know what's in store for them. In fact, without that context, they won't have any reason to keep caring about the numbers."

Randy said, "We understand this is just another step in fully implementing the Game. We also acknowledge that getting everybody involved in putting the Game's annual plan together is a huge task. We probably won't get it right the first year, but we'll make a point to take the time to educate everybody on the process, giving them the tools they need to contribute and involving as many people as possible. The first step is to get buy-in on the top line. To do that, we've scheduled our sales and marketing presentations a month from now to address that. People are already clamoring to pull together information and they're gathering all the competitive intelligence they can find. It's really exciting to be a part of!" Randy almost choked up.

As the session time was ending, Tom asked for one final question from the audience; as hands shot up, someone shouted from the back, "What ever happened to Gerald?" Everybody laughed, because Sam had mentioned in the presentation that not everyone had been on board through their implementation.

Randy tried to contain a smile, but it didn't work. "Gerald hung in there. But by spring, it was pretty clear that the more transparency and accountability we embraced, the less it looked like a place Gerald wanted to work. He self-selected out and took another job. Fortunately, with our competitor." Everybody laughed out loud.

Tom couldn't resist adding, "So where would you invest your money . . . in a company full of Randy's people, or a company full of 'Geralds'?"

Sam spoke up, "But seriously, it created an opportunity for Meredith, the assistant manager, to step up and take the reins at the Dry Cleaning operation."

There was laughter and applause from the audience as they congratulated and thanked Randy and the panel for the amazing story. Offers to help and requests to visit flooded in as the session ended and people left the meeting room. Randy was certain of one thing. He was going to call his dad. That weekend, they'd be laughing in that bass boat together.

OVERVIEW OF THE PRINCIPLES AND PRACTICES OF THE GREAT GAME OF BUSINESS

THE GOAL

Improve business results and the lives of the people who drive those results . . .

THE STRATEGY

. . . by creating a "business of businesspeople" who "think, act, and feel like owners"

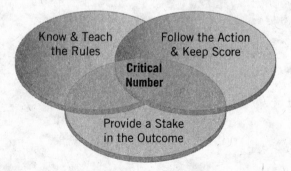

THE PRINCIPLES OF THE GREAT GAME OF BUSINESS

EVERY EMPLOYEE . . .

• should be given the measures of business success and taught to understand them:

Know and Teach the Rules

• should be expected and enabled to act on their knowledge to improve performance:

Follow the Action and Keep Score

• should have a direct stake in the company's success and risk of failure:

Provide a Stake in the Outcome

THE PRACTICES OF THE GREAT GAME OF BUSINESS

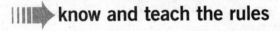 know and teach the rules

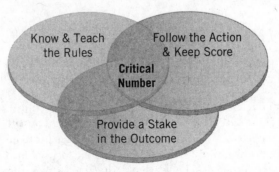

Financial Transparency and Education

The financials are often the only report card in the company that shows the collective contribution of each and every department and individual in the company. So why not use them to bring people together?

If the strategy is to create a "Business of Businesspeople," it follows that employees must learn the language of business—the financials. Nothing can duplicate the informal, practical learning that comes with keeping score and following the real numbers day in and day out. But there is definitely a place for formal *financial transparency and training*—if it is done right.

High-Involvement Planning

When the Game is created with broad participation—specifically the people who are closest to the action and who understand the realities—it creates a level of commitment and alignment that just can't be matched. *High-involvement planning* helps companies transform their planning process from an annual, time-consuming ritual to a highly informative, educational journey that involves everybody at every level of the company in understanding the big picture and the importance of looking forward into the marketplace.

The Critical Number

Focusing on the *Critical Number* is an essential step to getting everybody focused and accountable for results. The Critical Number defines winning. It rallies people around a common goal and a focus on what's most important and critical to the company's success. When the Critical Number is correctly identified, targeted, and tied to a reward—the rules of the Game have been set. The Critical Number becomes the focus of the Game.

Once your people know what's critical to success, they must then understand what they can do to drive that success. Identifying the right drivers helps everybody begin to understand what they can do, both individually and as a team, to influence the Critical Number and bottom-line financial results.

ⅢⅢ▶ follow the action and keep score

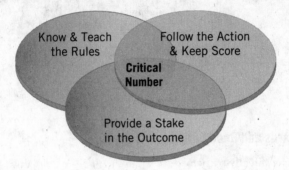

Keep Score

Winners are fanatics about *keeping score*. They understand, if you're not keeping score, it's just practice. The primary objective of keeping score is to simply and consistently inform the players if they are winning or losing and who is accountable.

Follow the Action

Following the action through a series of Huddles provides a rhythm of communication where everybody is kept informed, involved, and engaged in moving the company forward.

Forward Forecasting

You can't change history. *Forward forecasting* is the fundamental way in which Great Game of Business companies communicate the numbers and create forward-looking, educational, and results-focused Huddles.

⫸ provide a stake in the outcome

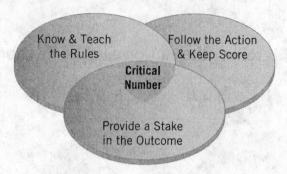

Rewards and Recognition

All who directly participate in strengthening the company likely do so because they have some form of *a stake in the outcome*. They come to work to win, because they know their work will result in significant *reward, recognition, and ownership* in the outcome.

MiniGames

MiniGames are short-term, intensely continuous focused, improvement campaigns designed to effect a change, correct a weakness, or pursue an opportunity within the company. There is a team goal, a scoreboard, and a reward for winning.

Ownership

Not all who play the Great Game of Business can or will share equity. Those who do share equity understand that employee ownership doesn't guarantee success. But experience and research have shown that employee-owners have a different attitude about their company, their job, and their responsibilities that increases the likelihood that their company will be successful. For more information on employee *ownership*, contact the National Center for Employee Ownership at nceo.org.

ACKNOWLEDGMENTS ...

I wish to thank all the people who trained and guided me to do this book. I'll never forget my parents driving our family past the factory where my father worked, and my mom telling her four little children to bow their heads and "thank God your daddy has a job." Or the three to four jobs my dad took every year at Christmastime along with my mom, who went to work at the post office, so their children would have gifts under the tree. My family taught me self-reliance, respect for one another, love of God, and the wonderful feeling of trust. For this, I will forever be grateful.

I want to thank all the people I worked for and with at Melrose Park. They were truly great people trying to survive tough times. For them to be still standing and still in business is remarkable. From the time I arrived there to the time I left, survival was in doubt every day, but with sheer determination, teamwork, and a burning desire to win they are still there, and I am proud to have been a part of that team.

To my partners, associates, and friends at SRC, I wish to thank you for the many years we have worked together to make dreams come true. It hasn't been easy but it has been fun. I appreciate all your enthusiasm, your interest in making the world better, your quest for knowledge, and your respect for one another. I hope we can attain those dreams, putting a little bit in everyone's pocket and leaving our environment better than when we used it.

Finally, to the people who worked and sacrificed to produce this book, thank you for all your blood, sweat, and tears. Thanks to Harriet Rubin of Currency, who first saw a book in the Game and who has been our faithful guide ever since. Thanks to her Currency associates, Janet Coleman and Lynn Fenwick, who kept the train on the tracks when it seemed on the verge of being derailed. Thanks to Pat Pascale, Janet Hill, and Lorraine Hyland of Doubleday for the heroic work they did to get this book published in record time. Thanks to Peter Kruzan and Marysarah Quinn, who combined their formidable talents and skills to come up with an arresting package and design.

Thanks to Kathy Robbins, Elizabeth Mackey, and the other members of The Robbins Office for being there when we needed them, and for making sure we all kept our eyes on the ball.

Thanks to Betsy and the kids for keeping the faith, and for keeping me going, through the many ups and downs. Thanks to my sister, Margaret Lombardi, for deciphering what I was trying to say on hours of tape recordings. Thanks to Dennis Sheppard for preparing us for what lies ahead, to Becky Lane for handling everything that comes along, and to Richard Cunningham for his unswerving support from beginning to end. Thanks to Lucien Rhodes for his early contributions.

Last, but surely not least, a standing ovation to Lisa Burlingham for her patience and fortitude and to Bo Burlingham for providing the talent and enthusiasm required to help me get this all down on paper. There would be no book without him.

As you can tell by now, the original book has been kept in its classic form, with the exception of the new introduction, and the "Get in the Game" guide to getting started.

This twentieth anniversary edition was the brainchild of Roger Scholl at Crown Business and Steve Baker of the Great Game of Business, who recognized the impact the book has had on people's lives and knew we needed to reach a whole new generation of business leaders. Rich Armstrong, president of the Great Game, deserves a commendation for building a team, an organization, and a growing community of practitioners dedicated to supporting the principles and values of the book.

Donna Coppock is, by far, the most celebrated, enthusiastic, and energized teacher I know when it comes to teaching the principles of the book in all walks of life.

And, finally, I want to acknowledge all the Great Game coaches; without their belief and devotion toward the philosophies of the book, there would be no twentieth anniversary. Tom Samsel, Rich Armstrong, Steve Baker, Bill Collier, and Patrick Carpenter are just a few of the Great Game coaches who have spent a significant part of their lives helping people prosper and grow. They have validated the concepts by teaching people how to create a better world.

ACKNOWLEDGMENTS 2.0

There is real power in putting something down in writing. Once you write a book, you grow your circle of friends and open yourself up to new opportunities. It becomes part of your life and your legacy. But it is you, our readers, who deserve the acknowledgment for leading us on a spectacular journey over the past thirty years.

A heck of a lot of people have touched our lives because of this book. It was almost as if when we opened up the doors to our company, we extended an invitation to people all over the world to begin sharing their ideas about how to do the right thing. It's been a wonderful privilege to sit at the center of a movement and watch people use the Great Game of Business system and improve upon it over the years.

We want to sincerely thank all the practitioners, associates, writers, families, and others who have helped validate the message of *The Great Game of Business*. Without all of you, this would have become just another pile of paper gathering dust on a shelf. Books, like movies, are nothing without an audience to support them.

Many of you read this book and said, "Wow, this is a tool that can change people's lives." Perhaps it gave you permission to listen to your heart and run a business the way others said couldn't be done. You're the ones who had the courage to give this leadership system a try and see if it worked. And by doing so, you changed lives, companies, and communities.

One of my greatest thrills in life is watching somebody use this system to become an entrepreneur—somebody who evolves from just showing up to do a job into somebody who understands how to run a business. That's a level of involvement that changes somebody's life forever. You think differently. You see people who were insecure or who doubted their talents develop the confidence, spirit, and creativity to build a home and start a family, and maybe even start a company that employs six or seven of their neighbors.

Call it the American Dream if you want, a path to prosperity, or even a kinder form of capitalism where everybody has an opportunity to live an equitable and satisfying life. Whatever name you give it, something good is created as a result.

But it is you who make it all happen. Thank you for the positive impact you've had on the lives of others, as well as your own. By working together, you've made the world a better place.

ABOUT THE AUTHORS

JACK STACK is founder, CEO, and president of SRC Holdings Corporation, a pioneer of the leadership model known as Open Book Management. He is the author of two books on the subject, *The Great Game of Business* and *A Stake in the Outcome*. His expertise in using the open book model has helped SRC Holdings Corporation start, acquire, and own over sixty small and medium businesses since 1983. In addition, SRC Holdings Corporation has increased its stock value 292,000 percent since 1983. SRC was also named one of the Top 100 Companies to Work for in America.

Jack has been called the "smartest strategist in America" by *Inc. Magazine* and one of the "top ten minds in small business" by *Fortune Small Business* magazine. Jack is a contributing editor for *Inc.* magazine and a contributing business writer for the *New York Times*. He is a popular public speaker and a practitioner of the open book model. He is the father of five children and grandfather of six.

BO BURLINGHAM is editor-at-large—and former executive editor—of *Inc.* magazine and chairman of the Small Giants Community (www.smallgiants.org). His book *Small Giants: Companies That Choose to Be Great Instead of Big* was a finalist for the 2006 *Financial Times*/Goldman

Sachs Business Book of the Year award. His most recent book, coauthored with Norm Brodsky, is *Street Smarts: An All-Purpose Tool Kit for Entrepreneurs.*

Bo has also written two books with Jack Stack. The first, *The Great Game of Business*, was named one of 100 best business books of all time. The second, *A Stake in the Outcome*, has been called "the first management classic of the new millennium." Burlingham is currently working on a book about exits. He lives in Oakland, California, with his wife of forty-one years, Lisa. They have two children and three grandchildren.

STEVE BAKER is vice president of The Great Game of Business Inc., a division of employee-owned SRC Holdings Corporation. He coauthored the update to *The Great Game of Business* 20th Anniversary Edition, "Get in the Game: The Interactive Guide," with GGOB president Rich Armstrong. Known for his high-energy and engaging message, he has become a top-rated and sought-after speaker, author, and coach on topics of Open Book Management, strategy and execution, business literacy, and employee engagement.

Steve has served on the board of directors of the National Center for Employee Ownership and SRC's Ownership Culture Steering Committee. He holds a design degree from Missouri State University and spent two decades working in marketing and branding roles before joining SRC, and is an award-winning designer. He lives in Springfield, Missouri, with his wife, JoAnn, and their three children.

RICH ARMSTRONG is the president of The Great Game of Business Inc. and a 20-plus-year veteran of SRC Holdings Corporation. He coauthored the update to *The Great Game of Business*, 20th Anniversary Edition, "Get in the Game: The Interactive Guide," with GGOB vice president Steve Baker.

Rich has been instrumental in the ongoing design and development of the GGOB methodology because of his practical, firsthand experience running businesses at SRC—experience that has enabled him to successfully apply the practices of GGOB in both small- and large-scale company implementations around the world. Known for his engaging, down-to-earth, and authentic style, Rich is a popular, versatile speaker and business coach for audiences ranging from executive leadership to frontline employees.

Rich holds a degree in business from Pittsburg State University and serves on the board of Court Appointed Special Advocates for children (CASA) and the National Center for Employee Ownership (NCEO). Combined with the love and enjoyment of his family, including two wonderful children, Ryan and Rylee, Rich is an avid musician and will often be found enjoying music in his home studio.